UNEVEN
INNOVATION

UNEVEN INNOVATION

THE WORK OF SMART CITIES

JENNIFER CLARK

Columbia University Press   *New York*

Columbia University Press
Publishers Since 1893
New York   Chichester, West Sussex
cup.columbia.edu
Copyright © 2020 Columbia University Press

Library of Congress Cataloging-in-Publication Data
Names: Clark, Jennifer, 1972– author.
Title: Uneven innovation : the work of smart cities / Jennifer Clark.
Description: 1st Edition. | New York : Columbia University Press, 2020. |
Includes bibliographical references and index.
Identifiers: LCCN 2019026398 (print) | LCCN 2019026399 (ebook) |
ISBN 9780231184960 (cloth) | ISBN 9780231184977 (paperback) |
ISBN 9780231545785 (ebook)
Subjects: LCSH: Cities and towns—Technological innovations. |
City planning—Technological innovations. | Cities and towns—Growth.
Classification: LCC HT153 .C583 2020 (print) | LCC HT153 (ebook) |
DDC 307.76—dc23
LC record available at https://lccn.loc.gov/2019026398
LC e-book record available at https://lccn.loc.gov/2019026399

Cover design and illustration: Henry Sene Yee
Scaffolding image: © Shutterstock

CONTENTS

ILLUSTRATIONS

FIGURES

TABLES

PREFACE

THE smart cities project—as a discourse and a practice—first came on the popular scene with initiatives such as IBM Smarter Cities in the early 2010s. As with many technology initiatives, the novelty of the smart cities project captured the public's imagination. Technology firms, the auto industry, and business consultants and advisers argued that self-driving cars would soon disrupt urban transportation systems and reshape the built environment as we know it. Soon policy makers, urban planners, and urban designers came to see the smart cities project as an opportunity to integrate the new technologies that were changing industries, including advanced manufacturing, energy, into the infrastructure and operations of cities. The resulting intelligent infrastructure, it was thought, would then serve as the platform for sustained economic growth. The smart cities project thus became an economic development project.

In February 2016, the President's Council of Advisors on Science and Technology (PCAST) released a major report, "Technology and the Future of Cities," which outlined a strategy to guide federal investment and engagement in smart cities initiatives. Although the future of smart cities initiatives and the policy impact of the original PCAST report remains uncertain, the report itself was revealing. Only a small number of the more than 100 contributors to the report represented the perspective or expertise of the social sciences that are dedicated to cities and the urban scale: urban policy, urban planning, urban geography, urban history, urban economics, or urban administration.

The growing interest in smart cities and the expansion of smart cities programs and projects has thus presented some interesting questions for the academic community: where does one learn about smart cities? Who teaches about smart cities? What discipline or degree programs prepare students to design, implement, and evaluate smart cities? Increasingly, the smart cities project is challenging the established social science disciplines to rethink their own boundaries and knowledge claims. The question then becomes, who will define what is required to be a participant in or an analyst of the smart cities project? Who will define the processes and practices that govern the future profession of urban innovation?

Ultimately, the smart cities project is rarely seen for what it is: a technology diffusion challenge operating in a dynamic and contested space between the public and the private sector. Technology development is the easy part; the real challenge is that the design and deployment of these models into this liminal space where governance, regulation, access, participation, and representation are unclear and the "operating standards" are yet to be fully articulated.

In this book, I tackle that challenge by providing a framework for analyzing the smart cities project that is grounded in the analysis of economic development and embedded in economic geography's established discourse on uneven development. The result is a way of thinking about urban innovation that recenters the analysis on scale, markets, and regulation. The book produces this framework for analyzing uneven innovation and proposes potential interventions in the smart cities project in order to shape a more equitable outcome.

A book project like this one takes a considerable amount of time, energy, expertise, resources, and collaboration. In particular, this work emerges from my experience as director of the Center for Urban Innovation at the Georgia Institute of Technology. As director of that research center, I conducted a number of empirical projects on the emerging smart cities project in collaboration with a team of research scientists, postdoctoral fellows, graduate students, and faculty colleagues. In addition to the projects we conducted, I had the opportunity to observe many other projects first hand through our participation in the MetroLab Network, the National Institute of Science and Technology's Global Cities Team Challenge, and conferences, convenings, and summits with professionals from other cities, universities, and companies engaged in producing and analyzing the smart cities project.

Specifically, I want to recognize the work of Thomas Lodato and Emma French, each of whom worked with the Center for Urban Innovation for several years. The projects they worked on are referenced throughout the book. I also appreciate the research contributions of the postdoctoral fellows and graduate students who supported the center's research, including Supraja Sudharsan, Chris Thayer, Taylor Shelton, Sarah Carnes, Greg Giuffrida, MacKenzie Wood, and Caroline Golin.

I also thank colleagues who contributed to my thinking about this book, how to frame it, and how to present this topic through the lens of economic geography and uneven development and with an eye toward the future of urban planning practice. Those colleagues include the external reviewers who were kind enough to provide comments on the book; my editors at Columbia University Press, Eric Schwartz and Lowell Frye; and students in my courses on urban and regional policy. In addition, I am grateful to the following colleagues for their advice, insights, and support: Elizabeth Mynatt, Nichola Lowe, Laura Wolf-Powers, Greg Schrock, Marc Doussard, Harley Etienne, Rachel Weber, Karen Chapple, Amy Glasmeier, Dieter Kogler, David Bailey, Robyn Dowling, Scott Campbell, John-Paul Addie, Helen Lawton Smith, Dieter Kogler, and Jamie Peck. I am also grateful to the American Association of Geographers and the Regional Studies Association for their recognition of my work.

I would also like to thank Benjamin Flowers who—again—put life on hold while I pursued another all-consuming book project. I am grateful for that patience and for the unwavering belief in my capacities. Finally, a special note of appreciation to my parents, Don and Linda Clark; and my adviser, Susan Christopherson. I am nothing if not well-trained. And that is because of them.

UNEVEN
INNOVATION

1

UNEVEN INNOVATION

The Evolution of the Urban Technology Project

T HERE is a robust tradition of technocratic solutions to
urban policy challenges in urban planning and engineering.
That history is characterized by wide pendulum swings
back and forth between solutions and the backlash against them.
This pattern is perhaps most familiar in the oft-cited and certainly
overstylized conflict narrative of autocratic public administrator
Robert Moses and organic community organizer Jane Jacobs.[1]
The more accurate story of the backlash pattern in urban planning against the urban renewal programs of the mid-twentieth
century—with its multilane highways, (new) Brutalist multiblock
government centers, and, later, its hyper-historicized festival
marketplaces—is better told in books like *After the Planners*.[2] If
urban planning practice proves any inescapable reality, it is that
large-scale interventions in the urban landscape are often, if not
always, controversial. Whether it is Baron Haussmann's Paris,
Nicolae Ceausescu's Bucharest, or Robert Moses's New York City,
such interventions rarely reconcile the issue of scale—city and
community, neighborhood and nation-state, people and place.

And so, the smart cities conversation starts in the early twenty-
first century by trying to shake off the weight of this heavy
baggage about how technology intervenes in the city. The initial

challenge for the smart cities project lies in producing a narrative that allows for the active consideration of big urban interventions without triggering the "after the planners" backlash of the last half century. To date, the great accomplishment of the smart cities project is in achieving this rhetorical goal. This is why the smart cities project should be taken seriously as a policy project.

The smart cities project cleared this first rhetorical hurdle for two important reasons. First is the absence of a compelling counter-narrative to the expansion of urban innovations. The second is a conceptual flexibility within the smart cities project that allows for its impact to be framed as substantial and its implementation as iterative and incremental; that is, as discrete projects rather than as physical interventions in the built environment.

Further, smart cities are difficult to define. Almost every discussion of smart cities begins with an effort to define the term or to assert that no definition is possible or necessary. The resulting "fuzzy concept" is reminiscent of Ann Markusen's classic critique of such terms across the development and policy literature. Markusen argued that such terms obscure the role of specific actors and identifiable processes, leading to analyses and subsequent conclusions that lack both rigor and policy relevance. To apply Markusen's argument here, if one cannot identify who are the actors in the smart cities project and the processes pushing the project forward, then one cannot identify where policy interventions can make a difference in how the project proceeds.[3]

Then, as now, there are a number of possible responses to the proliferation of fuzzy concepts. The call for additional empirical and comparative work is one common response.[4] Several recent books respond to this appeal with case studies and examples of smart cities programs and projects.[5] This emerging body of research responds to Markusen's call for specificity, formal identification, and categorization. In so doing, those works draw boundaries around earlier vague and amorphous understandings of smart cities deployments. However, like the response to Markusen's original critique of fuzzy concepts in the context of regional development, the resulting case studies provide specificity at the cost of generalizability. In the smart cities case in particular, the ability to implement smart cities programs increases as their individual characteristics are analyzed and understood. But replication is only one goal of the research. By studying smart cities projects as they unfold, the research focuses on the presence of smart cities efforts rather than their absence. In other words, the approach spotlights urban innovations. This book pulls that light back and shines it at a different scale, one the exposes the actors and processes involved in producing uneven innovation. In other words, this book places the smart cities project in its broader context.

. . .

A critique of the smart cities model might be expected from professionals with expertise in urban planning and policy. After all, it was those in community economic development who proposed the most comprehensive alternative to previous large-scale technocratic interventions in the built environment concentrating on small-scale, continuous, and incremental investments in people and places driven and defined by communities themselves.[6] However, after two decades of both disinterest and disinvestment in community economic development, urban planning has lost much of its capacity to launch a sustained response to an urban technology project of the scale of smart cities. The slow starvation of community development, a subfield of urban planning that emerged from the backlash against urban renewal, resulted in a failure to replace the academics and practitioners who brought us participatory planning and a theoretical discourse about planning in the face of political and economic power.[7] As a consequence, the most substantial critique of smart cities has developed in urban geography, not urban planning, focusing on the generation, acquisition, use of, and access to smart cities data (critical data studies), which is a piece of the puzzle but not the whole picture.[8]

The smart cities project has mapped out a path toward implementation by effectively capturing the conversation and working around the history of technocratic approaches to urban policy and planning. The question now is what form that implementation will take, not whether this new urban technology project will move forward. In other words, the question now is whether the smart cities objects, systems, and platforms, and the data that are derived from and empowers them, will be owned and governed by private companies or by cities themselves.

In reality, there are many possible paths toward the promise of smart cities, and some of them align with community economic development practice and public participation. However, other paths replicate a pattern of development and redevelopment reminiscent of those practices that brought about the backlash against urban renewal in the first place. That is, projects that are too big, too fast, and too uneven and that give far too little thought to the existing built environment and the people who live in it and, simultaneously, too much consideration for the so-called revenue potential of places and what can be extracted from them.

In many ways, then, smart cities are a new approach to an old question: how to remake cities for the purposes of further and continued economic development with the functional consent (if not the real support) of the people who actually live there. In analyzing the smart cities project, then, it is essential to sort out what is new or novel about this urban development strategy— what is actually innovative about either the processes producing smart cities or the products and services deployed in smart cities. And, what is decidedly both old and path-dependent about the smart cities project—its goals and practices. Thus far, the combination of these novel processes and known practices has produced a predictable outcome: *uneven innovation.*

My research on smart cities led me to question several assumptions behind the project—both what it means for cities and what it does to them. The result is an alternative framework for thinking about smart cities as an economic development project with implications for labor and work, participation and engagement, infrastructure and real estate investment, inter-jurisdictional cooperation and competition, and the relationship between public and private interests. This framework is captured in five key premises about how, under the novelty of the smart cities project, we must ask the same core questions about the private development of public assets; namely, cities.

PREMISE ONE

Uneven innovation is both where we have been and where we are going.

A core argument in this book is that urban innovation is producing uneven innovation. Effectively, the smart cities project is following the patterns and practices that produced contemporary uneven development in the first place. The result is a technologically uneven landscape where places within cities and between cities have different resources, access, opportunities, and outcomes. There are multiple reasons for this. Primary among them is the explanation laid out in chapter 2—that urban problems are generated not by characteristics of the city but by characteristics of the economy. This is, of course, a way of updating what Neil Smith said about the relationship between uneven development and the economy in 1984.

> The point is that uneven development is the hallmark of the geography of capitalism. It is not just that capitalism fails to develop evenly, that due to accidental and random factors the geographical development of capitalism represents some stochastic deviation from a generally even process. The uneven development of capitalism is structural rather than statistical. The resulting geographical patterns are thoroughly determinate (as opposed to "determinist") and are thus unique to capitalism.[9]

Simply put, uneven innovation is a technologically enhanced articulation of uneven development that is accelerated and enabled through these new technologies and the distribution of the platforms and systems that enabled them. The underlying inequities produced, however, should be understood as a feature and not a "bug" in the economic operating system that produces and reproduces those inequalities.

A second explanation for uneven innovation is that the smart cities project is simply not intended to provide equal access or manage market failures (see chapter 3). Smart cities are an industry-driven rather than a public-driven project. As a consequence, the project is principally designed to create consumers rather than serve citizens. The market is thus differentiated in response to variations in the resources and capacities of different localities and consumers. Smart cities projects are intended to capitalize on variations, not to mitigate them. In other words, the smart cities industry is designed to make and serve distinct markets with the ability and the willingness to pay for products and services.

A third argument is that the smart cities industry is driving new forms of urban entrepreneurialism both for cities and for citizens (see chapter 4). For cities, the result is an emerging form of inter-jurisdictional competition in which cities compete for primacy as technology centers rather than as hubs for specific industrial specializations. This form of interjurisdictional competition serves to pit all places in competition with one another and to push cities to take a permissive approach to technological experimentation. The examples of Sidewalk Labs in Toronto (Alphabet/Google), Amazon's H_2 competition, and Uber's search for cities in which to pilot its autonomous vehicle experiments illustrate the point. Less well understood is the way in which smart cities accelerate a form of urban entrepreneurialism that fundamentally reconfigures work space, thus enabling labor flexibility and providing an alternative framework for precarious work arrangements embedded and reflected in the built environment itself.[10]

These three arguments about the origins of urban problems, the evolution of smart cities firms' strategies, and a new urban entrepreneurialism harken back to the broader conversation within economic geography about uneven development. Smart cities provide a contemporary empirical example of what has become largely a theoretical construct in urban and economic geography in the decades since the conceptual framework was introduced. What is identified as uneven development, particularly in modern capitalist economies, is often (though not always) the outcome of market failures rather than of an analysis of the processes behind those failures. Thus, this discourse is heavy with a critique of local and national governments for shirking their responsibility to manage and mitigate these failures on behalf of the citizens and residents they represent. It is all too often a conversation about the outcomes of uneven development and not its origins. Consequently, the policy remedies implicitly accept these outcomes, leaving the processes that produce them largely uncontested.

The smart cities project, however, actually operates within an existing set of neoliberal practices that drive devolution, deregulation, and privatization.[11] The novelty of smart cities—to the extent it exists—is not in its orientation toward questions of equity, distribution, or civic participation. As an industry-driven project, smart cities should be expected to produce outcomes that serve the priorities of the firms and industries invested in the industry's growth and expansion—like any other industry. It should not be expected that smart cities have some inherent progressive orientation because they seek to partner with cities to develop their products and services. Without an effort to intentionally design the smart cities project to mitigate rather than exacerbate existing inequalities, there is little chance that the project will result in a different outcome than any other kind of development pursued in the past.

PREMISE TWO

The tech sector needs the city as a source of subsidy and risk reduction; it exploits uneven innovation and maintains it.

One of the questions surrounding the smart cities project is why the technology sector selected the city as a scale of action and engagement. Until very recently, technology firms—especially those for whom the collection of data is at the core of their business model—have operated rhetorically, if not actually, as deterritorialized entities. The second premise in this alternative framework is that the technology sector needs the city as a source of both subsidy and risk reduction for its innovation process.

Like firms in other sectors, tech firms select specific jurisdictions to achieve discrete operational goals. For example, to avoid tax liabilities, Apple located operations in Ireland.[12] Likewise, in order to minimize labor costs and employment commitments, technology firms have developed a division of labor that carves out core and peripheral work functions and outsources noncore functions to large, minimally regulated labor markets—both within industrialized countries and to developing economies. Specialist firms such as Cognizant Technology Solutions exist to manage the dynamics of this spatial division of labor. And, to retain core functions and core employees who perform them, technology firms are well known for providing attractive corporate campuses in regions that appeal to those valued employees.[13] Agglomeration economies persist, as in the classic case of Silicon Valley, but with a distinctive pattern of spatial separation between innovation and production functions.[14] Even Amazon's effort to select a location for a second corporate campus outside its original Seattle headquarters followed an established practice of investing in multiple sites of production in order to limit the power of any one jurisdiction in negotiations over the terms and conditions of taxation and regulation.[15] Equally predictably, Amazon's search was explicitly framed against the backdrop of a dispute with its hometown, Seattle, over the costs of its corporate citizenship and the extent of its civic responsibilities. That was a battle Amazon ultimately won.

These are established locational strategies among large, modern corporations.[16] Although technology firms are often singled out for their innovative and disruptive strategies, these locational practices are more typical than exceptional.[17] The practices are intended to hold down the costs of production that are affected by regulations and costs imposed or incurred by specific jurisdictions. What has been geographically distinctive about technology firms was never the geography of their production but, rather, the geographic claims about their markets. Many technology firms claim that there are no significant geographic barriers to their market expansion. The functional limits lie in their ability to understand the scope and extent of the market: who can afford to buy their products and services and under what conditions. The urban technology project faces the same challenge as the rest of the sector: developing and scaling the revenue model. The firms are limited only by their internal capacity to reliably gather appropriate market intelligence and scale fast enough to meet demand. As the tech sector has discovered cities, geography, to an increasing extent, matters for defining markets as well as for production strategies. And notably, it is the same geography that has risen to prominence: the city.

So, why cities? Why did the technology industry, which has been so successful so quickly, operating explicitly as a de-territorialized project, suddenly develop an interest in cities in the 2010s? From an economic geography perspective, there are many potential reasons for the technology sector to choose urban agglomerations.[18] However, for technology advocates and CEOs who have made consistent arguments about the diminishing importance of national boundaries and antiquated notions of governmental regulations and administration, the interest in cities is curious. It is also underexplored. Because urban policy and planning debates in the United States have centered on regionalism for decades, the explicit positioning of the city as the center of the urban innovation conversation is more than just unexpected.[19] The turn toward smart cities by the technology sector suggests an increasing recognition of the importance of urban agglomerations to the future of the innovation process and the identification of markets.

So, in one sense, the city is cast as a customer or a client. Cities buy smart cities objects, systems, and platforms and provide services and infrastructure to citizens. In this sense, "the city" acts as an administrative unit (cities, counties, regional authorities, special districts) engaged in service delivery in each jurisdiction or territory. In a second sense, the city is administrative territory tasked with managing services. But cities are also designated and regulated places where potential smart cities clients and customers are aggregated and where firms can find them. In both senses, the city provides an organizing logic—a distinct and delineated geography—for collecting information on the characteristics and behaviors of people and organizations in the built environment. Also, the city serves as a market space for selling the objects, systems, and platforms developed by the smart cities project. Whether it is the city purchasing a system for managing public services or individual customers or citizens purchasing services to optimize their individual behaviors, the city provides a scoping mechanism for product development and deployment. Thus, the smart cities project operates as an enabling industry to sell technologies both *to cities* and *in cities*.

The smart cities project operates in both a contested policy space and an emerging market space, sitting somewhere between the private, public, and third sectors. Smart cities, as an industry, are focused on the design, development, and deployment of an emerging class of cross-platform, service-integrated technology products that enhance infrastructure performance and expand services. This process of technology diffusion into the public sector focuses on "upgrading," efficiency, and broadening access and opportunity on a platform of open innovation.

That is the promise. The reality is that the smart cities project is entering a market space where the distinction between citizen and consumer is actively contested. The functional difference between vendors selling a solution and a city providing services is rarely specified. The criteria that determine the difference between public and private spaces are also unstated. Thus, cities serve as a site of both subsidy and risk reduction for a range of products and services that extend well beyond those designed for smart cities applications alone.

Among the most important contributions of smart cities programs and projects is the integration of locational data with other policy-relevant data that, in the past, have been collected and/or analyzed without geography as a central variable.[20] Urban geographers engaged in critical data studies have argued effectively for academics to increase methodological and theoretical attention on the use and interpretation of locational data from these projects and programs, for both research and policy.[21] Other researchers coming from digital media and computing fields also have begun to engage questions about location and scale in data collection, analysis, and use by the technology sector.[22]

The next step, then, is to turn analytical attention toward the locational choices of the smart cities industry as it constructs the logic behind its own emerging economic geography. Scholars have extensively critiqued the ambiguity and even underlying arrogance of the term *smart city* emphasizing how the word *smart* belies a limited understanding of real-world places, the people who live in them, and the systems that make them work.[23] And to some, the scale of the city for the smart cities project is simply viewed as a rhetorical move based in marketing. However, the selection of the city scale can also be seen as a deliberate locational decision by an industry collocating innovation, production, and consumption in the same place as an intentional firm strategy.[24] That is, the city serves as a site of production and a site of consumption in the smart cities project, as well as a site where new products, systems, and platforms are identified, designed, and prototyped. Thus, the city is a strategic site for the collocation of the entire production process, from innovation through consumption for an industry (the tech sector) that has long argued that it operates beyond the territorial boundaries and the benefits of proximities that govern the locational logic of legacy industries.

PREMISE THREE

The smart cities project is enabled through "fast policy," a combination of devolution and policy mobilities that circumvents traditional models of policy transfer.

The rapid proliferation of smart cities programs and projects raises questions about how places are determining what experiments and partnerships to pursue. The third premise in this book is that "fast policy" process provides an essential rationale for the exchange of so-called best practices outside of the standard processes of policy transfer, and it explains an otherwise inexplicable avoidance of evaluation of projects and programs before their broader diffusion. Recently developed urban innovation networks serve as the key intermediaries promoting technological solutions ranging from open data to civic participation to mobility solutions. These networks facilitate information exchange among cities and increase the capacity of cities to collect and implement smart cities projects.

What makes the fast policy process and the networks that facilitate it problematic is the proliferation of new programs and projects that lack systematic evaluation or validation. Public policies are generally assessed after a pilot phase and evaluated to determine whether outcomes align with goals. These questions include concerns about coverage (who benefits?), effectiveness, and cost. Rapid and direct policy transfer based on best practices rather than validated models that are subject to assessment circumvents the ability of cities (and other stakeholders) to evaluate alternatives against one another. In other words, fast policy feeds the taken-for-granted assumption that technology offers solutions to urban problems (chapter 2) and that the only question is which solution to choose. Urban innovation networks provide the menu of solutions; technology partners provide the services selected (see chapter 6).

PREMISE FOUR

The smart cities project exacerbates and amplifies precarious work, embedding labor flexibility in the production and operations of the built environment.

The smart cities project builds on and extends the signature trends of neoliberalism: privatization, devolution, and deregulation.[25] Derivative of these trends is the increase in labor flexibility and precarious work. In recent decades, labor flexibility has resulted in a decline in long-term employment arrangements and an increase in contingent employment arrangements.[26] The rise of ride-hailing services is one example of how smart cities platforms (ride-hailing cell phone applications) extend labor flexibility and increase the simultaneous privatization and casualization of work space (the private car rather than fleets of vehicles or public transport).

The smart cities project and the infrastructure and connectivity it requires turn the city into a platform for new forms of flexibility and enable the expansion of precarious work within the existing systems of labor and consumer regulations. Advocating for a technology-enabled service platform capable of providing the tools and connectivity once offered in an office and by an employer changes the landscape of work in cities. In other words, just as employers once offered health insurance, pensions, and skill training, so too did employers once offer desks, computers, Internet connections, and access to a bathroom. The smart cities project allows for the work in smart cities to be performed outside both the traditional employment relationship and the traditional work space. Just as the burden for health care, social security, and labor market reproduction has shifted away from firms and toward the state and the individual, so, too, has the burden for providing the platform for performing work shifted to city and the worker.

As Alex Rosenblat noted in her 2018 study of Uber's business practices: "Uber does treat drivers both like consumers and like workers. By blurring these lines, Uber creates a legacy for how we all identify as workers or consumers. Uber benefits from this strategic ambiguity because it is hard to decide which rules apply to its model."[27] In other words, the smart cities project destabilizes more than the boundaries between employer and employee, further eroding the psychological contract. The smart cities industry also disputes the boundaries between worker and consumer and the rights and responsibilities that accrue differently to each role. The rights and responsibilities of citizens and residents are equally ambiguous and increasingly precarious.

PREMISE FIVE

The data are the product, and the
revenue model is under construction.

The original smart cities project imagined by IBM and other early advocates identified a set of applications of new technologies for what was considered to be a large and potentially predictable new market associated with the territory and function of cities.[28] More recently, however, things have gotten complicated for the smart cities industry. Where once the city seemed to present a large, predictable, and conveniently delineated market, administratively and geographically, it has become increasingly less obvious where the value and where the revenue in the smart cities project lie. The smart cities business model could once be summarized as (1) extract the data of the city from the city, and, if possible, sell it back to the city, while simultaneously (2) developing smart cities objects, systems, and platforms for cities, firms, and consumers or users. Today, that strategy seems less certain. Among the challenges in estimating the size of the smart cities market is understanding the value of smart cities data and the costs of acquiring, curating, managing, and marketing it.[29]

This uncertainty, however, has not stifled experimentation. The case of Sidewalk Labs in Toronto remains an active example of real-time strategies as a technology company assembles a firm-specific and largely privatized urban economic development model merging real estate, data-harvesting, and creative class practices.[30] This example involves a division of one of the leading and largest technology firms, Alphabet, the parent company of Google, designing an ever-expanding plan for Toronto's waterfront. These plans include a whole array of proposed innovations to the relationship between developers and cities and resulting models of urban governance. It is about more than technology.

The distribution of the costs and benefits of such neighborhood-scale smart cities projects and their long-term economic value to cities and to firms are difficult to assess, in part, because standards for data ownership and use remain ambiguous, dynamic, and increasingly varied from place to place.[31] In other words, the size of the required subsidy remains uncertain, as is the need for public subsidy at all. With all the promises of data innovation and the Internet of Things, three key issues prevent the accurate evaluation of the size and value of these markets and, thus, the level of private and public investment or subsidy justified to access them: (a) the connectivity requirements and the distribution of those requirements among actors, (b) the governance of data (privacy, security, ownership, and access), and (c) the distribution of the risks and responsibilities among actors; ultimately, the exchange and use value of smart cities data.

Even with these uncertainties, many investors and observers are convinced of the value of the data collected, aggregated, and analyzed from smart cities programs and projects for the purposes of future and continuous product development. Much of the business discussion about smart cities concentrates on these possibilities: interfaces and visualization tools to make data accessible to communities of users, to customers. Among the most interesting contributions of smart cities programs and projects is their explicit integration of locational data with other policy-relevant data that have, in the past, been collected and/or analyzed without geography as a central variable.[32] Urban geographers engaged in critical data studies have argued effectively for academics to increase methodological and theoretical attention on the use and interpretation of locational data from these projects and programs, for both research and policy.[33] Now industry is paying attention.

CHALLENGING THE TECHNOLOGY DISCOURSE: FROM UNEVEN DEVELOPMENT TO UNEVEN INNOVATION

There is, of course, a role for the public sector in enabling or minimizing uneven development. However, it is important to understand the scope and extent to which uneven investment is not exclusively (or even primarily) a consequence of public sector decision making (or its absence). The proposition that local governments can significantly slow the processes that generate inequalities operating across land, labor, and capital markets governed and regulated at national and international scales (when they are regulated at all) is optimistic at best. This is a persistent issue in public policy and, specifically, in urban policy and is discussed in detail in chapter 2. Promising and effective possible policy interventions are discussed in this chapter and in chapters 5 and 6. But, in any case, a focus on the city's capacity to mitigate the effects of uneven development addresses the symptoms and not the disease. Gentrification and displacement are the outcomes of uneven development. Uneven investment is the core problem.

In the smart cities context, establishing this distinction is not simply a rhetorical exercise. Because the smart cities project is fundamentally a project defining the ways in which new technologies will be distributed in and across cities today and in the future, the focus on distribution in the deployment design is critical. One potential of smart cities is the opportunity to force a reckoning with past development practices—and to design a new model of infrastructure investment at the city scale. The uneven development critique may not be able to produce a public-sector intervention that resolves the existing manifestations of the economy problem in cities, but it may be able to motivate the design of new policy models that break the cycle of complicity between the public and private sectors in decisions about infrastructure investments. And, if smart cities are indeed a platform that will guide and govern economic development (read: private and public investment in place) going forward, that one intervention matters a great deal.

Despite attempts to argue otherwise, urban agglomerations remain central to social reproduction and economic development in the contemporary world economy. Indeed, much of recent urban theory has concentrated on how to conceptualize this central role of cities in the global economy and what that means for people, places, and production.[34] Consistent among these explanatory frameworks is the acknowledgment that cities are distinct socially constructed spaces.[35] Cities are concentrations of people and processes forming an uneven landscape both within their own boundaries and compared with spaces beyond their territories.

Cities remain perhaps the clearest evidence of uneven development. Smart cities are further evidence. Cities are aggregations of people and activities into geographic concentrations that both facilitate transactions and minimize their cost. Although the smart cities conversation is often weighted toward the definition and operationalization of *smart*, the conversation is fundamentally about *cities* and the benefits that accrue to urban agglomerations and the ways in which those benefits are particularly important for the development, deployment, and adoption of disruptive technologies.[36] The production of smart cities, then, is best understood through an explanation of the processes and actors that produce urban agglomerations in the first instance. It has long been argued that cities provide particular evidence of the ways in which space is socially constructed and, with that, the capacity for cities to produce economic value and establish and embed political power.[37]

The purpose of this book is to sift through the buzz about smart cities and provide a needed critical perspective, highlighting both the potential of these emerging technologies and their attendant capacity to exacerbate existing inequalities and even produce new ones. The book presents the smart cities project as what it is: a technology diffusion challenge operating in a dynamic and contested space between the public sector and the private market. A central argument in the book is that technology development is the easy part; it is the design *for* and deployment *into* this liminal space—twenty-first century cities, where governance, regulation, access, participation, and representation are all complex and highly localized—that is the real challenge. In other words, it is the city, not the technology, that must be better understood to pursue the potential of the smart cities project.

The distinctive—and perhaps unique—contribution of this book is in unpacking the discussion about smart cities as a new and wholly novel experience for cities and embedding it in the long and complex trajectory of uneven development in cities and regions. In addition, the book offers a critique that leads to substantive and specific policy prescriptions. The intention here is to both analyze the smart cities project as it stands and present a path toward an alternative future in which smart cities lead to more efficient, open, sustainable, and equitable places. The book also contributes to the socioeconomic analysis of cities and regions and particularly to urban policy and technology-led economic development.

To accomplish this, I analyze the smart cities project from a number of vantage points across six thematic chapters. Unlike many of the recent works on smart cities, this book is not a discussion or a critique of projects in various world cities.[38] Nor is it a discussion of the smart cities experience in a particular city. Instead, this book lays out an approach to thinking about the smart cities project more broadly, across cases and places. Once we understand smart cities as an emerging market and an enabling industry, the next step is to analyze how its products, processes, actors, markets, work, and governance are arranged and organized.

Chapter 2 places the smart cities project in the context of the long history of *technocratic solutions* to urban policy challenges: projects, programs, and products. Advocates of smart cities objects, systems, and platforms argue that the tools and services they enable can offer solutions to "urban problems"; some are so-called people problems, and others are urban systems problems. Many of the most prominent smart cities applications fall into this discourse: predictive policing, traffic signal coordination, storm sewer monitoring, and human services tracking. All of these applications are effectively new ways of observing urban problems; they are not solutions. This is in part because the origins of these problems lie not with some characteristic of the city but, rather, with characteristics of the economy.[39] And, as has been the case in the past, blaming cities for problems generated by the economy is an effort to assign agency to places so they can bear both the cost and the responsibility for negative externalities generated by choices made elsewhere.[40] Redesigning the built environment doesn't fix structural economic problems. It does, however, rearrange structures that can provide economic development opportunities across the uneven landscapes that emerge. In other words, it does provide a platform.

As chapter 2 establishes that the smart cities project is a continuation of a pattern of engineering and technology interventions in cities, chapter 3 shows how the smart cities project fits a pattern of market-making in the technology sector. The smart cities project itself is an effort to create a distinct industry for which cities are both the institutional customer for smart cities objects, systems, platforms, and data and the geographic container defining and scoping the consumer market for smart cities products and services sold to individuals, institutions, and other firms. The smart cities project is engaged in a market-making exercise that remains publicly agnostic about whether it is designing services for citizens or products for consumers, although that distinction makes a difference.

It is difficult to understand a market without clarifying who is purchasing products and services and for what purpose, particularly if there is a perceived public purpose. The extent to which public sector subsidies are required or requested to facilitate the smart cities project rests, in part, on whether and to what extent the industry serves not only public versus private interests but also localized versus de-territorialized economic interests. Cities tend to make economic development investments to benefit actors or activities within their jurisdiction. The smart cities project continues to be ambiguous about contributions to urban and regional economies beyond an argument about increased efficiencies and interjurisdictional competition.

Chapter 4 picks up the conversation about interjurisdictional competition and casts it within a longer historical narrative about urban entrepreneurialism. Although the smart cities project is clearly about marketing cities as platforms for technology-driven economic development, it is also about some more nuanced forms of urban entrepreneurialism. First, chapter 4 lays out how the interjurisdictional competition in the smart cities project is rooted in a need to compel cities to comply with technological experimentation and data extraction. Among the novel elements of this urban entrepreneurialism is the elimination of competition based on localized specialization or embedded competencies. Instead, as the Amazon headquarters selection episode demonstrated in 2018–19, competition has become an undifferentiated notion about making cities attractive places for the technology sector rather than a story about technical specializations such as biotechnology, advanced manufacturing, or financial services.

Second, chapter 4 analyzes another type of urban entrepreneurialism: the work in smart cities. The smart cities project builds on and extends labor flexibility. It supports flexible work practices by producing flexible work spaces. Labor flexibility has, in recent decades, resulted in less long-term employment and more contingent and precarious employment arrangements. One recent example, noted earlier, is the development of ride-hailing driving as a specific occupational category. The smart cities project extends labor flexibility by extending the casualization of work to work space. Advocating for a technology-enabled urban platform capable of providing the tools and connectivities once offered with an office and by the employer changes the landscape of work in cities. In other words, just as employers once offered health insurance, pensions, and skill training, they also once offered work space and the tools required to perform work tasks. The smart cities project provides an opportunity for the work in smart cities to be performed effectively outside an office space as well as outside the employment relationship.

A core argument in the book is that there is less novelty in the smart cities project than its advocates suggest; however, there are new processes at work. Positioning the smart cities project in its historical context makes what is distinct about smart cities more evident. Chapter 5 focuses on one new factor: the development of multiple urban innovation networks. These networks enable collaboration among cities and the transfer of policy knowledge through horizontal networks rather than top-down hierarchies. The networks build capacity within cities to conduct the increasingly specialized and highly technical work of smart cities and underscore the importance of embedding expertise within cities. They also produce a new third sector that participates in urban governance and policy design and the acceleration of policy mobilities. There is both potential and risk with these emerging urban innovation networks. But, whether presenting potential or risk, their presence is altering how technology decisions are understood among participating cities and how the work of assessing the adoption and expansion of smart cities projects and programs is conducted.

Chapter 6 analyzes how the smart cities project expands civic engagement. Again, positioning the claims about expanded citizen participation within the history of participatory planning reveals both the potential of smart cities to result in so-called smart citizenship and the barriers present in the current project that prevent that outcome without further intentional interventions. Smart citizenship depends on two factors: the ownership of the data extracted and collected on the characteristics and behaviors of people in cities, and the design and expansion of participatory planning practices made possible through new tools and technologies.

Chapter 7 completes the critique of present patterns and presentation of alternative proposals. The smart cities project acts as a series of mechanisms for exacerbating *uneven development*. This is largely because the smart cities project does nothing to change the processes and conditions described in the first four chapters and implicated in the antecedent iterations of uneven development. Chapter 7 analyzes how uneven development is producing uneven innovation and suggests where the public sector has a possible role in preventing that progression. That chapter reconsiders uneven development as more than an aggregation of its symptoms (as with gentrification) and the inadequate policy responses designed to mitigate them. And, in the process, chapter 7 begins to analyze where cities can exercise their existing power to design an alternative future for smart cities.

Chapter 8 ties these arguments together to propose concrete policy solutions to significant urban problems exacerbated by the smart cities project. These policy proposals are directed at cities themselves as they consider their own smart cities programs and projects. The first proposal is to rethink what the work of smart cities requires and embed innovation capacity within cities to institutionalize programs and invest in their persistent rather than episodic evaluation. The second proposal is to revisit how property rights are assigned to the data on individual characteristics and behaviors extracted from smart cities projects, systems, and platforms. The third proposal is to redesign the scope and coverage of participatory planning practices, given new technologies that can mitigate transportation and communication costs.

Ultimately, communities should be careful not to concede the progress made in forming institutionalized forums where citizens can influence policies and the applications of them (for example, neighborhood planning units). Building on these accomplishments expands citizen decision making, not just civic participation. Proposals around smart citizenship are far more likely to move beyond the performative if they are framed as upgrades to participatory planning practices rather than as substitute formats for civic engagement.

WHY SMART CITIES MATTER

In this book, I argue that the conversation about smart cities is a conversation about urban planning and policy. It requires two types of expertise to make clear judgments, plans, and policies to take urban innovation forward. First is expertise on cities. That is, knowledge about the functions, operations, histories, cultures, systems, politics, and geographies of cities is necessary. This point may seem obvious. However, as will be seen time and again in this book, the conversation about smart cities is situated as a technology discussion.

Cities, in this discussion, are flat, undifferentiated terrains. There are reasons for this construction. For a technology project, the local is the enemy: specificity, difference, variation—all require tailoring. Tailoring requires time, knowledge, and money. The persistent use of language about cities as testbeds is telling, as are the references to so-called urban operating systems. In this construction, the nuances of these cities are annoyances complicating the analytics. In fact, it is the acquisition of massive amounts of data that flattens the specific and smooths over the outliers. Conversely, professionals in the fields with domain knowledge about cities strive to document, understand, and categorize these nuances. The effort is made to identify variations and develop typologies that describe and explain complex urban systems but do not obscure or eliminate them.

The second type of expertise necessary to analyze smart cities is the ability to analyze how and why economic activities evolve and diffuse differently in and across different places. Because the smart cities project explicitly implicates space, its analysis requires a spatial analysis. In short, analyzing smart cities requires some knowledge of economic geography. The smart cities project is a discussion about rearranging the resources and assets in cities and regions and how and whether those assets and services are available and to whom. Whether the issue is new services or better services or publicly or privately provisioning these new or enhanced assets and services, an understanding of spatial economies is necessary.

This is not to say that economics provides the necessary clarity; rather, an understanding of how economies operate in specific places is needed. This means that the conversation required touches on many elements of proximity: organizational, institutional, technological, and geographic. Further, the understanding of how space constrains and amplifies economic systems and outcomes is necessary to understand how smart cities change these arrangements and opportunities. In no small way, the smart cities project parallels transitions and changes in other industries, thus placing its analysis squarely within the boundaries and expertise of economic geography.

The recent attention paid to cities—especially the attention aimed at better governance and administration—is surprisingly disconnected from the last century of in-depth urban scholarship. Today, urban knowledge is focused on the ability to gather, construct, process, and analyze massive datasets about any number of urban (or not-so-urban) phenomena. The urban social sciences are playing a backseat role in the development of smart cities initiatives. Instead, the emerging field of urban science is setting policy priorities and determining use cases for the smart cities project. In fact, most of the scholarship on smart cities has taken this form, focusing on case studies of smart cities programs and projects as interventions in the built environment or with urban communities, or in the operations of city government.[41] The absence of established critical disciplines—for example, urban geography, urban sociology, urban history, urban economics, urban anthropology, and urban planning and policy—in the development of the smart cities project is conspicuous.

This absence is not for lack of some experience in these disciplines with the development and diffusion of technologies. Urban and economic geographers have long studied innovation as part of the broader disciplinary project of mapping and analyzing the spatial distribution of economic activities within and across cities, regions, and countries. In recent years, technology and innovation have gained privileged positions of prominence in these industry analyses. Researchers are particularly focused on processes of technology diffusion and policy mobilities and how regional economic ecosystems absorb new technologies and incorporate them into existing complexes of firms, industries, and industrial specializations. In other words, they focus on how incumbent systems incorporate new processes, products, materials, and actors. From a regional economic policy perspective, this effort isolates the factors that contribute to or detract from economic development—which places become the next Silicon Valley or the next Detroit.

In this book, I argue that uneven innovation is a consequence of uneven development. Uneven development is both a historically contingent consequence of past practices and a dynamic process driven by contemporary choices. The common critique of the public sector's role in the production of uneven development greatly overestimates the level of agency that (local) public officials and public institutions have to intervene in the investment and disinvestment processes that produce uneven development and the possible impact those interventions would have on the landscape. Uneven development is a multiscalar process, and the ability of cities to mitigate the consequences is significantly constrained. The smart cities project, however, is rapidly changing the impact of those constraints. In particular, the role of data in the smart cities project is shifting processes of public sector privatization while revealing new opportunities for cities to act.

As noted earlier, technology diffusion is certainly not a challenge unique to the smart cities industry. It is often the case with new technologies—particularly new systems technologies—that diffusion proves to be problematic. Innovation policy in general, as well as innovative firms individually, struggle with this challenge.[42] New materials, processes, and products often face surprisingly slow adoption rates. Incumbent systems are difficult to dislodge even when there is clear evidence that a new system—or elements of it—would produce a greener, faster, or safer production system, service, or product. This can be observed across multiple sectors, including energy, transportation, and manufacturing. The smart cities project faces similar challenges.

There are many barriers to technology absorption. First, incumbent systems often represent large sunk costs. Replacing them is viewed as more expensive in the short run regardless of the long-run efficiencies that ultimately might accrue. Visualizing this issue of incumbent costs and legacy systems in the smart cities context can be overwhelming: roads, sidewalks, signs, telephone poles, streetlights, and electricity grids all require upgrading, modification, or replacement.

Second, there are often regulatory barriers to technology diffusion in industries with strong standards and certification regimes. Again, applied to the smart city, the challenge of meeting standards in a public sector context is daunting. The standards are also not uniform across localities. In addition, these are not always policy barriers. It is important to note that many of the standards and certifications that limit what materials and processes are acceptable in production processes are industry self-regulations, not public policies imposed by government regulators. In other words, industries themselves are slow to absorb new technologies because of the barriers to entry they impose on themselves.

Third, one of the most compelling cases for technology adoption is about lost competition. Because the adoption of new technology is costly and risky, the motivation to do so is often cast in notions of being left behind. This parallels the arguments behind the interjurisdictional competition driving urban entrepreneurialism described in chapter 4. There is a narrow boundary between an incumbent system and an antiquated system. One is a conservative business choice, and the other is a strategic disadvantage already on the road to decline. When the standards are not set and the market is not clearly defined, it is difficult to determine whether the costs of consistency are actually a choice about obsolescence.

The smart cities project matters because it shapes how technology diffusion and adoption happen in the public sector in the twenty-first century. That may not be its goal, but that will be its effect. The stakes, then, are high for places and for people. How industry establishes the rules of the game for how new technologies influence and define regulations, ownership, distribution, and, ultimately, the subsequent expectations surrounding choices made by the public sector on behalf of citizens and residents matters a great deal. The power of technocratic solutions is that they gloss over choices and scope the range of alternatives to fall within the tolerances of the proposed solution. The question is how a solution will be deployed, not whether it should be at all. The smart cities discourse, as chapters 3 and 4 demonstrate, is designed specifically to minimize the ability of cities and communities to implement the most powerful alternative they hold: the power to say no and bargain for an alternative future.

2

SMART CITIES AS SOLUTIONS

THE smart cities project is often presented as a set of solutions to what is a largely unspecified "urban problem." In a recent article by Wanda Lau in *Architect* magazine, Anthony Townsend, author of one of the first major books on smart cities, *Smart Cities: Big Data, Civic Hackers, and the Quest for a New Utopia* (2013), summarized this position:

> To me, it's a movement that's about using digital technology to solve the timeless problems of cities—the same problems that mayors in Ancient Rome had to solve: How do you collect the trash? How do you secure the streets? How do you address chariot congestion in the center of the city? Now it's Ubers, but it's still ride for hire. We have solutions for urban problems but often they're too costly or there's political gridlock that prevents the solutions we have from being implemented. And sometimes these new digital tools provide shortcuts.[1]

The urban problem, as it is perceived by some technologists, has something to do with failures of the administration, management, and design of cities. These failures are in both capacity and the choices and priorities set by cities for infrastructure and investment. As the argument goes, for all the energy, infrastructure, talent, markets, and money concentrated in cities, they remain challenging places for firms to do business and for people to be productive. Fundamentally, cities are inefficient, expensive, congested, and difficult to navigate. Cities have problems. Technology has solutions.

Turning again to Townsend, "What they [cities] need from technologists are solutions to the problems they identify."[2] In other words, implicit in the smart cities project is an assumption that cities—and urban policy more broadly—cannot and do not have the ability to design technology solutions internally, nor can they select among alternative solutions developed externally. Ironically, forty years on, the smart cities project has flipped the old Ronald Reagan joke on its head: "The nine most terrifying words in the English language are: 'I'm from the government and I'm here to help.'" The smart cities project proposes a new version of this quip: "I'm from a multinational technology firm and I'm here to help." Cities just need to identify their problems; technology will develop the solutions.

• • •

Unfortunately, problem identification is never so easy. In the quest to identify urban problems for which technology is the solution, the arguments of smart cities advocates collide with longstanding debates about the purpose and function of cities. The question is whether cities provide and manage services or whether they do more for their citizens, serving as reflections of the visions and values of the communities they represent. That normative question has been at the heart of debates about urban economic development for a half century and the tension between managerialism and several forms of urban entrepreneurialism[3].

It is not clear whether this collision between the service provider role and the community economic developer role for local government is intentional or inadvertent in the smart cities project. Regardless, the result is that identifying the problem in the public-sector context, in the urban context, is far more complicated than simply proposing technology solutions in pursuit of optimized services or interoperable systems.

It is precisely the vagueness in defining the scope of the urban problem that opens the door to smart cities as the potential solution. In order to provide the specificity required for further analysis, in this chapter, I place the smart cities project within the historical context of proposed technology solutions to urban policy challenges and the debate about cities as active participants in urban economic development. The emphasis here is on what is new and distinct about the smart cities discussion and what are replications of previous proposals for simple technocratic solutions to what are complex economic problems.

In the matter of technical policy analysis, it is crucial to define the problem and to make the case for intervention and investment. In teaching policy and planning analysis, professors drill this methodological approach into urban planning and public policy students: define the scope of the problem and then identify alternative solutions. Indeed, in *Basic Methods of Policy Analysis and Planning*, I and coauthors Patton and Sawicki emphasized the "classical rational problem-solving process": define the problem, determine evaluation criteria, identify alternative policies, evaluate alternative policies, select the preferred policy, and implement the preferred policy.[4] The presumption that these six steps reflect the reality of actual practice is, of course, naive. As Norman Krumholtz pointed out in his 1999 article, "Equitable Approaches to Local Economic Development," the models taught in the classroom are far from the "actually existing" practice of urban economic development.[5] Instead, we observe the increasing dominance of policy transfer practices, the horizontal policy mobilities between cities that short-circuit any established model of a deliberative decision-making and design process (see chapter 5).[6]

The smart cities project has developed in this widening gap between formal models and practice largely independent of broader debates and anxieties about policy process and planning approaches. In a significant way, the argument about smart cities as a public-sector case of technology diffusion follows the case that has been made for the need for these new technologies in the private sector; in short, the widely held and modestly evidenced belief that more technology will enhance performance and productivity a priori.[7] That is, it is less essential to know how all these benefits will accrue to cities than simply to believe that they will.

The smart cities project promises to integrate advances in information and communications technologies (ICT) into urban infrastructure to both upgrade existing services (roads, electric grids, water systems, waste management) and provide new services through the deployment of new systems and platforms (5G, fiber networks, coordinated multimodal transit systems; see figure 2.1). Smart cities propose a new baseline standard of accessibility, intraurban mobility, and a platform for an array of business services provided by (or perhaps through) cities themselves. In effect, the smart cities project is an effort to rethink connectivity in cities and of cities in the broadest sense: as high-tech, geographically bounded platforms produced to support commercial and, to a lesser extent, civic activities. The proposition is that smart cities—through a set of services, products, process, and programs—solve an underlying problem.

Cities face service delivery challenges for which technology can be (and always has been) part of the solution. The Pew Research Center predicts that the U.S. millennial generation

FIGURE 2.1 "Intelligent infrastructure": the backbone of urban innovation. Installation of fiber-optic cables in Strasbourg, France, 2018.

(*Source*: Hadrian/Shutterstock)

(born between 1981 and 1996) will outnumber the nation's baby boomer generation (born between 1946 and 1964) in 2019.[8] This demographic transition highlights the importance of viewing widespread technologies such as handheld devices, Web portals, messaging apps, social media, and a wide range of technology-enhanced interfaces as important tools for expanding public participation. These platforms provide recognizable forums for civic engagement for a new cohort of citizens and residents in a way that in-person public meetings and zoning hearings do not.

This generational transition includes a shift in expectations about public services. The standards for interoperability among functions, platforms, and devices are set to enhance private-sector performance (or perhaps, more to the point, private-sector marketing). Citizens and residents of this younger generation expect public transit smart cards to be contactless and interoperable across multiple modes (metro, bus, train, bicycle, scooter, taxi, and

FIGURE 2.2 Smart-card systems for public transit can facilitate integrated and multimodal public transit. Kuala Lumpur, Malaysia.

(*Source:* Travel Man/Shutterstock)

ride sharing; see figure 2.2). These smart cards are expected to connect to smart phone applications that provide real-time location and scheduling information and that can be connected to a credit card or bank account. This expectation is set by the tech sector's marketing themes around mobility and interoperability despite the exceedingly limited number of real-world examples in which this level of service exists.

How these heightened expectations of a service-embedded city are to be met remains a challenge. Further, whether and to what extent these integrated mobility platforms emerge from the private sector and interface with public services remains uncertain.[9] The questions of how opportunity and access—to the smart cities market and to smart cities–enabled services—are to be distributed and their costs financed remain unanswered. Ambiguity about specifically what problem is being solved and for whom persists. It is this debate that revisits the long history of pendulum swings between technocratic solutions to urban challenges and grassroots efforts to shape the choices made in and about the form and function of cities. One recalls the robust response to urban renewal of participatory planning scholars and activists.[10]

Interestingly, the emphasis in the smart cities conversation remains on the ability of innovations to provide technocratic solutions to deeply entrenched urban infrastructure and design challenges, rather than to provide for enhanced access, opportunity, and participation—as if it were the absence of appropriate technology that limited connectivity, equitable access, and mobility and not political and economic choices.

The question, then, is, in the midst all this buzz, what are the factors contributing to the rapid adoption of the smart cities vision and, simultaneously, the slow implementation of smart cities solutions? Many analysts argue that it is lack of resources— put simply, money—that has delayed implementation. Public funding for infrastructure and upgrading is often inadequate. But there is also a lack of consensus around core questions about coverage and access—specifically, about the distribution of urban innovations—that has slowed momentum and is likely to limit implementation going forward. This debate becomes more nuanced as people elaborate on its causes. For example, one argument is that the revenue model for smart cities solutions is not clear and that the value proposition is thus uncertain. This argument assumes that public services are intended to generate revenue for cities as if they were firms. It overlooks a foundation behind public service(s).

Further, the appropriate allocation of risks and responsibilities between the public and private sectors has not been codified. Indeed, the conversation about pursuing public–private partnerships to push out smart cities technologies appears entirely disconnected from four decades of urban planning and policy literature on validated models and practices; rather, it appears to be associated with underanalyzed experiments.[11] In addition, the lack of formal certifications and accepted industry standards makes the development of interoperable and interconnected urban systems nearly impossible. In effect, the smart cities project cannot move from the individual project scale to the systems scale because it is designed as a set of discrete technology solutions to identifiable problems and not as a systematic shift in practices or process.

Although all these factors affect the speed of adoption (resources, partnership models, and standards and certification), they do not tell the whole story. No government, institution, or industry has emerged to finance what is a complex set of operational and initial capital expenses. And without that economic investment, the questions around partnership models and certifications remain secondary concerns. In the absence of clarity about the resource problem, there remains little discussion of who pays and who benefits from what is essentially a massive systems-upgrading proposal across multiple domains that are, themselves, deployed across an uneven landscape.

Critiques on equity, distribution, and access include, among other things, close readings of the rhetoric around smart cities discussions and analyses of who shows up to the table (or, more often, a critique of who is invited to participate) to engage in those discussions.[12] In other words, the critique surrounds the question of representation in planning smart cities and the absence of marginalized communities in the larger discussion (see figure 2.3).[13] These critiques are elaborations on not only the specifics of the lack of representation and equity in the design and deployment of the smart cities project but also

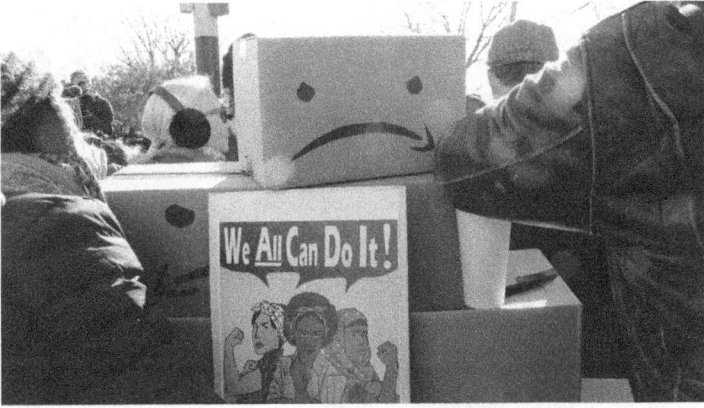

FIGURE 2.3 Turning the Amazon logo upside down. Protest in Queens, New York, against public subsidies for private development: Opposition to the selection of Long Island City, New York, in the Amazon competition for a second headquarters, 2018.

(*Source*: Scootercaster/Shutterstock)

the services and infrastructure in cities (and elsewhere) over time and across places.[14] That is, the argument that smart cities decision making is not representative of the voices of the marginalized and the interests of the disenfranchised does not shed light on smart cities in specifically. It does, however, act as a reminder of the pervasive and intractable inability of many governance regimes to incorporate practices of participatory and deliberative planning into decision making about public-sector services and infrastructure sixty years after the backlash against large-scale technocratic infrastructure planning began (see figure 2.4).

Here we run into an interesting dimension of the smart cities conversation: its striking lack of historical context. When speaking about participatory planning as a response to technocratic infrastructure policies one may visualize Jane Jacobs

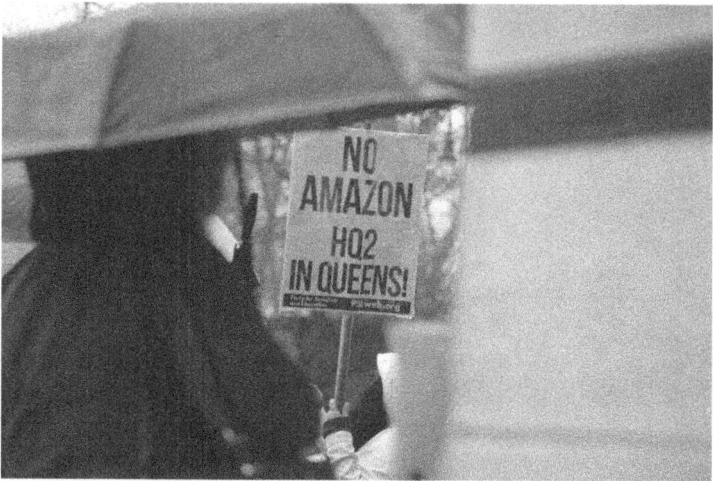

FIGURE 2.4 Public opposition to subsidies for private development: Protest in front on the New York State Governor's Mansion against the selection of Long Island City, New York, in the Amazon competition for a second headquarters, 2018.

(*Source*: Scootercaster/Shutterstock)

confronting Robert Moses: a stylized clash between community and bureaucracy. This begs the question, to what is the smart cities project a reaction? The critiques cited earlier underscore the complexity of the smart cities project—and ultimately question its intentionality as well as its intentions. The smart cities project is an intentional reframing of a very old question in a very old debate: how to provision services in cities. This leads to two follow-up questions. First, what happened to the debate about whether and to what extent cities are service providers and to what extent are they agenda setters? Do smart cities simply provide more services more efficiently, or do they enable citizens to design a shared vision for place and community and enable cities to develop that vision? The second question, perhaps related to the first, is, why is the smart cities project explicitly ahistorical? Why is it important for the smart cities project to elicit a conversation about cities that is divorced from what we already know about cities, seemingly disembodied in both time and space?

To answer these questions, I turn to the first omission in the piecemeal methodological approaches to the smart cities project: defining and scoping the actual problem to which smart cities are the proposed solution. As it turns out, the rhetoric about technology solutions to urban problems is more than a bit jejune; it denies the real problems and the need for real solutions (see figure 2.5).

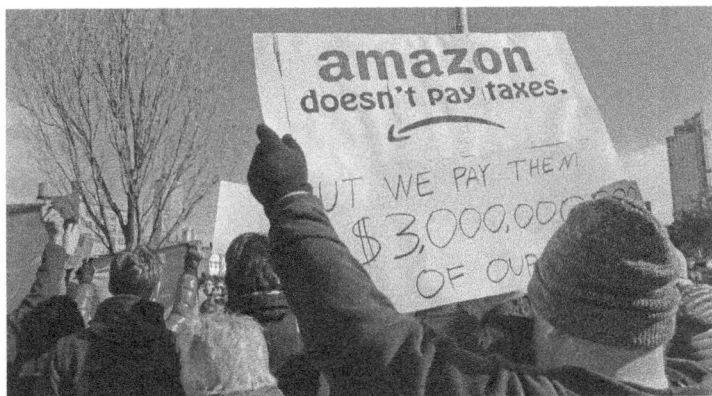

FIGURE 2.5 Connecting the tech sector's tax avoidance strategies to local expectations about corporate citizenship. Protest in Queens, New York, to public subsidies for private development: Opposition to the selection of Long Island City, New York, in the Amazon competition for a second headquarters, 2018.

(*Source*: Scootercaster/Shutterstock)

THE URBAN PROBLEM

Cities have long been both much maligned and much celebrated. Even before Jacob Riis's photographs of the squalor of New York City tenements in the nineteenth century and the Kerner Commission's report documenting extensive urban inequality in the twentieth, the problems of cities motivated a series of regulatory and market interventions that included zoning, neighborhood policing, and the rise of private, gated communities.[15] Recent years have witnessed a return to the city after a century in which the word *urban* was seen largely as an undesirable adjective implying a problem to be solved: the "urban problem." In the twentieth century, urban development patterns—especially in the United States—featured a fear of cities and abandonment of both density and the neighborhood scale.[16] Urban renewal programs emerged out of the post–World War II era as one attempt at modernization through infrastructure. Urban policies more broadly became not about the value of cities—their economic role, cultural importance, and social capital—but about managing the seemingly inevitable descent of cities into decline. It was the suburbs where one wanted to live and go to school.[17] Cities were to be passed through on the way to and from the office building downtown—that is, if one was not instead traveling to new office developments in an "edge city" or to the sprawling lawns of a bucolic corporate campus.[18]

The academic and popular literature on the challenges of the metropolis from this period in U.S. history consistently cast the city as a place of problems. Its neighborhoods were islands of concentrated poverty, and in the exceptional cases where there were pockets of wealth, these only highlighted growing inequalities. The housing stock was either substandard or too expensive, and sometimes both. City services—water, waste management, electricity, gas, policing—were simultaneously more expensive than suburban alternatives and less reliable.

Perhaps the clearest discussion of how and why the city was assigned such a vast array of social and economic problems is found John Kenneth Galbraith's 1977 *The Age of Uncertainty* in a chapter titled, "The Metropolis." It was written when these narratives about the urban problem were reaching an apex in the national consensus.[19]

> Since it is there that people live, the problems of the industrial civilization are seen as the problems of the city. What should be blamed on expanding income and output, the changing composition of product, higher and different consumption, the modern role of unions, the unwillingness of people peacefully to starve gets blamed instead on the way the city is governed. The modern big city mayor is a most convenient figure in our time. He gets, and in his innocence largely accepts, the responsibility for the tensions, discomforts, maladjustments and failures of the industrial system. It follows that to understand that system nothing is so important as an understanding of its urban life. This, like most things, must be examined in some historical depth. For the word city itself, in its singular form, is misleading. There is not one kind of city but several, and all are combined, in varying mix and form, in the great metropolis.[20]

Galbraith's insight in 1977 was to highlight the extent to which the city was absorbing the outcomes—the market failures—of a system of production and mode of capital accumulation that was not of the city but of the economy. In other words, the city was the spatialization of the inequalities generated through the geographically and socially uneven distribution of gains and losses, winners and losers of a particular economic system. The city was not the cause but the site of the urban problem.

The capacity for cities and their leaders to accept the premise of the critique that this is an urban problem with city-scale solutions also did not escape Galbraith's attention. Thus, the urban administration and urban policy literature is full of articles and books framing and reframing the scope and dimensions of the urban problem.[21] For many years, the conversation centered on the question of whether the urban problem was, in actuality, a regional or metropolitan problem requiring the buy-in and engagement not only of cities but also of suburbs and surrounding jurisdictions to "share the burden" of financing the services and distributing operations across the regional economy.[22]

Subsequently, the policy intervention most frequently advocated involved pooling tax revenues and redistributing poor people—and the negative outcomes their presence seems inevitably to produce (limited tax base for schools and services)—more evenly across the regional landscape. These policy interventions were, and still are, largely unpopular. Resistance to these policy solutions by jurisdictions that can continue to opt out of paying their fair share for the market failures of the industrial (and now industrial *and* knowledge) system is entrenched. The movement to adopt metropolitan governance regimes such as the Metropolitan Council in Minnesota (Minneapolis/St. Paul region) essentially has been stalled for four decades.[23]

Still, political inertia is not an excuse for ignorance of the specifics. Galbraith pointed out that understanding how the city operates is essential for understanding the broader economic system that produces it. It is important to embed this understanding in economic and urban history as well. It is interesting to note that a great deal of the modern discussion of smart cities is convened not only without a sense of the history of cities, urbanization, and urban governance but also without a broader conversation about the mechanics of urban and regional economies or previous debates about regional governance. The emphasis on (largely) undefined technology solutions to provide a new array of urban services that are historically disconnected and culturally neutral, and that hold both socially ambiguous and economically unspecified value, seems increasingly out of place in the context of Galbraith's commentary on the metropolis in the industrial economy. For what reason did the smart cities project emerge and take root in the popular discourse independent of the experts and established expertise on cities? What difference does it make to position the smart cities project as a conversation about technology rather than cities?

THE ECONOMY PROBLEM

This book contains a great deal of discussion about the role and function of scale. Scale operates to delineate the geographies of smart cities actions (the individual, the building, the neighborhood/community, the testbed/campus/installation, the city, the region, the nation), and it operates to signal levels of magnitude, the perceived or actual size of the problem or intervention at hand. Distinguishing between an economy problem and an urban problem implicates both types of scale: where the problem is located and how large the problem is. The determination of location and magnitude subsequently influences the assignment of responsibility for the problem and the ability of the actors who are assigned the responsibility to exercise agency in addressing the problem. Scales do not always match: sometimes the scale of the problem does not align with the scale of the solution.

Galbraith's commentary reveals a subtext that has haunted the discussion of solutions to urban problems for the last fifty years: governance. The scale of governance—the city—does not meet the scale of the problem—the economy. This is a fundamental thesis in economic theory and is often used in economic geography: the regime of accumulation operates at scale that is mismatched with the mode of regulation. It is unclear whether a set of technology solutions can have an impact on resolving that mismatch in the scales of action. An argument can be made that multiscalar coalitions are essential for any next steps, whether those steps stop at mitigation of urban problems or evolve to confront the broader market failures around housing and work.[24] That said, the absence of a historicized and nuanced conversation about labor markets and housing markets, and about privatization and devolution, is not encouraging. Although critiques exist about smart cities as a discourse, there are few discussions about how smart cities fit into a longer conversation about the spatial distribution of economic activities within and across cities. And, ultimately, there are few discussions about how smart cities may change the locational calculus that determines competitive advantages on the ground, thus defining both winners and losers and the scope and scale of the urban problem going forward.

Agency is a critical concept that operates in the emerging smart cities discourse and in the established discussions about urban and regional economies. In the smart cities discourse, there is a naively optimistic strain of discussion about technology and civic engagement. This is a conversation about how technology can operate through a number of intermediate actions—for example, data transparency and small-scale sensor deployments—to expand the array of actions and interventions available to citizens and communities. The urban problem can be tackled—or at least confronted—by small-scale interventions at the city scale. In other words, the intractable challenges confounding cities can be recast and reframed as bite-sized problems and distributed solutions. The localized civic engagement conversation is largely agnostic as to the magnitude of the problem (urban vs. economy), because the scale of its interventions is circumscribed to citizens and communities (the project scale) and operates independent of scales of policy, governance, and administration (see chapter 6).

A second emergent smart cities discourse also focuses on increased membership and participation in networks and partnerships (see chapter 5). This discourse operates not at the individual or neighborhood scale but at the scale of cities, regions, and nations by creating networks of cities with shared solutions to the urban-scale manifestations of the economy problem. These cities band together in networks to diffuse policies and to sway interventions at multiple scales of decision making. This globalized civic engagement discourse parallels the localized smart cities civic engagement discourse, but it acknowledges that these are not bite-sized problems.

There is considerably less naïveté about the viability of a crowd-sourced solution to the market failures of the broader economic system. Instead, the global smart cities networks discourse, which is allied with sustainability and resilience networks such as the Rockefeller Foundation's 100 Resilient Cities, identify policy actions and engagements across scales—wherever individual cities or sets of cities can identify a scale for policy action. This discourse accepts the magnitude of the economy problem and tries to confront it with a diffuse coalition of urban-scale actors and facilitating policy mobilities.

In the more established conversation about urban and regional economies dominated by fields such as economic geography, there is far less optimism about the ability of places (individual cities and regions) to confront the economy problem on their own. This conversation is anchored in the same critique of the broader economic system that is present in Galbraith's discussion of the metropolis. In the conversation about urban and regional economies, there are two key conclusions about scale that dampen the optimism seen in the smart cities civic engagement conversation. First, there is a mismatch in the scale of policy action. Because it is an economy problem and not an urban problem alone, this mismatch operates across scales of potential policy intervention. The problem is one of market, not governance failures; it follows the distribution of economic activities irrespective of jurisdictional boundaries. Second, the scale mismatch exists in the magnitude of the problem. The economy problem produces a big problem requiring a big solution. Put another way, it is not cities that are poor (when they are poor); it is the people who live in them who are poor. That is fundamentally a function of income. The condition is influenced, but not determined, by location.

Interesting conclusions emerge from a treatment of the two key scale questions I have identified: scope of agency and magnitude. First, smart cities solutions are not solutions to the urban problem; they are mitigation efforts. The conversation about solutions is yet to be had. It is possible that the smart cities discourse will evolve into a discussion of the economy problem, but that has not happened yet either. Second, smart cities solutions are not big; they are actually small. Smart cities solutions— with the exception of a number of major systems overhauls (energy, transportation)—follow a pattern seen in public works over the last fifteen years, when national infrastructure budgets become especially anemic: build small, incremental projects. The emblematic example of this is the High Line in New York City. Cities are engaged in shrinking the interventions they pursue, scaling down infrastructure investments to the levels of their own agency, to fit within their capacity to act.

These two conclusions about the scale of the economy problem thus affect the agency assigned to cities through either smart cities tactics or conventional means to act to identify and implement solutions. In a parallel to Galbraith's argument that urban problems are not the problems *of* the city but *in* the city, in 1979, Doreen Massey made a similar argument about the effects of deindustrialization and globalization on cities and regions in the article, "In What Sense a Regional Problem?" In Massey's analysis, the Regional Problem is akin to Galbraith's urban problem.[25] It is an economy problem assigned to place without the power to solve the problem. Massey's conclusion makes this point:

[I]f the regional problem is not a problem produced by regions, but by the organization of production itself, neither is its solution simply a technical question. If production for profit may actually both imply and require such inequality, the issue of policy must be "who pays?" There is a need to make explicit political choices. Finally, the implication of this analysis is that intervention in the spatial distribution cannot be divorced from issues of intervention at the level of production. To see regional policy and regional problems as simply questions of spatial distribution is completely inadequate.[26]

It is probably no surprise that the pessimism in Massey's and Galbraith's diagnoses of the challenges faced by places and within urban and regional economies has generated a constituency of advocates smaller than the group of advocates who hold the optimistic view of increased agency proposed in the smart cities conversation. But it is still important to understand these smart city solutions in a broader historical context. In 1975, the

New York Daily News reported the headline, "Ford to New York City: Drop Dead," describing New York's effort to leverage the federal government's assistance in resolving a fiscal crisis caused by an imbalance between services and revenues. Today, U.S. cities have no more revenue assistance from federal or state governments than they did in 1975; indeed, they have less.[27] Further, municipal debt levels increased substantially between 1980 and 2015 in the United States. As a percentage of gross domestic product, municipal debt stood at almost 14 percent of GDP in 1980. U.S. municipal debt as a percentage of GDP had risen to 20.7 percent by 2015, after declining from a high point of 25.2 percent in 2009. The prevalence of austerity policies and the shrinking of the public sector is a subject of significant commentary and concern, particularly in light of the proposed expansion and upgrading of services implicated in the smart cities project.[28]

Even if the state and federal governments were to take on a greater share of the costs of city services, that would not resolve the issue highlighted by Galbraith and Massey. It would be an effort to mitigate the urban problem, not solve the economy problem. Arguably, what we see in other advanced industrial economies to varying degrees (Germany, Japan, Canada, the United Kingdom) are simply greater efforts to mitigate the urban problem than seen in the United States. And, without getting into an extended discussion about the whiplash experienced by cities and regions in the United Kingdom as the national government implements endless variations on placed-based economic development strategies, suffice it to say that these are explicit political choices about the policies that determine who pays to which Massey refers.

What seems increasingly clear is that no one wants to talk about the economy problem. And so, the smart cities project exists as an explicitly geographic conversation (the city) with a specified scale of governance and administration (the city) presented strangely as apolitical, ahistorical, and deterritorialized. This is a difficult task to accomplish, and it is notably one of the great achievements of the smart cities project thus far: to talk about cities without implicating either the urban problem or the long-standing debates about regionalism as a solution. The smart cities project argues that technology is the solution. The problem, however, remains unspecified.

THE OTHER SCALE PROBLEM

Advocates of smart cities solutions frequently discuss the issue of scaling. This conversation about scale is largely about the question of how to move (presumably successful) smart cities demonstration projects and programs from the prototype or testbed phase to larger deployments. In other words, the intention is to expand the coverage of these programs and services to provide for a broader population than the initial communities that were served. Again, turning to the policy analysis literature, one would anticipate that successful programs in specific places would be analyzed and evaluated and then incrementally scaled to serve more places and more people. The next step would be to expand the scope of coverage of programs to provide for more access, opportunity, and equity. Scaling up is not merely a question of preferences; it is a question of fairness or distributional equity.

It is here that we see another way in which scale is a critical challenge for the smart cities project. Scale is the real problem. If these deployments are not scalable, they will contribute to and significantly exacerbate existing inequalities within and across cities by providing an uneven distribution of services to citizens.

Smart cities would not be a solution to the urban problem, then, but a new manifestation of the economy problem. The path of the smart cities project would be to move from uneven development to uneven innovation.

Among the many ways in which the scaling problem plagues smart cities is one that can be traced to its implementation models. Once it became clear that large-scale smart cities investments in systems-level or platform-level interventions were unlikely because of resource challenges (neither the amount of investment required appeared forthcoming, nor the lead actors who were needed to leverage that investment obvious), the smart cities project turned to a different innovation diffusion model, one borrowed from the high-tech start-up world: if you cannot find a single sponsor for your design and deployment, then distribute the solution. Initiate a contest, competition, or challenge. Solicit volunteers and pick a winner. Note here that in the shift to a distributed solution, the antecedent research activity is dropped from the research, design, and deployment framework, to say nothing of the absence of any evaluation of capacity.

Consequently, smart cities deployments have gravitated toward small-scale implementations that are distributed and deprofessionalized. Cities and the smart cities intermediaries who collaborate with them have defaulted to a menu of activities that is well known in the high-tech space around the notion of competitions. Civic intermediaries such as Code for America (national scale) or Code for Atlanta (as a local affiliate) sponsor hack-a-thons to build apps for citizens to access public information.[29] Cities and their civic entrepreneurship partners put out requests for crowdsourced solutions. Universities sponsor student competitions that are integrated into courses and offer scholarships and technical assistance as prizes to move prototypes into commercialization. Projects such as Data Science for Social Good mobilize students and researchers to tackle technical problems in the civic domain, often taking complex data series that are inaccessible but publicly available in city halls, cleaning and coding them to make them available through portals and applications.[30]

The results of these competitions highlight the scale challenge yet again. The outcomes of this hack-a-thon–inspired approach to city services are layers of unrelated efforts built on platforms that lack not only intentionality but also interoperability. Each project may have its own internal logic and its own elegant design, and the projects also are frequently legitimate efforts to use data for social good, providing greater access and transparency for an array of use-case scenarios. However, they remain ahistorical, apolitical, and deterritorialized. They are artifacts of the circumstances of their own creation. Who maintains the data in these platforms and portals? Who updates them? Who checks them for accuracy? Who reviews them to ensure alignment with standard practices and information from other projects? Who is the aggregator, the editor, the curator, and the redactor? How is it that these one-off smart cities projects become a smart cities program for the cities and citizens that need these platforms and this information to build a better, safer city? A city where citizens in a high-rise apartment fire can receive information about what to do in such an emergency, rather than simply use their cell phones to call out to friends and family the desperate circumstances of their current locations? The job of smart cities is making data accessible, legible, and meaningful and making intentional, deliberative, and ethical decisions about the use of those data. In chapter 5, I discuss how to develop this capability within cities instead of crowdsourcing or outsourcing it.

Cities are complex systems. They are organized to deliver highly routinized, consistent, and necessary services and highly specific and intermittent emergency services that are equally necessary in the moments when they are required. In the past, public administrators designed cities as silos of action that function effectively without interdependence. To function properly, they must be able to work independently. To a significant degree, information integration is an administrative luxury, not an operational necessity. The advocates of smart cities as civic innovation assume that data transparency and access are shared values motivating policy makers to invest in the choices that support advocates' efforts. This is the case on a small-scale basis: at the scale of one project, one competition, one contest, one hack-a-thon at a time.

It is important to understand why scale in the smart cities project is not simply a rhetorical challenge but an actual problem. Perhaps it *is* the problem. This chapter presented scale as both a question of designated geographies of smart cities actions (the individual, the building, the neighborhood/community, the testbed/campus/installation, the city, the region, the nation) and a signaling about magnitude, the perceived or actual size of the problem or intervention at hand. The scaling up of the smart cities project is where these two ideas of scale intersect. As we have seen, the trend in the smart cities project in recent years has been not to scale up services and expand coverage but, rather, to scale down projects and concentrate on highly targeted efforts that have discrete boundaries in terms of both jurisdiction and project scope.

This is true of projects that are explicitly seen as smart cities efforts and those that are running on a parallel (and sometimes intersecting) track. In the first category are the civic projects discussed earlier. The whole array of smart cities sensor deployments that begin at the testbed scale with the anticipated outcome of broader coverage fall into this category as well. Rather than creating islands of technology advantage within cities—what the

Technology and the Future of Cities report called "urban development districts"—these projects are perceived as stepping-stones toward large-scale implementation.[31]

In the interest of historical context, it is important to note that distinct spaces within cities with differential access and opportunity are not a new phenomenon. Cities throughout the United States have neighborhoods with substantial variation in access and advantage. For example, school districts can vary dramatically in quality across districts in the same city and across schools in the same district.[32] The effectiveness of storm sewers, park maintenance, policing, and—as we have been reminded in recent years—the quality of the pipes that bring water into homes can vary significantly within and across cities.[33] So, it should be no surprise that access to the technologies promised by the smart cities project might be unevenly distributed as well. This is, again, an outcome of an economy problem manifesting as an urban problem. Cities don't create inequality; they provide a landscape on which it plays out.

It is worth noting that projects that are not explicitly labeled as smart cities efforts also have been affected by the rescaling of urban investments to match the scale of intervention available to cities in the current period. We have moved from an era in which "make no small plans" was the theme behind the audacity of the urban renewal projects of the 1960s, to an era in which "big ideas" such as livability and connectivity substitute for large-scale interventions. After working their way from urban renewal through festival marketplaces, cities have landed on a category of much smaller projects and a host of leveraged "P3" approaches, which is shorthand for emerging public–private partnerships. Driving this approach is the need to rescale urban regeneration projects to adapt to the organization of the funding mechanism. Small-scale and big idea infrastructure investments are conducted not by the city itself but with the city as a partner. And, increasingly, these smaller-scale interventions have the effect of exacerbating uneven development by driving both densification and gentrification and leveraging branding and design narratives to "place-make" in one corner of the city while postponing investments in other corners until a private partner makes a move.

Subsequent chapters analyze how and in what ways the smart cities project plays into the partnerships of urban entrepreneurialism (chapter 4) and the practices of local economic development (chapter 3) that are familiar to many urban geographers and economic development scholars. To conclude the discussion here, it is important to underscore several key points. First, the smart cities project has emerged as an ahistorical, apolitical, and deterritorialized discourse about places that are defined by their geography, jurisdictions and governance, and history.

Second, it is necessary to discuss the problem for which smart cities is the solution. It is important to avoid defaulting to defining the problem as the urban problem. It was a mistake to do so fifty years ago, and it is a mistake to do so now. That mistake is highlighted by the fact that the problem in question—unequal access to opportunity—remains stubbornly in place, though not exclusively in cities. Whether the smart cities project can mitigate or even provide a potential solution to the economy problem has yet to be determined. What is clear is that for the smart cities project to avoid contributing to the inequalities that crisscross the urban landscape, there must be a deliberate and intentional effort to understand the spatial distribution of the opportunities provided through the design, development, and deployment of the smart cities project.

3

SMART CITIES
AS EMERGING MARKETS

WHEN considering smart cities as an emerging and enabling industry and not simply as a discourse or movement, it is important to analyze how technology diffusion operates when a city is a client and also a site of innovation, production, distribution, and consumption. Economic geographers have long studied innovation and production processes within and across industries as part of the broader disciplinary project of mapping and analyzing the spatial distribution of economic activities within and across cities, regions, and nation–states.[1] These patterns of technology diffusion and industry change are responses to emerging markets and the effects of new materials, processes, or products that enable better, faster, safer, or greener alternatives.

What is distinct about the smart cities project is how the technology industry uses space—in this case, the city—as a site of the entire production process, from innovation through consumption. The demarcation of the city as the exclusive territory of production presents a stark contrast in a world economy that is full of global production networks and distributed supply chains. The hyperlocalization of the smart cities project places the city at the center of technological innovation, product design, and consumption.

The result is a heightened risk of exploitation as well as a rare moment of leverage.

The development of Sidewalk Toronto serves as an illustration of how cities "present firms with a set of strategic options along with production locations."[2] Sidewalk Toronto is a smart cities redevelopment project begun in 2017 in an industrial waterfront neighborhood in Toronto, Canada. It is a public–private partnership led by Sidewalk Labs, a subsidiary of Google's parent company, Alphabet. The project combines several aspects of recent urban development strategies (specifically, development led by real estate and industry) to forge a model for development led by the tech sector that underscores how cities present firms with a set of strategic options for production. Sidewalk Toronto enables Sidewalk Labs to create a prototype of a model for an urban development district as a site of innovation, production, distribution, and consumption of smart cities products and services.[3] As reported in *Intercept* in 2019, Sidewalk Labs plans to use the data gathered from Sidewalk Toronto to develop Replica, a software program for cities (and other parties) to model patterns based on locational data on the individual characteristics and behaviors of people who pass through the urban development district.[4] Sidewalk Toronto highlights how the urban scale "is becoming more important—as a source of subsidy and risk reduction to firms competing in global markets," particularly as it pertains to the ongoing question of data governance around such developments and the revenue models that support them.[5]

Through the lens of economic geography, the smart cities project can be seen as an industry with a diverse set of actors, processes, and markets that is not unlike other enabling and emerging industries associated with application-driven high-tech sectors of the last two decades (e.g., biotechnology, nano-technology, additive manufacturing).[6] This analysis draws on the geographic concept of scale to develop a typology describing how the city operates as a market for the smart cities project in multiple ways. In one sense, the city is a customer or client. Cities buy smart cities objects, systems, and platforms and provide services and infrastructure for citizens. In this sense, the city acts as an administrative unit (cities, counties, regional authorities, special districts) engaged in service delivery in each jurisdiction or territory.

In a second sense, the city is administrative territory. Cities are designated and regulated places where potential smart cities clients and customers are aggregated and where firms can find them. In both senses, the city provides an organizing logic— a delineated geography—for collecting information about the characteristics and behaviors of people and organizations. Also, the city serves as a market for the consumption of objects, systems, and platforms. Whether it is the city purchasing a system for managing public services or individual customers or citizens buying services to optimize their own activities, the city provides a scoping mechanism. The city offers a marketplace; an aggregation of customers with predictable demands for products and services. At the same time, the city provides a platform for innovation and design.

In the beginning, the smart cities project was essentially an effort to brand a collection of technology applications for a new market: cities.[7] The smart cities project identified a set of new applications for technologies to apply to a large and potentially predictable emerging market.[8] The effort to define a smart cities industry—the products, services, firms, and customers involved in the production and consumption of smart cities technologies— is distinct from the urban entrepreneurship effort, discussed in chapter 4, to sell the city itself to citizens and firms as a place of production and as a development partner. In this chapter, I analyze the smart cities project from an industry perspective, identifying the processes and actors involved in making the smart cities market. In addition, I analyze how the smart cities project operates as an emerging industry to sell technologies *to cities* and *in cities*. I describe how cities became the target market for the platforms, products, and services of a set of firms that self-identify as stakeholders in the smart cities project.

LOCATING SMART CITIES: GENERATING DEMAND

The smart cities project employs a narrative about emerging markets to build demand for technology products and services. Scale shapes this narrative as well. Again, an understanding of how shifts in scale redefine jurisdictions and, subsequently, markets is critical for understanding why smart cities constitute more than an innovation narrative that proposes technology solutions to urban problems but also represent a sustained effort to build new market opportunities for an emerging industry at a variety of interconnected and mutually dependent scales of action and production.

Thinking about cities as new markets is not a novel idea. Economists, urban planners, and policy makers have used emerging market language to describe the unmet market opportunities in cities for some time. This language was particularly prevalent in the 1990s, when, in the United States, the Clinton administration's urban policies advocated for enterprise zones that designated central cities locations as spaces of preferential tax treatment to help stimulate private investment in cities.[9] Although urban planners objected to enterprise zones in their previous iterations proposed by both the Reagan administration and the Thatcher government in the United Kingdom, the U.S. policy models continued to gain ground[10]—ground they continue to hold today. At the same time, Michael Porter adapted his *Competitive Advantage of Nations* (1990) to an article titled "The Competitive Advantage of the Inner City" (1995), which identified a series of potential market opportunities for central cities.[11]

Throughout the 1990s and 2000s, these conversations about cities as emerging markets paralleled conversations about developing national economies that were popular among advocates of globalization, free trade, and other neoliberal policy priorities. The argument was that there were indeed private market opportunities to be had—money to be made—in places where people were not themselves wealthy. Rapid development—including urbanization—was driving rising incomes in countries with large populations (for example, Brazil, Russia, India, and China), and these consumers would gradually "come online" to the services and products of the global economy. Whether the product was a cell phone requiring connectivity or an automobile requiring gas, the market was there and the opportunity was growing, and that opportunity involved a network of products and services. By identifying the competitive advantage of a place, one could carve out economic opportunities for new firms using new models of enterprise development.

As the competitive advantage framework shifted from a national to a subnational application (from nation to city), it also shifted away from emphasizing production advantages and toward targeting concentrations of consumers. In this consumption-based construction of place-specific market opportunities, density defined demand as well as wealth and income. As with the global economy as a whole, the tide turned toward consumption.[12]

This approach to economic development amounted to parsing out opportunities for private enterprise while leaving the truly intractable market failures in land, labor, and capital markets to be mitigated and managed by an ever-shirking public sector. Academics in the 1990s observed that the logic of this sort of enterprise development seemed to operate in parallel in international and urban development. The concern remained that cities would continue to serve as the landscape on which the economy problem played out, even if in slightly different ways. In other words, the urban problem would simply be rearranged, not solved, through this approach to enterprise development.

Since the 1990s, the conversation about cities as emerging markets has changed, and the smart cities project has evolved in this context. The narrative about who lives in cities and whether they constitute a wealthy or disadvantaged target market shifted dramatically when Richard Florida began to strategically remind a new generation of policy makers and real estate professionals that cities were the site of the "creative class" (2002) and not merely the "truly disadvantaged."[13] Florida, writing about urban development for a broad audience, recast the story of cities away from the urban problem. Even after Florida's work about the creative class gained traction, much as had Porter's work on competitive advantage a decade earlier, the policy proposals from the UK and U.S. governments continued to position cities as remedial market spaces requiring targeted incentives and special programs such as promise, enterprise, and empowerment zones. In the policy parlance of the European Union, cities were understood as "lagging regions" requiring public programs to stimulate private investment. Thus, the practice of offering public subsidies for private development in cities became further normalized, seen as both standard practice and expected.

At this point the parallel between urban economies in industrialized countries and the economies of newly industrialized countries begins to unwind in important ways that are related to governance: subsidy and regulation. Unlike developing countries transitioning to modern capitalist economies, cities in industrialized countries are already the construct of modern capitalist economies.[14] They have clear property rights, institutional norms, governance regimes, and well-established actors and interest groups. In other words, the smart cities project depends on considering the city as a different kind of emerging market than the enterprise zones of the 1990s. Unlike the inner cities of the 1980s and 1990s, the cities of the creative class are not truly disadvantaged but, instead, serve as a dense and distinct aggregation of first movers in terms of taste and technology.

Understanding the power of the creative class as market makers was the essential shift necessary for the smart cities project to take hold. It took fifteen years after Florida convincingly asserted that urban policy makers and the private sector had misunderstood the economic value of the people living and working in cities for the technology sector to develop a strategy to harness that value. The economic opportunity identified in the smart cities project is both *about the city* and *about who is in the city*. It is about access to people, firms, and institutions that require an impressive and ever-expanding array of interoperable services and products, and it is about access to the data about the characteristics and behaviors of those people.

SCALING SMART CITIES: CONSUMERS AND USERS

Fundamentally, the smart cities project identifies the city as both a customer and a location for the innovation, production, distribution, and consumption of the products and services it designs and develops. Smart cities interventions—the products and services, systems, and platforms—do not operate exclusively at the scale of the city. The city is not the only customer, nor is urban the only potential scale at which these interventions can be (and are) deployed. But urban is the preferred scale. Understanding the scale of the smart cities production process is an important first step in analyzing the actors and processes involved in the industry.[15]

In this section, I present a typology to describe the target market of the technologies that are self-defined as part of, or related to, the implementation, operation, and design of smart cities. In this typology are five scales of target markets, which are distinguished largely by whether and to what extent decision making operates at a distinct and definitive scale of authority. At what scale the industry chooses to direct its market making is an issue of clarity in terms of authority, geography, and the anticipated value of the market. In other words, the selected scale for market making in the smart cities project is both a strategic and an economic decision.

The typology begins with products and services directed at *individuals*, defined as both citizens and consumers. This is primarily a market for smart cities objects rather than complex and interconnected systems of platforms. Smart cities objects are often directed at this user scale because it is individuals who acquire these objects and the services that enable their connectivity: wearables such as fitness trackers and smart phones—in other words, things. Individual consumers, however, are not the only market for user-scale smart cities objects. These objects also can be targeted to local governments and institutions to purchase at a larger scale and subsequently provide as a service to individuals (see figures 3.1 and 3.2).

FIGURE 3.1 Smart cities objects providing public services and forming a fixed urban sensor system. Big Belly Trash Can (solar powered and Wi-Fi enabled) without advertising in Melbourne, Australia.

(*Source*: Galexia/Shutterstock)

This leads to the next distinct scale in the smart cities market: *the building scale*. At this second scale is a set of technologies that produce a networked building, home, or office populated by smart cities objects and systems. These systems include smart thermostats, internet-connected appliances, and home-operating systems.

FIGURE 3.2 Smart cities objects providing public services and forming a fixed urban sensor system. Big Belly Trash Can (solar powered and WiFi enabled) with controversial public service advertising message in Nottingham, England, 2016.

(*Source*: Jason Batterham/Shutterstock)

The third smart cities market scale is effectively a networked variation on the building scale. This scale aligns with ideas of the smart campus in the broadest sense, including universities, corporate campuses and production facilities, military installations, and other institutional configurations. In addition, *smart neighborhoods* can be included in this category, such as neighborhoods with a formal governing body. Examples include business improvement districts (BID) or innovation districts where a private entity representing a local membership makes decisions about provisioning services and purchasing assets. What is distinctive about all three of these scales is that the decision about service levels and the selection of vendors are made by an identifiable actor—a consumer, a citizen, a membership organization, a corporation, or an institution.

It is important to note that smart cities initiatives also target markets where decision making is not centralized but, rather, is diffused over a network of actors representing multiple constituencies. The first scale in this category is that of community. *Community* in this sense parallels the notion of user community that is often discussed within the technology industry, as well as the concept of the community that is familiar to urban planners and policy makers. One could even argue that this community parallels the identity communities or communities of interest as they are understood in political science and social policy. At this scale, the community does not have a governing jurisdictional authority making decisions about services and products. Rarely are these communities in the business of providing public services. That said, they are clearly identifiable use communities, and as such, they remain a target market in the sense that smart cities products and services are tailored to these specified user communities with specified characteristics and behaviors.

The second distinct scale of the smart cities market with diffused decision making is the region or the metropolitan area. In this case, the scale represents both distributed jurisdictional authority and dynamic spatial definitions. Neither the authority nor the geography is fixed. However, the metropolitan or regional scale is that of many of the platforms required for smart cities deployment: transit, energy, and connectivity. The autonomous vehicle or the smart grid or the 5G network does not stop at the jurisdictional boundaries of the city. The functionality of these platforms requires that they operate beyond municipal boundaries and implicates planning at the regional scale.

The final scale of the smart cities market, of course, is the scale of the city itself. Here, we begin to understand why the smart cities project was initially targeted at the urban scale. The city scale is categorized by both a jurisdictional boundary (the administrative boundaries of the city) and an identifiable decision-making authority that determines not only the level of services provided but also the regulatory framework that governs the design and implementation of those products and services (including data acquisition and use). The city is the largest geographic unit (and, thus, market) that allows for the implementation of objects, systems, and platforms and operates under a defined jurisdictional authority that determines the terms of data collection, extraction, and use. Thus, the embrace of the city should be seen not merely as a rhetorical exercise but as a firm strategy. However, it is not a recognition (or consideration) by the technology sector of the city as a complex, nuanced, and historically contingent sociotechnical system. It is simply the signal of an enabling industry's awareness of the city as a suitable site for product development and an emerging target market that eventually allows access to all five smart cities markets in the long run. In the short run, the city scale determines the point of entry, not the scale of the industry's ambitions for the urban technology project (see table 3.1).

Across these five categories, what distinguishes the scale of the city is that it incorporates a single decision-making authority within a bounded and fixed geography. There is a predictable process to decision making in cities and a predictable territory in which those decisions are applied. Cities are governed, administered, and regulated. Although cities in industrialized

TABLE 3.1 The scales of smart cities markets

Examples	Jurisdiction	Authority	Markets			
			Data	Objects	Systems	Platforms
Individual						
Smart watch; fitness tracker	Defined	Centralized	Yes	Yes	No	No
Building or home						
Smart thermostats; IoT appliances	Defined	Centralized	Yes	Yes	Yes	No
Community or neighborhood						
User community portals and platforms	Ambiguous	Diffused	Yes	Yes	Maybe	No
City, campus, or enterprise (firm)						
Smart trash cans; Environmental sensor deployments	Defined	Centralized	Yes	Yes	Yes	Yes
City-region or metropolitan area (or larger region)						
Smart energy grids	Ambiguous	Diffused	Yes	Yes	Yes	Yes

countries are dynamic and diverse, they are also developed as a matter through a process of governance. The investment boom in developing countries in the 1990s was followed by institutional and political failures that forced investors to confront the wisdom of relying on the (un)predictability of domestic practices in places with weak (and sometimes seemingly arbitrary) governance regimes. Thus, investors began to weigh two questions when considering emerging markets: how uncertain is the economic opportunity, and, equally, how uncertain is the political environment?

From an emerging markets perspective, the city scale is a knowable market space, whereas the community and regional scales are significantly more fluidly defined. Moreover, they change over time. The city provides a landscape to rethink private market opportunities with clear governance practices and territorial demarcations. The city, then, is not a scaled-down analog to a developing economy, as the discourse in the 1990s proposed. It is more as David Harvey once described it: a particular site of capital accumulation in capitalist market economies. The interesting issue in the smart cities project is the change in direction that the technology sector has taken in aligning its firm strategies with urbanization processes and the benefits derived from urban agglomerations.

Even with the increased certainties that cities bring to the urban technology project in terms of governance and geography, there remain many uncertainties about the revenue models and value of the smart cities project. How predictable is an emerging market opportunity given the uncertain ecological environment? Strong governance and predictable institutions are likely to matter more as climate change reshapes the political and economic landscape and creates both new markets and attendant new risks.

It is into this uncertainty that cities in advanced industrial nations present an opportunity for the smart cities project.

Cities hold agency, institutions, and territory. They possess the established mechanisms for independent economic and political action. They can make investments, provide services, and engage in redistribution.[16] That capacity, coupled with an enormous share of people and capital, motivates the smart cities project to see the city as the strategic scale for its target market. The effort, then, is to create demand—to make the market—for smart cities systems and objects as a mechanism for managing uncertainties and generating revenue from change.

Having established how and why the city scale serves a strategic purpose as the preferred geography for the smart cities project, the next task is to identify the industry's array of products, services, platforms, and systems. As described in chapter 2, the smart cities narrative principally sells solutions. In effect, the core idea is that the urban problem has a technology solution—or at least a discrete, scalable, and repeatable technology intervention. In addition, as noted earlier, smart cities as a discourse sells the city itself—as a site for private, public, and personal investment. This is a story about how urban and regional competition builds and extends on a type of urban entrepreneurialism that has characterized economic development policy and practice since the 1980s (see chapter 4). However, the products and services developed by the emerging smart cities industry in order to serve the smart cities market are a different issue. In other words, this is an examination of the demand side of the industry. Again, scale dominates the discussion and shapes the necessary typology.

As noted earlier, there are three major categories of customers for smart cities objects, systems, and platforms: consumers or citizens, institutions and firms, and cities (jurisdictions). For each of these customers, the package of products and services is somewhat different and, in important ways, interdependent. Cities, institutions, and firms are positioned to purchase networks of services and objects. Thus, they are the target markets for the sensor arrays and systems of services that form the backbone of smart cities deployments. These include the prototypes of systems that are developed by research institutions. Perhaps the best-known example is the Array of Things (AoT), which is an urban (primarily environmental) system of sensors developed by a project team that includes the University of Chicago, the Argonne National Lab, the School of the Art Institute of Chicago, and the Computation Institute's Urban Center for Computation and Data (UrbanCCD); it was initially funded through the National Science Foundation. The systems and sensors that are commonly understood as smart cities deployments constitute the leading demonstration products for the smart cities industry. The smart cities project is designed around the deployment of these scalable networks. Further, these are the constituent parts of the urban operating system into which all other services and objects must "plug." Much as the case in the industrial and office markets, if you own the operating system, you own the market.

It is here in particular that understanding smart cities as an enabling industry is analytically useful. Smart cities deployments are frequently sold as packages produced by a consortium of vendors. In chapter 5, I discuss the implications of these urban innovation networks in greater detail. What is important to note here is that few firms specialize in producing integrated smart cities solutions by themselves. Incumbent firms operate within an existing legacy market. For example, communication providers such as AT&T and Verizon work on connectivity, whereas firms such as Siemens and GE work on sensor networks. In order to deliver these connected systems, firms are setting up partnerships and consortia to develop and access the emerging smart cities market. In part, this is a hedge against the risks that are inherent in expansion into new markets. But it is also an effort to strategically stake out market space and lock in path dependencies by establishing technical standards and practices that weave in critical barriers to entry for nonpartner firms. These corporate consortia thus produce competitive advantages based on technological interoperability, the proprietary standards that are employed in designing and defining an emerging market in the absence of open standards and requirements about cross-platform compatibility.

This is another aspect of the smart cities market in which the public sector plays a critical role in the development of emerging industries and enabling technologies: the definition of technical standards. After thirty years of systematic disinvestment, city governments are not equipped with the technology expertise to evaluate the novel and often untested smart cities objects and systems that are marketed to them by private-sector vendors. This is less a question of domain expertise as it is an issue of unclear and unspecified technical standards. A relatively little-known federal agency, the National Institute of Standards and Technology (NIST), is often the leader in defining standards for new technological developments and their applications. NIST serves a critical public function in the rollout of new technologies for both the private and public sectors by establishing baseline industry standards ensuring safety, privacy, and, in some cases, interoperability. These standards then set out the terms for competition by minimizing information asymmetries and the impacts of proprietary practices on an emerging industry.

Often, formal, technical standards act as a barrier to entry into new markets, especially for small and medium-sized firms with fewer resources to pursue certifications before entering the market. In recent years, NIST has partnered with private firms and research institutions in the development of the smart cities industry, particularly in technical areas where there is some clear public interest. For example, NIST has been concerned specifically with interoperability of communications systems for emergency response coordination across agencies and firms. However, the federal government has not yet stepped in to place guardrails (technological or competitive) on the industry by defining best practices or defining common standards. NIST and other federal agencies are having a conversation about the smart cities project rather than exercising authority over it. As a consequence, cities are left to manage issues of privacy and security at the local level with little guidance from the federal government but a great deal of input from the tech sector. The result is uneven implementation of not only smart cities projects and programs but the standards and practices guiding their implementation.

This is particularly problematic when it comes to sequencing smart cities project deployments. For example, effective planning for the management of smart cities data or the integration of those data with legacy data systems does not—but should—precede the implementation of systems and objects that collect and aggregate such data. The result is a chaotic and highly localized approach to the implementation of the overall smart cities project, as evidenced by the spring 2018 hacking of the city of Atlanta and subsequent demand for its stolen data.[17]

PROTOTYPING SMART CITIES: FROM PRODUCTS TO PLATFORMS

Just as the technical standards for the smart cities project remain in flux, so, too, do the goals of the project in terms of who the smart city project serves. There is an ongoing conversation in the fields of urban geography and urban policy about the citizens of smart cities and citizenship in smart cities.[18] This discourse focuses on the language around smart cities and their purpose. The central question is, smart cities for whom? This discourse critiques smart cities as a project that fails to address real and existing urban problems such as housing affordability, gentrification, displacement, and homelessness, and it neither engages nor mitigates discriminatory practices such as environmental racism and residential segregation.

This critique of the smart cities project often falls back into the path dependencies established in the conversation about the urban problem. The response, then, is to adapt smart cities solutions to these particular urban problems. The result is the development of smart cities solutions that purport to engage problems such as homelessness, neighborhood air quality, and public health and safety. These efforts to find technological interventions to mitigate systematic socioeconomic problems rarely touch on what is at the core of any robust smart cities critique: it is not ultimately a question of *for whom the smart city?* but *who owns the smart city?* That is, there is an antecedent question to consider that sits squarely at the intersections of privatization and austerity: who owns and operates the smart cities products, systems, and platforms that are deployed in cities, as well as the data that both facilitate and are extracted from them? The challenge is to see smart citizens and the cities in which they live as more than the passive receivers of smart cities systems but as owners and designers of those services and systems.

Cities provide services to citizens. Vendors provide products and services to customers. Customers purchase access to and use of spaces, products, and services. Citizens gain access through their citizenship, not through their purchasing power. City services are provided to citizens and financed through some combination of fees and taxes. The costs of these services and products are not necessarily (or even often) the same as market prices.

There are several reasons for this. The first is that city services are delivered on the platform of a complex, contingent, and layered built environment. This includes a road system, a utilities network, street lights and traffic signals, networks of parks and libraries and hospitals, and an entire interconnected system of social and cultural services. Smart cities objects plug into that platform of connectivity, and smart cities systems sit on top of that existing platform of infrastructure. The smart cities industry does not, however, build and maintain that infrastructure—at least not yet.

The smart cities project represents a set of technologies that are grafted onto incumbent urban infrastructure. That infrastructure serves as the platform for smart cities development and subsidizes it. The reason citizens do not pay the market price for city services is that these are generally (though not always) a representation of operating costs. Large capital projects are spread out over long periods through bond issues and other financing mechanisms. It is only when large capital expenditures for infrastructure become necessary—a new sewage treatment plant, a project to separate storm and sanitary sewers, the replacement of the municipality's entire network of water pipes—that the price of services substantially increases.

The technical infrastructure required as the platform for the broad implementation of the smart cities project is one of these large capital expenditures. A key challenge for the smart cities project lies in resolving the question of how this urban platform becomes more than what it currently is—an antecedent condition, an antiquated backdrop behind the uneven implementation of smart cities objects and systems innovations. Who, then, upgrades the platform on which smart cities systems and objects operate and on which, and about which, data about the characteristics and behaviors of citizens are collected? The issue here is how the costs of the smart cities platform are distributed between cities and their citizens and between vendors and their consumers.

Perhaps the most familiar example of how this challenge has been articulated is autonomous vehicles. Both the public and the private sector have embraced the idea of upgrading from fleets of traditional operator-driven cars to fleets of autonomous vehicles. The 2016 U.S. Department of Transportation Smart Cities Challenge highlighted the promise of autonomous vehicles.[19] The entire typology of smart cities deployments—data, object, system, platform—is implicated in the autonomous vehicle project. Unlike some smart cities objects, such as device-charging solar park benches or traffic-monitoring systems, autonomous vehicles require investments in a smart cities platform to create the market for the smart cities object: the autonomous vehicle. And so the autonomous vehicle case provides an ongoing example of the complexity of the smart cities project in practice and the market case for the smart cities project, and why it depends on public investment to be realized.

Autonomous vehicles present as a disruptive technology. They are perceived as a change in the way life is lived, the way cities are designed, and the way firms develop their business strategies in sectors that include automobiles and software. However, as is typical with this sort of technological transition, the change is more incremental than it is disruptive. What is happening with autonomous vehicles is that a product is getting an upgrade. In this case, the individual vehicle remains the fundamental product platform. However, it becomes extensively interconnected through the addition of information and communication technologies (ICT) that take driving out of the hands of individual drivers. In other words, the car is completing an incremental transition from a discrete manufactured object to a service-embedded good. Autonomous vehicles are cars with an additional service contract, expanding the array of revenue streams they produce beyond the already existing markets for insurance, debt financing, and maintenance.

Indeed, automobiles are key examples of service-embedded consumer goods. The car connects to a growing network of financial services, including warranties, leases, loans, and insurance. Most manufacturers offer information and communication services that include real-time customer service, streaming radio, and navigation and traffic information systems. Recognition of the incremental innovation behind the autonomous vehicle informed the U.S. National Highway Traffic Safety Administration's approach to its guidelines for autonomous vehicle testing and deployment. The guidelines describe *self-driving* in stages rather than as one giant, disruptive leap from operator-driven to autonomous vehicles.

The autonomous vehicle case has gained prominence because it both affects and appeals to a large constituency: people who drive cars, people who ride in cars, and people who manufacture cars and the ICTs linked to them. Autonomous vehicles affect the production processes and supply chains for two major global industries, autos and ICT. Autonomous vehicles appeal to consumers because they might significantly save commuting time, mitigate the costs and challenges of parking, and potentially improve safety, although there is some evidence that these promises are not likely to be fulfilled in the short run.

Autonomous vehicles appeal to the smart cities industry as a test case of the smart cities project that does not necessarily disrupt the current operations of the automobile or the information and communications industry while pushing the public sector toward investment in the smart cities platform. It is important to note that autonomous vehicles enable firms to pursue a market expansion strategy that focuses on existing customers and is subsidized by the public sector, not only in research but in implementation. The data-driven technological innovations within these incumbent industries allow for three types of new revenue generation: (a) the optimization of existing products or services (which conserves revenues), (b) the development of new services and products for existing customers (which sustains revenues), and (c) the development of new services or products for new customers (which expands revenues).

Among the revenue opportunities created by autonomous vehicles is one that both automakers and connectivity companies can monetize: a customer base captured in a specific location with embedded connectivity—people riding in their cars. People on a commute or errand with reliable connectivity and without the distraction of driving are a new target market. This is a whole new, undistracted audience to view ads, use software, and consume media content during a part of the day that is largely lost to the ICT industry under current conditions. It is also a whole new community of users from which to extract data on individual characteristics, behaviors, travel patterns, and choices. Autonomous vehicles enable the auto and ICT industries to conserve and sustain revenues while creating a strategy for expanding revenues. Autonomous vehicles provide an alternative to facing the combined effects of increasing urbanization and public investments in public transportation networks. They represent an alternative path that points to a declining market for individual cars.

In addition, autonomous vehicles might influence the design of cities going forward. They might decrease demand for convenient parking places and increase demand for waiting spaces for cars on curbs rather than "staying" places in parking garages (see figures 3.3 and 3.4). Cities, of course, can manage these shifts in demand by altering the number of parking spaces required for residential and commercial businesses in zoning regulations and designing new curb cuts and lane lines. These interventions all fall within current practices and programs. They are modifications to the current transportation platform, not a transformation of it.

FIGURE 3.3 Smart cities objects: A typical ICT integrated urban parking system with payment connected to smart phones, Montreal, Canada, 2015.

(*Source*: Jennifer Clark)

FIGURE 3.4 Example of smart cities solutions operating at the building scale. Illustration of the uses of real-time data for car parks.

(*Source*: Akarat Phasura/Shutterstock)

That said, the investments that autonomous vehicles require to move past the demonstration phase are much more significant. Autonomous vehicles require the full-scale redeployment of transportation and connectivity platforms in cities. Curb cuts are not enough. Indeed, efforts to create testbeds for autonomous vehicles have demonstrated that it is their interactions with the existing environment that limits their successful implementation. It is not the level of the car's autonomy that matters; it is the character of the built environment in which it is deployed—the clarity of the lane lines, the speed of the information the car acquires (and sends and processes), the behavior of other actors in the external environment. In other words, under current conditions, when autonomous vehicles move beyond their primary state as a smart cities object and are deployed in the city, they fail to integrate effectively into the existing urban transportation and communication systems. They are, then, simply objects searching for an interoperable platform into which to plug. The platform they require is well beyond that for which there is a plan to provide. And like a pet who reaches the edge of an invisible fence, the territory over which autonomous vehicles can roam is functionally restricted; in this case, to the boundaries of its tailored testbed rather than to the lot lines of the backyard.

Don Clark, in the *New York Times*, summarized the current state of autonomous vehicle deployments as follows:

> Today's internet-connected car may be able to get driving directions sent to it, but it is essentially the same as getting email: the one-way transportation of pre-existing information. The autonomous car is something vastly different, in which the 5G network allows computers to orchestrate a flood of information from multitudes of input sensors for real time, on-the-fly decision-making.[20]

Because autonomous vehicles are designed as upgraded products for an existing market, they reflect specificities (and histories) of that market. Predictably, autonomous vehicles are designed to be attractive to current clients and customers. That market is not currently asked to consider (or significantly share) the cost of the urban environment in which the vehicle operates. Those costs and characteristics are borne and determined by the cities and jurisdictions that provide the transportation platforms on which the city and its citizens conduct myriad individual and collective activities every day. Autonomous vehicles are effectively incompatible with the city as is because they were designed on the assumption that the smart cities platform would be provided for them, just as the antecedent urban transportation platform was developed to accommodate driver-operated cars.

This, of course, is an untenable situation under current conditions. Although vendors can provide smart cities systems and objects to both cities and consumers, they cannot provide the platforms on which the smart city operates: the energy grid, the networked connectivity, the transportation network, the roads, bridges, and highways. Or, more precisely, vendors do not, for the most part, offer those platforms now. In some cases, utilities provide energy systems, but they do so in a highly regulated environment, especially within municipalities. All this is to say that the private provisioning of urban infrastructure—particularly at the platform rather than the project scale—would be a new phase and new form of privatization. And this is an important point: how the smart cities project implicates further and future privatization.

Perhaps even more ubiquitous than autonomous vehicles in the smart cities project is the proliferation of navigation software as services in cars and smart phone applications. The design and deployment of such software is itself an instructive example of how the smart cities industry relies on urban data and uses the city not only as a subsidized platform for product development but also a site of extraction from which to collect the data necessary for the products and services it offers.

Regarding the technology industry, which has denied the importance of territory at all, a demonstrated attention to geography deserves some analytical attention. The objects, systems, and platforms in the smart cities industry require data about activities and behaviors in cities. They also produce data about activities and behaviors in cities. Data sit at the beginning and the end of the production process. Cities subsidize the smart cities project through the allocation of infrastructure and the allocation of rights and regulation of activities—or, perhaps more clearly, in the failure to do so.

Navigation software applications are generally a subscription service. They are developed by competing software firms based on publicly available data about the built environment and transportation systems, coupled with a dynamic and proprietary service grafted onto that base of public information. The subscription service is available to users who are interested in the information through a registration system. The data on users that are collected and aggregated then provide that essential real-time information back to the software to enhance the interface.

Navigation software highlights the three elements that constitute the basic framework for the design of smart cities applications. These elements illustrate the ways in which smart cities firms function as "controllers and processors" of data on the characteristics and behaviors of individuals.[21] First, users provide continuous information on their behavior through the use of the software. This enables the proprietary and dynamic element of the software that distinguishes it from the basic, public information that underlies it. In effect, the user of the service provides the content. Second, the user enables firms to gather (collect and analyze) information about his or her behavior and characteristics over time and across space. This locationally enhanced information may be of future interest to the software developer or to another firm that is interested in designing and developing future products or marketing additional services to users with a given set of behaviors or characteristics. Third, the navigation software functions as a platform on which the provider or a third party can market services and products (or information) to a user of the navigation app that is tailored to the behaviors and characteristics revealed by the data.

The revenue model of navigation software depends on the balance between these three uses of the data and their relative value. And this balance changes over time. For example, if advertising on the platform substantially reduces the number of users, the ability to collect the behavioral information necessary for the software's essential functions can be affected. Excessive advertising thus constrains the value of the data collected for subsequent product development. Balancing the value of the service to the user against the need to extract data from that user or to convey information across the platform is an essential calculus in the tech industry. The constant rebalancing between extracting and providing is not unfamiliar to people who are in the industry or observers of it.

At least two elements of this business model depend directly on the rules that cities choose to govern data use and ownership. For the firms that are developing smart cities services and products, the importance of the terms of use and ownership affect the production side of the equation. The navigation software example demonstrates two key ways in which cities subsidize the production of smart cities products and services. First, information is provided on the characteristics of the place—for example, the street grid in this case. That information is gathered from public sources. And although this is widely understood it, few characterize navigation software as a publicly subsidized commercial product. More often, such software applications are thought of as examples of technology-driven entrepreneurship. It is, of course, one of the functions of urban entrepreneurialism to provide a platform for private (and public) innovation. However, the design and operation of that platform are not without cost. Thus, residents (and taxpayers) significantly subsidize both the platform and the information generated from it. Said another way, cities provide not only the streets but also the map, the signifier of the streets.

In the navigation software example, the value of user data for the design of smart cities products and services is in its *additionality*. That additionality is the dynamic data collected from drivers and projected onto the map of the city to provide information to inform choices. To design the service, however, there must be a strategy for harvesting those data and a platform on which to project them. The city becomes the laboratory for that product design. Time, like geography, influences the value of the data. This meaning, importance, and, ultimately, demand for navigational data is highly specific in both time and space. Data about traffic volume on highway I-395 means something to someone caught on the Capital Beltway in northern Virginia who is trying to make it on time to a performance at the Kennedy Center. But that same information means nothing to a driver on the Connector who is trying to catch a flight at Atlanta's Hartsfield–Jackson airport. The market value of the data is highly contextualized. The stored data, however—the record of routes and individual behaviors and characteristics—have much broader applications. Those data might be valuable for multiple research and marketing applications. And that information generates a great deal of attention in the smart cities industry and should be a focus of urban policy makers.

In effect, smart cities firms do not pay for the two essential inputs to the products and services they produce: the base information or the user data they graft onto it. By way of comparison, there are many technology and innovation-intensive industries operating across the economy. To put the navigation software into context, the pharmaceutical industry relies heavily on publicly subsidized basic research. In that industry, time to market, internal research and development, and identification of the target market are all far more expensive activities and hold greater potential liability and risk in data acquisition, monitoring, and testing. Although product development and examinations of research on market demand are publicly subsidized in both the smart cities and the pharmaceuticals industries, the development process for pharmaceuticals and medical devices is more complex, uncertain, and expensive. In a competitive investment environment, smart cities look light on initial capital investment, fast to commercialization, and large in the market and thus a lower cost investment with a potentially higher return.

Whether smart cities are the application or the intention that ushers in that new phase of privatization remains unclear. Thus far, the smart cities conversation has not acknowledged the magnitude of the distinction between contracting out to vendors for city services and systems and privatizing urban infrastructure or smart cities platforms. The absence of this conversation—even in most critiques of smart cities—is telling. It is, in part, revealing about how far the conversation about what sits in the public sector and what sits in the private sector has evolved in the wake of the broader neoliberal projects of devolution and privatization.[22] The withdrawal of the public sector from domains it previously occupied disregards the erosion of a previous doctrine that justified public investment in public goods to provide a level playing field for private development. What has emerged in place of that argument is an alternative practice, if not a competing argument. Instead of a level playing field provided by the public sector, there is now decidedly uneven investment by the public sector, determined on a case-by-case basis, in specific private partnerships. The practice, then, has moved away from creating the normatively neutral conditions for private development toward the differential selection of private development proposals in terms of both the projects chosen and who has the opportunity to pursue them.

In economic development, there has long been a prohibition against the public sector picking winners and losers, privileging one provider over another. Procurement practices by cities have guarded against this practice through the process of requesting multiple proposals for services and then selecting among them based on stated and transparent criteria. The smart cities project challenges these models in significant ways. The autonomous vehicles example illustrates that the conceptual and operational distinction between the role of the citizen and the function of a consumer in smart cities implementation requires disambiguation. By imagining that there is no difference between the design of a system for a citizen and one for a consumer, and suggesting that the ownership of infrastructure follows the same rationale and review as the ownership of an object, the smart cities project demonstrates an impressive level of ignorance of both cities and economies.

MONETIZING SMART CITIES: PUBLIC PLATFORMS FOR PRIVATE ENTERPRISE

If the platform makes the smart cities market, then the data make the smart cities product. Data are among the most conceptually complex elements of the urban innovation conversation. This is not because the data are large in scale or complicated in character, but because they constitute unqueried information with an unknown value. Additionally, the emergence of data as a commodity is by no means restricted to the smart cities discourse.[23] The valuation (and evaluation) of data has emerged as central to the technology sector as a whole and to incumbent industries as they struggle to develop new revenue models that are capable of competing with the emerging technology sector.[24] That competition is conducted not only in the market but also in the world of public policies that support two very different industry structures—one with significant path dependencies, legacy costs, market power, and substantial assets, and the other with flexibility, capital, and emergent rather than established organizational behaviors.

Some commentators have begun to refer aspirationally to data as "the new oil."[25] There is much speculation as to the potential value of data as a tradeable commodity and its future role as the "fuel" of a knowledge economy. There is less attention to the aspects of this metaphor for data commodification that are far more troubling, including its extractive nature and its potential for geopolitical destabilization. An emergent economic geography of data commodification is becoming increasingly evident, delineated both by the national and regional variations in governance as well as in underlying regional capacities and the spatial organization of incumbent industries (and their dynamic supply chains and global value networks). Smart cities data make up only one of the conversations about data ownership, access, value, quality, and meaning. In many ways, the smart cities data conversation is more complicated than the data conversation in other industries because of the porous boundaries between the public and private sectors in the current operations of cities.

In contexts such as smart manufacturing and energy, which are dominated by private-sector actors, the question of data valuation

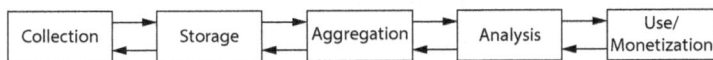

FIGURE 3.5 Industrial data production process.

and commodification can be understood using established analytical techniques borrowed from economic and urban geography and industry studies.[26] For that reason, my research group started our work on industrial data rather than the production of smart cities data, identifying the production circuit for industrial data as the collection, storage, aggregation, analysis, and use or monetization of the data generated in the production of industrial objects or in the general operations of an industrial object (see figure 3.5).[27]

A premise of our approach is that if data constitute a production process, then the actors, processes, geographies, and objects produced through the commodification of data should be identifiable within and across sectors. That said, it is important to distinguish how and in what ways data production in the smart cities domain is distinct from the production of data in the private sector. It would be far more straightforward to say that smart cities data are produced, consumed, or applied in the public sector—in, for, and by a city. However, this is not the case. Smart cities data are generated, collected, stored, aggregated, analyzed, and used (including sold) by a dynamic collection of private- and public-sector actors. This reality has complicated the production of an open data framework in the implementation of smart cities strategies. It is not entirely clear what constitutes public data when private firms, not cities, are providing public services that generate and collect the information.

Context matters. Again, understanding the character and conditions of the incumbent industry into which a new technology is diffused is critical for predicting the patterns and practices that will emerge from that diffusion process. Effective public policies that are intended to direct and support urban innovation require some basic conceptualization of the underlying structures of the existing industry. In the case of smart cities, the relative dearth of domain expertise in urban policy or planning in what is largely a technology conversation reveals itself in the absence of this analysis. Cities (and most local governments) are engaged in a great deal of outsourcing. City services are performed by a network of private-sector actors that include utilities, asset maintenance, waste management, telecommunications, social services, and others. The levels of outsourcing vary by national and regional context, thus complicating how the smart cities project develops as a model for data collection and extraction.

As an asset, data have three levels of potential value for existing operators. These three levels hold across industries. First, data are valuable because they provide potential insights about the optimization of existing operations. In other words, data enable an operator (manufacturer, service provider) to do what it does better—faster, cheaper, more sustainably. Second, data are valuable because they provide the opportunity to identify and develop new services (or products) for an existing client base. In the first instance, data allow for an operator to operate better; and in the second instance, data enable the operator to expand beyond current offerings. In the former, the operator saves money; in the latter, the operator develops an additional revenue stream from an existing market. Third, data are valuable because they enable an operator to expand beyond current services (or products) to a new market altogether. The data make a new market.

For cities, the value of data begins with the potential for optimizing existing services provided to citizens and then moves on to facilitating the creation of new services. These new services can be the result of an integration of existing services or innovations into new services altogether. For example, the provisioning of municipal wireless or small cell services fits the category of new smart cities services provided to existing citizens.

Using the data they have collected, cities can develop new products that can be provided to clients or customers beyond the base of the cities' citizens. These products could be new smart cities objects, systems, platforms, or data. The product could be raw data, or, following the oil metaphor, the product or service could emerge from refined data that have moved further through the production process and developed a discrete new use (an object, system, or platform). Thus, an aspirational goal of urban innovation for cities is to develop and provide the new technology services and products that emerge from the integration of emerging innovations into city services and operations: the objects, systems, and platforms.

The reality is that the design and delivery of city services is not a public project; rather, it is a hybrid public–private space. In other words, the smart cities project is not merely unfolding on an uneven physical landscape in terms of what services are provided; it is also emerging on an uneven organizational landscape in terms of who provides particular services. In some cities, waste management services are provided by a third-party vendor, just as in some places, water services or streetlights are managed and maintained by third-party contractors. Further, cities frequently contract out for services for a fixed period. A city might enter a contract for the management of its parking services and then, at the end of that contract, chose to bring those services back under city management. This process of contracting in and out is part of the regular operations of city services.[28]

In short, public-sector privatization is a dynamic rather than a static condition. The uneven distribution of services and capabilities in technology-enabled services and in the underlying basic services themselves varies across time and space. Innovation is uneven, and so is privatization.

For the smart cities industry, all these factors—including data access and ownership and the scope and timing of public subsidy—have complicated the market calculus. Simply put, it is not obvious where the value (and the revenue) lies. Among the challenges in estimating the size of the smart cities market is understanding the value of smart cities data and the costs of acquiring, curating, managing, and marketing that information.[29] The costs and value are difficult to assess because ownership and access standards remain unclear. With all the discussion of the promises of data innovation and the Internet of Things, there are three key issues preventing the accurate evaluation of the size and value of these markets and, thus, the level of private and public investment justified to access it: (a) the connectivity requirements and the distribution of those requirements among actors; (b) the governance of data (privacy, security, ownership, and access) and the distribution of the risks and responsibilities among actors; and (c) the exchange and use value of smart cities data. Ultimately, the challenge in defining the market is the ambiguity in pricing and distribution of its component costs.

As with many emerging industries, the smart cities industry requires infrastructure investments to take hold. In addition, it requires investments in research and development. The public sector thus becomes implicated in the development of smart cities from several directions. First, as I have discussed, cities are the client for many smart cities products and services. Public investment is required to secure that demand for smart cities systems. Second, cities, states, and public authorities are responsible for the deployment of the infrastructure that forms the foundation for smart cities systems (connectivity, energy, transportation, etc.). Finally, the public sector frequently finances some measure of precommercial research and development for smart cities technologies. From a demand perspective, a governance perspective, or a technology development perspective, the public sector plays an essential role in the financing and management of the smart cities industry. Therefore, the question of the balance between public- and private-sector engagement is particularly critical in the development of this industry. The public-sector subsidizes both the demand and supply sides of the smart cities project, as it does in the defense and health care industries. It is not an unprecedented arrangement, but it is also not often clearly articulated.

Unlike the evolving industries and emerging markets in the (primarily) private sector, the smart cities industry operates largely within the territorial boundaries of the city. That is, the required infrastructure for these deployments and the interoperability required for their functions is scoped to the city scale. The big "ask" of the smart cities industry is for cities to provide the platform and infrastructure foundation for the industry to operate its network of products and services. The real challenge that the smart cities project confronts, and the problem that the smart cities market makers hope that the public sector will solve for them, is the that of the platform. The emerging market that smart cities require is an upgraded urban platform on which to operate. What has developed in the smart cities conversation is an expanding role for the public sector in providing that platform for innovation (through connectivity, data, access), thus creating new economic opportunities. The increased availability of public data allows innovators (civic, social, private or public sector) to develop new services or products (including software, sensors, and data and service subscriptions), develop new processes for performance optimization to more efficiently provision existing public services, and upgrade infrastructure and urban design investments to contribute to either new data or enhanced performance, or both. But it is the platform that makes the market. And under current conditions, it is cities that are asked to provide it as part of the extended logic of urban entrepreneurialism.

4

SMART CITIES AS THE NEW
URBAN ENTREPRENEURSHIP

CITIES compete with one another for people and production. Cities work to attract residents and resources. This competition is not new. It is a feature and not a bug in the capitalist space economy.[1] In addition, cities are in direct competition because people, firms, and institutions all make choices about where to live and locate based on a set of preferences. Although interjurisdictional competition among places for economic activity and assets is common, the general public often seems surprised by the practices and policies behind that competition. The subject occasionally rises to public attention when there is a debate over the public funding of sports stadiums or other high-profile and overt interjurisdictional competitions such as the Amazon HQ2 request for proposals in 2018 or the Foxconn decision to locate a production facility in Wisconsin in 2017 (and the subsequent walking back of that deal in 2019).[2]

Interjurisdictional competition sets the stage for urban entrepreneurship. In other words, the competition for economic activity and assets among cities expands their role beyond simply managing and providing a commonly agreed-on level of public services and infrastructure to investing in differentiated—and, thus, differentiating—types of services and infrastructure.

These practices, and the trade-offs they require between basic services and tailored and targeted investments, are known as *urban entrepreneurship*. The urban entrepreneurship defined by David Harvey, and at the heart of the Lynne Sagalyn's "times square redux" paradigm, is the branding and entrepreneurial activity of the city itself.[3] The critique of urban regeneration projects and the "theme park" approach to urban redevelopment has received considerable attention. The smart cities project has adopted these practices, without any significant modification, in response to the concerns of academics or policy makers who have identified the ways in which these programs promote uneven development.[4]

In this chapter, I consider two broad categories of urban entrepreneurship operating in the smart cities project. These categories are distinguished from each other by the actors engaged in the entrepreneurial activity: in the first case, cities and private-sector firms, and in the second case, residents or workers who are both the subjects and the objects of the flexible work arrangements enabled by the smart cities platform. The second kind of urban entrepreneurship in the smart cities project has received far less extended discussion and is a new phenomenon ushered in by the smart cities project rather than the evolution of an old one. The smart cities project promotes and facilitates a new model of labor flexibility—a form of *individualized* urban entrepreneurship that grafts onto and spatializes the processes of labor flexibility that have developed in work practices over the last forty years.

It can be debated whether the institutions and intermediaries producing flexible work spaces in smart cities simply reflect the increasing labor flexibility of the last thirty years, or whether smart cities are actually dependent on flexible labor markets. In either case, the smart cities project promotes two types of urban entrepreneurialism: for places and for people. This chapter addresses both types of urban entrepreneurialism and, specifically, how the technological experiments of the smart cities project reshape cities and redefine work.

CITIES AS TESTBEDS: MARKETING TECHNOLOGY AND COMPETITIVE ADVANTAGE

Interjurisdictional competition and the zero-sum game it creates for cities and regions is a common and consistent part of academic economic development research.[5] The practice of economic development itself, however, remains predicated on the development of proposals and counterproposals to attract firms and economic activity to particular places. This practice is heavily critiqued but also firmly entrenched.[6] Few places resist the zero-sum game, and even fewer place restrictions on the subsidies and tax breaks that localities offer to firms. For cities, then, place branding is an aspect of competitive marketing that is carried out to draw comparisons with other cities and regions, rather than an isolated activity.

Cities and regions, especially as they emerged from the crises of the 1970s and 1980s, as characterized in chapter 2, largely stopped fighting interjurisdictional competition and began embracing urban entrepreneurialism and urban regeneration projects in the 1980s and 1990s.[7] The result has been what Frieden and Sagalyn referred to as "downtown, inc.," indicating an orientation toward rebranding cities as "festival marketplaces."[8] Simply put, the priority shifted toward urban regeneration projects that provide a safe space for consumption rather than a place for production. These priorities have changed central cities. They have facilitated the rebranding of many cities around consumption-oriented specializations rather than old production industries (see figures 4.1 and 4.2). Dropping the attributes of an industrial past and embracing a future of technology-driven knowledge services is now a well-established pattern. Indeed, if Pittsburgh can claim the transition from a steel center to a high-tech city, the trend is set.[9] Cities such as San Francisco and Seattle have embraced this practice rhetorically even as their urban economies made the transition incompletely, leaving vast gaps between incomes and housing prices as well as other symptoms of the partial and fundamentally inequitable outcomes of employing urban entrepreneurialism as a guiding strategy for civic investment.[10]

FIGURE 4.1 Showcasing urban entrepreneurialism: regeneration and reinvestment projects near Brindleyplace and Gas Street Basin, Birmingham, England, 2013.

(*Source*: Jennifer Clark)

FIGURE 4.2 Showcasing urban entrepreneurialism: regeneration and reinvestment projects near Brindleyplace and The Mailbox, Gas Street Basin, Birmingham, England, 2013.

(*Source*: Jennifer Clark)

Constructing narratives about cities is not a new practice. The rapid adoption of the smart cities discourse evolved from this underlying habit of "hyping" the city and creating buzz: its tourist attractions; sports teams; specialized infrastructure, technologies, or industries; and tailored business incentives and subsidies.[11] More recently, the selling of the city has extended to an expanding menu of civic amenities aimed at attracting and entertaining a "creative class" of workers who function as both residents and local consumers.[12] The smart cities project is a method that is used to define the city as a space specially tailored for innovative production and consumption activities, a platform on which workers and firms conduct their entrepreneurial high-tech activities.

Historically, defining a distinct regional identity is a marketing mechanism that is activated to attract both generalized and targeted economic investment. Regional identities are often associated with tourism strategies. For tourism-oriented cities such as Las Vegas, this branding is essential. For more diversified or historical cities, the branding tends to be more about an ethos or milieu rather than a specific function. "City of Lights" is a quintessential example. Such narratives also are associated with technology or industry specializations such as "Silicon Valley" or "Steel City." These regional economic identities were a common local economic development practice throughout the post–World War II era as cities and regions adopted explicitly export-oriented strategies in concert with their conventional real estate development investments in convention centers and stadiums.[13]

As noted in previous chapters, a set of emerging contemporary technology investments has redefined how cities compete in the new economy. Beyond the mains, drains, roads, and basic services essential for economic development, there is a growing set of expectations about connectivity and livability that influences the locational choices of firms, industries, entrepreneurs, and talent.[14] In the smart cities discourse, these building blocks of a competitive regional economy are provisioned and provided by the city, not the firms that operate in it. This discussion harkens back to David Harvey's 1989 commentary about urban entrepreneurialism and the meaning of those practices for interjurisdictional competition and the zero-sum outcomes that are the result of that process for people and places.[15]

In the smart cities context, there is an increasingly important distinction about how services are designed and how they are developed, and by whom. That distinction involves the porous boundary between the private and the public sector.[16] This distinction is further connected to questions about the growing flexibility of markets and market relationships that operate on the platform of capacities (integrated urban infrastructure) provisioned by the public sector. Through the rhetoric of smart cities, the responsibility for the underlying factors and conditions required for dynamic, high-tech entrepreneurial activity has subtly shifted from the private to the public sector. Connectivity—and all that it entails—is increasingly and newly defined as a public good necessary for the operation of not only the city but the economic, social, and civic activities that occur within it. In other words, it is becoming the mayor, not the CEO, who is perceived as responsible for the underlying technology infrastructure that supports everyday commercial and civic activities. It is the boundaries of the city, not the boundaries of the firm, that define that responsibility to provision the capacity to do high-tech work. However, the question of how this connectivity is appropriately provisioned has not been resolved and is the subject of many preliminary projects.[17] Ben Green's *The Smart Enough City* and Goldsmith and Crawford's *The Responsive City* catalog many of these projects in process.[18]

In part, the smart cities project has now become an essential branding exercise that is necessary for leveraging private-sector investment in technology and basic infrastructure. The buzz about smart cities drives local economic development and targeted real estate investments. A new vocabulary has emerged with terms such as *innovation district, coworking*, and *maker space* to describe places where infrastructure supports high-tech services and products that require enhanced connectivity and access. Real estate investors, commercial real estate firms, and cities themselves are working to label, brand, and sell these places in a competitive environment. These new entrepreneurial spaces are an evolution of a series of strategies and practices that have triggered critique from the initial inception of the basic model—enabling new types of entrepreneurial activities deployed on a platform of smart cities services rather than provisioned by individual firms.[19] Some of the emblematic examples of these trends include the Ponce City Market in Atlanta (see figures 4.3 and 4.4) and Brooklyn Navy Yards in New York City (figures 4.5 and 4.6).[20]

It is onto this landscape of redevelopment that the smart cities project is deployed. The smart cities project meets cities in the midst of their own entrepreneurial projects as they seek to brand and sell themselves as spaces of technological change and sites of production and consumption in the emergent knowledge economy. The mechanics of how cities make themselves attractive to people and firms in and for a new economy is far from straightforward. It is a work in progress. It is a model under construction. It is not clear what this new knowledge economy requires as a platform for entrepreneurship and economic expansion that is so different from platforms of previous eras. Narratives about the need for increased

FIGURE 4.3 New urban entrepreneurialism: redevelopment of a 2.1 million-square-foot former Sears Distribution Center along the East Side Trail of the Atlanta BeltLine by the developer of Chelsea Market in New York City, Jamestown. Dockless bicycle included at the BeltLine entrance to Ponce City Market, Atlanta, GA, 2018.

(*Source*: Adam Yesner/Shutterstock)

FIGURE 4.4 New urban entrepreneurialism: expanding the scope of mixed-use development to include manufacturing entrepreneurs: A "maker space" in The Ponce City Market, Atlanta, Georgia, 2019.

(*Source*: EQ Roy/Shutterstock)

FIGURE 4.5 New urban entrepreneurialism: "We used to launch ships; now we launch businesses." The beginnings of the redevelopment of the Brooklyn Navy Yard, Brooklyn, New York, 2014.

(*Source*: littleNY STOCK/Shutterstock)

FIGURE 4.6 New urban entrepreneurialism: Building 92 at the Brooklyn Navy Yard featuring coffee shop, museum, offices, and display of the products designed and manufactured in the maker spaces of the redeveloped Brooklyn Navy Yard, Brooklyn, New York, 2019.

(*Source*: Jennifer Clark)

connectivity and mobility dominate the discussion even as they lack specificity. The popularity of arguments about the creative class and lifestyle infrastructure investments highlight the ways in which strategies for economic development attraction and recruitment have been upended. For economic development analysis, it is no longer even clear if the unit of analysis is people or firms or some artifact of creative production such as a patent or an authentic place. Cities like Pittsburgh agree to serve as real-time technology testbeds in an effort to shed their industrial past and claim a new narrative that is focused on an as-yet-unknown future.[21] And cities like Atlanta rename themselves ("the ATL") to signal their emergent next-generational identities (see figure 4.7).

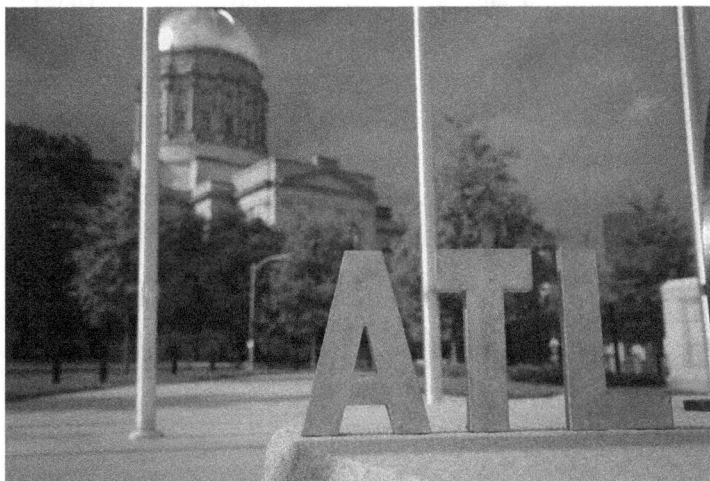

FIGURE 4.7 Branding Smart Cities: from Atlanta to "The ATL."
ATL Sign with the Georgia State Capitol's Gold Dome
in the background, Atlanta, Georgia, 2018.

(*Source*: TuckerBlade/Shutterstock)

As cities evaluate how to participate in the smart cities project, the reality of interjurisdictional competition influences their assessment. The scope of the smart cities project reaches well beyond the issue of casting or creating cities as "living labs" for technology experiments such as autonomous vehicles. Cities are becoming experimental spaces for all kinds of emergent flexibilities, including ride-hailing services and flexible work spaces. And it is here that urban entrepreneurialism converges with the smart cities project to reshape the physical landscape. But this convergence also redefines a practice as well as a place; ultimately, how the costs and risks of economic experimentation (entrepreneurialism) are distributed by and within cities among people, firms, and the public sector. Technology firms that are leading smart cities projects demand flexibility in regulatory regimes and also in land and labor markets, contracts, and relationships. They bargain for access to the city and the data they can derive from it in exchange for providing preliminary services in a piecemeal manner. Cities engage in this concession bargaining because of their limited ability to provide municipal services and the perceived necessity of these services to remain economically competitive. The example of LinkNYC information kiosks (see figures 4.8–4.10) and similar projects (see figure 4.11) serves

FIGURE 4.8 Evolution of the urban information kiosk: becoming a smart cities object and part of a fixed-sensor network. A LinkNYC kiosk integrates private advertising with public services, New York City, 2019.

(*Source*: Jennifer Clark)

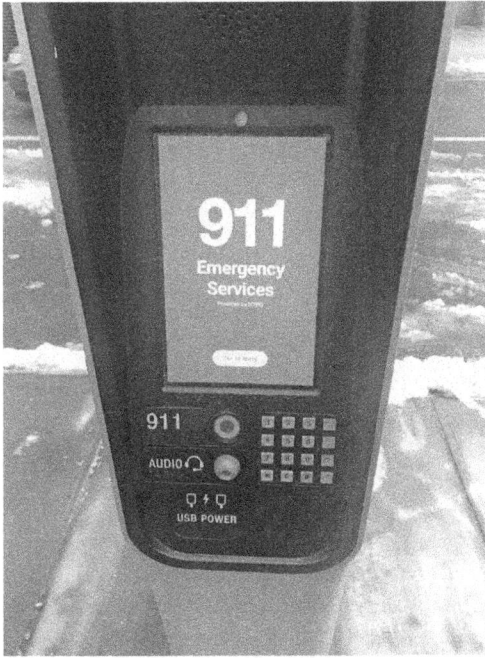

FIGURE 4.9 Evolution of the urban information kiosk:
becoming a smart cities object and part of a fixed-sensor network:
LinkNYC kiosk incorporates emergency public services:
911 reporting. New York City, 2019.

(*Source*: Jennifer Clark)

as a representative example of a private firm (Sidewalk Labs/
Alphabet) providing a municipal service—Wi-Fi—in exchange
for access to the locational and device data about users who
connect to the service.[22] The practice of swapping services for
access (to the city and its residents) is central to the design of
smart cities project deployments.

The evolution of these practices is not unexpected. Firms
often develop patterns and path dependencies in response to the

FIGURE 4.10 Evolution of the urban information kiosk: becoming a smart cities object and part of a fixed-sensor network: Just Plug In! LinkNYC kiosk combining public phone, public Wi-Fi, device-charging station, emergency services, and advertising, New York City, 2019.

(*Source*: Jennifer Clark)

FIGURE 4.11 Evolution of the urban information kiosk: a traditional kiosk providing one-way information flow and no connectivity at the Old Birmingham Central Library (demolished in 2016), Birmingham, England, 2014.

(*Source*: Jennifer Clark)

regulatory conditions from which the firms originally emerged.[23] For example, national labor market practices follow firms as they expand internationally as a set of practices and expectations that are hard wired into the firm's strategies, regardless of the regulatory regimes operating in the new locations.[24] The dominance of technology firms in the smart cities project has such effects. Tech companies come to the smart cities project with embedded expectations and strategies that were adopted from a time when their product development lived in a lab rather than a real place: an existing city. Much of product development and design in the tech sector occurs in a simulated or even completely virtual world. Computer modeling allows for experimentation based on estimated inputs and approximate outcomes using a language of scientific experimentation that conflates simulated spaces with actual places. The virtual spaces of technology experimentation are software platforms and portals: smartphone applications and Web interfaces. Such spaces facilitate user interactions and provide information. And, of course, they amass information extracted from users in the real world. However, because these objects and systems operate in virtual space—physically constrained and contained by that (virtual) reality—they provide users with information that influences user behavior in real space; for example, with wayfinding applications. But the action—the choice based on the information—remains at the discretion of the individual rather than at the direction of the application. It is that variation that makes the real-time observation of users in the real world so critical for the product design process.

Cities are no strangers to urban systems modeling. Urban planners have long used models to inform planning and policy decisions. Demographic and transportation models are fundamental project tools.[25] Analysts of economic development also use a series of tools to estimate the impacts of investments and ascertain the effects of particular changes.[26] These models are how planners test changes in assumptions and make projections about where to direct future investments. Planners adjust the parameters of the models to account for local conditions and past experience. Cities rarely use a planning model straight out of the box; rather, they tweak and adjust the tool according to the context and priorities of the communities they serve.

Cities engage in experimentation. However, that experimentation is largely confined to the policy analysis and design phases and does not often creep into program and project implementation. Since the 1960s, when large-scale computer models came into use, computer scientists and engineers have speculated about urban operating systems and the potential not only to automate the city—or, at least, many city systems—but also to use the city as a testbed for a whole array of other integrated systems.[27] The city, as noted in chapter 3, is a dense, rich space of human interaction with materials and machines, services and systems. The city is potentially the testbed that allows modeling to escape its virtual world and engage real-time spaces in order to observe the behaviors of people, institutions, objects, and systems in an environment where there are many alternative choices. In cities, there are many choices to make. To automate complex cyber physical systems, it is necessary to understand the vast number of layered and related potential decisions that are, or may be, possible.[28]

People who study and operate cities, unlike many of the computer scientists and engineers who guide the smart cities project, have remained skeptical of automated tools and the testing required to design and calibrate them. The argument in planning theory is that cities are about people making choices, not about computers making decisions.[29] That is one of the ethical presumptions operating within the practice and the discipline.[30]

And, in some key ways, this explains the absence of urban planners in debates about the smart cities project: automating the city is not an urban planning project; it is an engineering project. However, in the absence of domain experts on cities, the amateurs have moved forward with their new urban entrepreneurialism using the city as the testbed for everything from environmental sensor systems, to recycling-tracking systems, to audio detectors, to e-scooters, to driverless vehicles informing everything from predictive policing to vehicle routing.

The 2016 report issued by the U.S. Office of Science and Technology Policy, entitled "Technology and the Future of Cities," pushed the city as a technology testbed approach. This advocacy was explicitly geographic, focused on the creation of urban development districts as testbeds for the implementation of smart city ideas and technologies. The report essentially recommended that the development of smart cities happens not at the scale of the city but, rather, in "discrete regions within cities," where a "district does not necessarily have a predefined scale, nor must it fall within the political boundaries of a single city."[31] The report focused on these urban development districts; the authors argued that "districts offer larger cities the chance to take on these challenges in bite-sized stages."[32] There was no recognition of how an urban development strategy built entirely around these testbed sites contributed to continued uneven urban development.

As with all experiments in real places involving real people, there are real consequences. Autonomous vehicles now have a body count. Ride-hailing services have thrown traditional taxi services into sharp decline in the cities where they operate under new rules or no regulation.[33] Notably, ride-hailing services normalize and exacerbate evolving practices of labor flexibility and contingent employment. These new forms of transportation contribute to a dramatic rethinking of how to project and target investments in the built environment. The point is that real-time experimentation in cities has real-life effects beyond the scope of the project design. In an effort to appear technologically savvy, cities have allowed experimentation in their jurisdictions. This experimentation is cast as entrepreneurial and innovative, yet little of it is conducted by those small and local firms that are so often associated with an entrepreneurial ecosystem. Instead, most of the experimentation is conducted by large companies and corporate consortia or partnerships that are headquartered outside the region, simply using the territory as a testbed. Thus, the city is not a place of investment; it is a place of extraction.

WORK IN SMART CITIES: FLEXIBLE WORK/ FLEXIBLE WORK SPACES

This chapter reflects on how the new urban entrepreneurialism functions in two ways. First, such entrepreneurialism expands on the previous model by weaving the technology testbed approach into the selling and branding of the city as a whole. What is distinct in this new model is how urban innovation alters the brand. The smart city is not tailored to the specificities of places like Detroit as "the Motor City" or the Twin Cities' "medical device alley." Instead, the smart cities brand is the same across all places. The smart cities specialization is not a local capacity but, rather, a permissiveness in the face of technological experimentation, coupled with the policy environment that is required to enable it. Competitive advantage has now been cast as accessibility to technological experimentation.[34] Thus far, few cities have resisted the push of the technology industry to experiment with smart cities data, objects, systems, and platforms within their jurisdictions, although there are some indications—particularly in the Toronto waterfront case—that limitations may emerge.

Permissiveness toward experimentation results in an environment in which technological change plays out across land, labor, and capital markets without much in the way of systematic observation and assessment. There is also little active supervision to manage, direct, or curtail the adverse or unintended impacts of that technological change. The smart cities project has somehow managed to skirt systematic project evaluation, such as seen in environmental impact assessments, either before or after implementation.

Throughout this book there is evidence of the growing impacts of the smart cities project and the power asymmetries it influences and potentially rearranges between citizens and cities, consumers and technology service providers and producers, and the public and private sectors. The argument here is that these dynamic power asymmetries, operationalized and exacerbated through the smart cities project, may be evident in cities, but they are not caused by cities. These dynamics are produced by transitions in the operations, regulation, and distribution of economic activities within cities. The city is only one scale on which these activities operate, and the city is also only one scale of potential regulation. Thus, it is within this multiscalar regulatory context that the emerging new urban entrepreneurialism has affected the organization of work and the labor market as a whole. And this is the second way in which the new urban entrepreneurialism arising from the smart cities project functions: by producing flexible work spaces that incubate and facilitate (as well as reflect) labor flexibility.

The conversation about new entrepreneurial spaces predates the smart cities project, as does the conversation about urban entrepreneurialism. Discussions of such spaces originally characterized them as small business incubators, start-up accelerators, or corporate or university innovation centers. Sometimes these spaces were called *third spaces*, which were neither work nor home.

The institutional support for these spaces has always varied, and so, too, have their origin stories. Some were initiated by a university's facilitating technology transfer and start-up firms, and in other cases, the incubators and accelerators were initiated by a city or economic development agency, a company, or an industry advocacy organization. The accelerators and incubators associated with entrepreneurship typically house small firm start-ups as part of a broader effort to facilitate firm formation and scale-up.[35] The antecedents of these technology transfer and incubator efforts stretch back to the research parks of the 1980s. Evaluations of their efficacy have demonstrated uneven results over time.[36] However, as models of new urban entrepreneurial spaces, they have nevertheless firmly taken hold.

The relationship between these new entrepreneurial spaces and cities has remained fluid. Although established examples of corporate technology campuses such as Bell Labs and Xerox PARC are frequently suburban, in the 1990s and 2000s, creators of new innovation centers, incubators, and accelerators primarily chose city locations.[37] Driven by a discourse about spillover effects in innovation and a sense that proximity drove technological development, the incubators and accelerators were more and more likely to be urban rather than suburban and collocated with other, similar, initiatives.[38] This resulted in the identification of innovation districts in which cities and, often, universities collaborated to embed and attract entrepreneurial activity in central-city business districts.[39]

The innovation districts in particular are an explicitly territorialized part of the smart cities project.[40] They are characterized by agglomerations of technology firms, and the platforms and services designed to serve them, concentrated within specific parts of cities and regions. They are often anchored by major research institutions that maintain formal organizational structures, in contrast to the more flexible governance of nonuniversity incubators, accelerators, and innovation centers. The formal structures offered by universities, both organizationally and physically, maintain a continuity around which these highly flexible work arrangements can operate.

Innovation districts are only one form of the new urban entrepreneurialism. If the first wave was traditional research centers collocated with universities and research institutions, then the second wave was the more flexible incubators and accelerators that interfaced with individual entrepreneurs as well as with the nascent start-ups and the established corporate research partners who dominated the first wave of innovation districts. Maker spaces emerged as a third wave of urban entrepreneurial spaces; these focused on design-driven innovations explicitly aimed toward small-scale production rather than technology services.[41] The most recent wave of this sort of urban entrepreneurial work space is coworking spaces—the places where individuals lease work space from a coworking company such as WeWork rather than work in spaces provided by an employer. The new urban entrepreneurship narrative is built on a discourse that is connected to innovation districts and technology incubators and how they create spillover effects that people now purchase in provisioning their work spaces to better absorb the benefits of proximity. In other words, in the smart city, labor markets are self-aggregating on the supply side rather than responding to the geographies of demand that are defined by concentrations of employers. This is a shift not only in who provisions work spaces and how also but also where they do so in the regional economy.

Labor markets have long shaped cities. Indeed, one might argue that cities exist largely to organize and aggregate work, in addition to other economic activities.[42] That is, the urban form (and how it is deployed and redeployed) reflects a spatial organization of work and workplaces. From the company town to the industrialized city, the built environment serves as an organizing platform for work. In that case, it should come as no surprise that new organizational and institutional modes of work would produce new work spaces and new places. Coworking and the other new urban entrepreneurship institutional models underscore how the smart cities project has effectively translated flexibility as an emerging employment practice into a new physical norm. The smart city is a platform for providing flexible work spaces.

Flexibility is a key theme in the entrenched narratives of innovation systems, high-technology firms, smart cities, and urban entrepreneurialism. The argument for flexibility follows an anti-establishment notion that traditional forms of work organization, both contractual and physical, limit entrepreneurship and individualism. As the thinking goes, models of long-term employment, though perhaps appropriate in previous eras, are no longer desirable for either workers or employers. The old labor market intermediaries that managed employment relationships and defined occupations and established skill levels are too rigid and antiquated for these new entrepreneurial spaces and flexible workers.

It is well established that the proliferation of flexible work arrangements has changed work practices within firms and among workers. However, much less is known about how flexible work practices have produced and are producing flexible work spaces. Since the 1980s, economic geographers and scholars of industrial and labor relations have documented how flexible work practices led to the reorganization of external and internal labor markets, redistribution of work processes, and renegotiation of employment regulations.[43] These changes have affected how firms make strategic decisions about the spatial division of labor within the firm and how they deploy localized assets (work spaces) to manage an increasingly flexible workforce.

Labor flexibility is more than a new workplace practice; it has increasingly become the standard in the U.S. labor market and is on the rise in many other places.[44] The absence of a long-term employment relationship between an employee and employer is no longer considered unusual. Contingent work, part-time work, contractor work, self-employment—all these arrangements revolve around the same trends toward increasing labor flexibility and the absence of a long-term employment relationship. It should perhaps come as no surprise, then, that labor flexibility has a tangible impact on the urban landscape as well.

Most industries have a set of preferred labor practices. For the smart cities industry, the preferred practice appears to be independent contracting—in other words, no formal employment relationship at all. This aligns with the industry's origins in the technology sector. Whether it is a software designer or an Uber driver, the preferred work arrangement tends to be contracting rather than formal employment. Contractors work from project to project or call to call. The contracting arrangement enables the industry to eliminate labor costs from the list of its short-term obligations and potential long-term risks for pensions, health care, employment discrimination and harassment, or worker compensation.

As a consequence, workers are consistently finding themselves in a work world without a traditional workplace—or, at least, not a workplace provided by an employer with the features that are familiar from a shared psychological understanding of a workplace (coffee, a bathroom, a telephone, a desk, coworkers). The urban entrepreneurs in the smart city work in their cars, at the coffee shop or coworking spaces, or in their homes, enacting and reflecting the flexibilities in their psychological employment contracts. In other words, *precarious work* has become *precarious working*—facilitated and enabled by the smart cities project.[45]

It was into this context that Thomas Lodato and I decided to analyze the connection between smart cities and coworking spaces using data on the current state of the coworking industry.[46] In our research, we constructed a database of 662 active coworking spaces within the continental United States in 2016. From this sample, we analyzed the spatial distribution of coworking firms. From that set of 662 coworking spaces, we also created a geographically proportional subsample of 116 spaces on which to conduct more detailed research on the offerings, business models, and characteristics of coworking firms. We wanted to learn how and whether coworking spaces were functioning, not just as new entrepreneurial spaces but also as an emerging form of labor market intermediary.

Coworking is a relatively new form of work organization, so in order to conduct our analysis, we first developed both a working definition of coworking spaces and a typology for understanding the services provided. We defined coworking firms by the revenue models they used; that is, the firm strategies used to sell work space as a service for workers, customers, and members. Table 4.1 defines the four key value propositions we identified through our analysis of the firms in our dataset: (a) space as a service; (b) community, (c) professional network, and (d) labor flexibility. In our analysis, we found that 100 percent of coworking firms provided space as a service and 95 percent of coworking firms provided community. As a consequence, we used these two characteristics as the critical factors defining the coworking industry.

We were also interested in whether coworking was associated with creative class workers—the high-tech workers associated with narratives about workers who choose flexibility rather than permanent employment relationships. In addition, we were interested in whether simple population growth corresponded with the rise of coworking spaces in a given region. What we found was that neither the presence of creative class occupations nor the

TABLE 4.1 Work space as a service

Value proposition	Description
Space as a service	Access to affordable office space and office infrastructure (Wi-Fi, furniture, HVAC, mailboxes, etc.)
Space as community	Access to other workers who can provide social interaction for freelancers, remote workers, contract workers, and small businesses
Space as network	Access to a network of potential peers and clients, best practices and new skills, as well as input for finding investment and new business opportunities
Space as labor flexibility	Access to a work style that allows for labor flexibility and balance between personal and professional identity

pace of population growth in a given metro area fully explained the growth of coworking firms (see table 4.2).

Because we were interested in the connection between coworking spaces and smart cities, we first analyzed the locational distribution of coworking spaces. Of the 662 spaces in our database, only one was located outside a U.S. metro area. The vast majority of the remaining 661 spaces were located in large metro areas. Coworking firms, similar to other labor market intermediaries that have emerged in the era of increasing labor flexibility (such as temporary employment firms), concentrate in places with large labor markets.

Once we established that coworking is largely an urban industry, we turned to other characteristics of coworking firms; namely, their firm strategies and how their revenue models functioned. We found that there are two distinct types of firms:

TABLE 4.2 Testing explanations for the rise of flexible work spaces

Top 10 metropolitan statistical areas with high concentrations of coworking locations and their percentage of creative class occupations, 2016

Metropolitan statistical area	Number of coworking locations	Population, 2015 estimate (ranking)[*]	Population growth 2010–15[*]	Creative class Location quotient[**]	Supercreative core location quotient[**]
New York–Newark–Jersey City, NY-NJ-PA	65	20,182,305 (1st)	2.96%	1.12	1.10
San Francisco–Oakland–Hayward, CA	62	4,656,132 (11th)	7.15%	1.27	1.34
Seattle–Tacoma–Bellevue, WA	39	3,733,580 (15th)	8.26%	1.20	1.36
Los Angeles–Long Beach–Anaheim, CA	38	13,340,068 (2nd)	3.86%	1.06	1.08
Boston–Cambridge–Newton, MA-NH	32	4,774,321 (10th)	4.58%	1.21[***]	1.10[***]
Washington–Arlington–Alexandria–VA-MD-WV	32	6,097,684 (6th)	7.61%	1.48	1.53
Chicago–Naperville–Elgin, IL-IN-WI	28	9,551,031 (3rd)	0.84%	1.05	0.98
Denver–Aurora–Lakewood, CO	23	2,814,330 (19th)	10.17%	1.16	1.16
Nashville–Davidson–Murfreesboro–Franklin, TN	18	1,830,345 (36th)	9.21%	0.99	0.82
Atlanta–Sandy Springs–Roswell, GA	17	5,710,795 (9th)	7.67%	1.08	1.03
MSA Averages[#]	2[†]	329,894	1.62%[††]	0.92[‡]	0.92[#]

[*] Annual estimates of the resident population: April 1, 2010, to July 1, 2015. Source: U.S. Census Bureau, Population Division, Release Date: March 2016.

[**] Combination of reported counts for occupation categories originally specified by Florida (2012).

[***] Occupation data collected for the Boston–Cambridge–Nashua, MA–NH Metropolitan NECTA.

[#] MSA averages are calculated based on data available for all MSAs (LSAD M1), except for occupational reporting. Creative class and super creative core location quotients include a combination of MSAs and NECTAs (LSAD M5).

[†] Average number of coworking spaces includes MSAs where no coworking spaces were recorded. Actual calculated average value mean is 1.67 (median = 0; mode = 0).

[††] Median MSA population change: 0.86%.

[‡] Median creative class location quotient: 0.89.

[#] Median super creative core location quotient: 0.87.

Richard Florida, The Rise of the Creative Class, Revisited, 2nd ed. (New York: Basic Books, 2012).

single-location firms and multisited franchises. This parallels the organization of firms in the temporary employment services industry whereby large firms such as Adecco and Kelly Services set up global franchise operations, whereas local temporary service firms emerged in individual cities working in competition and collaboration with the larger, multisited firms in the industry.[47] And, similar to the case with temporary employment firms, we found some variation in the core services offered by different coworking firms, though not dramatic variation (see table 4.3). This is consistent with a new industry's sorting through the strategies for product differentiation beyond what is the core difference: location.

Cities have long balanced the distribution and management of life, work, and leisure spaces as settings where people, businesses, and flows of resources convene. As spaces of work and business, cities have been central to how and where work is organized, as industrial centers and as centers of information and knowledge production. Increasingly, however, cities are more than sites of collocation, density, and geographically specific resources. Instead, as work shifts from mass production models to hybrid and flexible systems that integrate service and production work, cities are transforming into places where flexible work happens. This trend parallels the emergence of service-embedded goods, niche and batch production enabled by technologies such as additive manufacturing, and the extensive and increasingly essential use of e-retailing for reaching customers for services and goods. The rise of coworking spaces, maker spaces, and other forms of new work spaces facilitates both high-tech service work and small-scale production. This work is often conducted by small businesses, freelance and contract workers, and remote employees.

Much has been made by smart cities observers and advocates about how the introduction of autonomous vehicles will change

TABLE 4.3 Common services provided by coworking firms

Frequency of common coworking offerings by firm and location, 2016

Coworking offering	By firm (percentage)	By individual site (percentage)
Office infrastructure (space as a service)	78 (100%)	116 (100%)
24/7 Access	60 (77%)	88 (76%)
Furniture	76 (97%)	114 (98%)
Wireless network access	77 (99%)	115 (99%)
Mailbox and/or mail services	45 (58%)	69 (59%)
Printing	61 (78%)	99 (85%)
Conference/meeting rooms	74 (95%)	112 (97%)
Meeting tools	61 (78%)	98 (84%)
Coffee and/or tea	73 (94%)	111 (96%)
Kitchen(ette) access	50 (64%)	86 (74%)
Community# (social interaction)	73 (94%)	110 (95%)
Professional development## (professional network)	54 (69%)	90 (78%)
Work-life support# (work-life balance)	49 (63%)	79 (68%)

"Social interaction" refers to language used by coworking firms about the benefit of proximity to other workers in terms of both company and collaboration.

"Professional development" includes informal learning (e.g., "lunch-and-learns"), professional panels, networking events (e.g., meet-ups), and members-only events.

"Work-life support" refers to listed amenities such as relaxation areas, gym access, bike storage, dog-friendliness, and wellness programs (i.e., on-site yoga or massage).

urban design practices and alter the built environment. However, the smart cities project has already changed the built environment in visible, if subtle, ways. The smart cities project has normalized labor flexibility through both the exercise of its preferred employment practices and the practices that embed in urban labor markets as a response to those norms. This is not to say that smart cities are responsible for labor flexibility; rather, it is the practices, products, and services of smart cities that support and facilitate labor flexibilities. Further, those labor flexibilities have produced a spatial reorganization of work space and the emergence of a whole new category of labor market intermediaries who sell space to new urban entrepreneurs. As a consequence, contingency and entrepreneurship have become rhetorically and spatially conflated.

The smart cities project depends on both forms of the new urban entrepreneurship: to convince and compel cities to serve as technology testbeds, and to organize the work of and in smart cities. Coworking is just one example of how the smart cities project is producing new forms of flexibility that are largely dependent on the development and deployment of business-grade infrastructure that is capable of supporting new levels of mobility and connectivity. Fundamentally, the design of the industrial city reflects the assumption of a daily journey to work or school. The assumptions about the level of mobility required reflect that underlying assumption about the organization of work. What smart cities propose is a reconfiguration of work that requires an increase in mobility and connectivity. What the smart cities project simultaneously proposes is a set of solutions to that challenge. As noted previously, the smart cities project seeks to provide the objects, systems, and platforms to meet the demand it creates. It is a market-making project.

The likely consequence of the increasing emphasis on mobility and connectivity is sustained investments in concentrated geographies based on a highly stylized narrative about the benefits of flexibility and the power of proximities. The acceptance of innovation districts indicates that there is little concern about how the clustering of new entrepreneurial spaces and the services that support them is producing an uneven economic geography.

And, in most cases, that innovation geography does not touch adjacent neighborhoods; rather, it facilitates concentrated commercial development much as the urban regeneration projects that served as the subject of the original critiques of urban entrepreneurialism. In this regard, the smart cities project is updating a process already in progress.

5

SMART CITIES AS URBAN
INNOVATION NETWORKS

T HROUGHOUT this book, the focus has been on distinguishing between what is new about the smart cities
project and what is not. The smart cities project follows
established and predictable paths, revealed through the lens of
economic geography and through combining the conceptual
models of uneven development and urban innovation. Once one
views the smart cities project through an economic geography
lens, the processes and actors operating fall into evolutionary
patterns of high-tech industries and technology-driven economic development policy.[1] In previous chapters, I concentrated
on the processes that produce smart cities and the established
actors that promote smart cities. The involvement of government and industry in technology-led economic development,
infrastructure investment, and urban entrepreneurialism is consistent with past practices and is even highlighted in the academic literature through discussions of the "triple helix" and
other innovation partnerships.[2] However, the emphasis on cities as the specific geographic scale of action is a shift in recent
practice, particularly in technology-led development and for the
tech industry.

This chapter describes urban innovation networks as new actors and processes that are involved in the design and implementation of the urban technology project. These networks are increasingly at the center of the policy work behind the development and diffusion of smart cities programs and projects. In this chapter, I look at how these distributed networks and institutional partnerships between and among cities function as policy intermediaries shaping both the smart cities project and urban policy more broadly. Subsequent chapters are elaborations on how civic participation processes also drive some smart cities program and project designs in limited, but potentially important, ways. Together, these chapters focus on a more optimistic interpretation of the urban technology project and incorporate policy recommendations that push that project toward a more equitable approach to urban innovation.

It may seem counterintuitive to claim that what is innovative about smart cities is not the technology but the policy processes behind its diffusion and the scale at which those processes operate. In other words, what is particularly novel about the spread of the most recent iteration of the urban technology project is the emergence of new intermediaries and the practices they employ to promote and facilitate multiscalar policy mobilities. The rising importance of institutional intermediaries aligns with other sectors and market segments and in many ways is predictable. However, in the case of public-sector governance and priority setting, the role of intermediaries deserves some analysis and perhaps greater scrutiny. Although these intermediaries provide both technical and material resources that are necessary for the diffusion of urban innovations, they are a temporary rather than a permanent replacement for a largely disengaged and absent federal and state government. The decision by the Rockefeller Foundation to retreat from its 100 Resilient Cities initiative in 2019 may serve as the best illustration of this reality.[3]

Returning the focus to the policy mobilities guiding the spread of the smart cities project underscores that most smart cities technologies are modified applications of technologies that have existed in other sectors and industries for some time, such as advanced manufacturing, supply chain and logistics management, health analytics, and defense and security. The technologies themselves are not new, but their application to the operations of cities is novel. The challenge has been, and remains, determining their relevance to cities and their citizens. This is both a question of delineating the scope of the market, as discussed in chapter 3, and one of determining the utility of these technologies for and in cities. As discussed in chapter 2, it is in part a question of determining how and whether these technology solutions effectively address an actual urban problem. Put another way, is crowdsourcing bicycle routes an act of technological design, an act of exerting political pressure intended to motivate government action (a form of civic engagement), or an artifact of amateur urban planning? Is mapping geotagged tweets about a given urban issue (#gentrification, for example) a test of the utility of a specific social media platform as an alternative, machine-searchable public document, or is it a poor substitute for established modes of analysis used for urban planning and policy design? That is, when are demonstrations of novel technologies evidence on which policy reasonably can be crafted, and when are such exercises something far less substantial—even, perhaps, superficial?

The public excitement about smart cities is driven by claims about how the built environment will be transformed by disruptive technologies.[4] Cities will no longer need parking lots to accommodate private cars. Citizens will have real-time and comprehensive access to information about their environment, whether traffic jams, air quality, transit schedules, public works and construction, or public safety. The vision of this emerging urban environment is one in which more information provides for more informed individual choices.

Here it becomes strongly evident that the primary unit of analysis in the disruptive technology narrative about smart cities is the customer rather than the citizen. In this narrative, choices are determined by individual decisions that are informed by increasing access to ever more detailed information. This is not only a world of rational decision making; it is also a flat world where equal access, equal capabilities, and equal opportunities define choices that are not contingent on or constrained by history, geography, income, or the form and function of the institutions and processes that produce variation among places. Thus, the role of institutions and intermediaries—both existing and emerging—rarely come up in the conversation about smart cities. And certainly, the complex interactions and interconnections between old and new institutions effectively fall outside this discussion. Here, the smart cities project is about a growing set of individual consumer choices rather than a complex array of social constructions.

In this way, a rational choice theory approach to smart cities misses what is actually disruptive and truly innovative about the smart cities project: the processes it has pioneered. The largely unconscious bias toward a consumer choice approach has obfuscated an emerging model of urban governance that is multiscalar and cross-national and driven by voluntary networks, not administrative hierarchies.[5] Previous chapters have emphasized the processes that produce smart cities and the geographic scales at which these processes operate, both economic and administrative.

Those chapters have focused on the governmental and industry actors shaping smart cities and pushing technologies.

In this chapter, I turn to the nongovernmental actors, the third-sector intermediaries that form urban innovation networks. These intermediaries are deeply involved in diffusing the smart cities project by designing a new model of policy mobility through city-to-city information exchange and collaboration. This is a distributed network model connecting cities to one another horizontally rather than relying on a traditional vertical or hierarchical model of policy replication.[6] The themes and priorities of these networks are not necessarily different from those of government or industry actors that are involved in the smart cities project, but they could be. The result is that the development of smart cities data, objects, systems, and platforms is influenced by a significant third-sector voice in both (a) the selection of use cases, meaning the key demonstration projects that define the smart cities discourse, scope, and capabilities; and (b) the design, implementation, and diffusion of those projects.

The policy goals that are prioritized and promoted by third-sector intermediaries—primarily philanthropies and nongovernmental organizations—are mediated not through the traditional policy diffusion process but through what is increasingly referred to as *policy mobility*.[7] However, the goals are designed to be interoperable with it. This network approach does not preclude other policy processes but coexists with them. This is not a question of top-down versus bottom-up policy design. In the United States, policy makers have long endorsed the idea of bottom-up policy development in everything from social services to economic development. The embrace of the idea of persistent, localized policy experimentation is perhaps best articulated by U.S. Supreme Court Justice Louis Brandeis's comments in 1932:

"a state may, if its citizens choose, serve as a laboratory; and try novel social and economic experiments without risk to the rest of the country."[8]

This "laboratories of democracy" approach has shaped U.S. public policy design and experimentation for most of the post-World War II period. The idea is that localities can and should conduct policy "experiments," which are then evaluated and assessed and, if deemed successful, launched into and across larger geographies. Thus, policies validated in a limited deployment can later be scaled up incrementally and deliberately to other jurisdictions, serving a broader public and establishing best practices. These policy experiments do not share the same tradition as smart cities testbed experiments; they are not technology tests but policy tests. The goals and evaluation criteria are specified and measured against alternatives. These alternatives are fully formed policy choices or simply the specified parameters of the status quo.[9]

Smart cities testbed experiments tend to be true experiments. They are efforts to observe the behaviors of individuals and institutions in the context of a technology intervention that is introduced into the environment. The assessment is not of the ability of the policy (intervention) to achieve a set of stated goals compared with the abilities of an alternative policy to do the same. Rather, smart cities interventions are not measured against alternatives; instead, their effects on users are observed: who uses the technology, in what manner, for how long, to what end? In this sense, the smart cities project has created an innovative approach to experimentation that is independent of the long history of formalized policy analysis and comparison among alternatives. Notably, no social impact assessment or environmental impact statement is required in advance of most smart cities interventions because such assessments remain outside the scope of formal policy interventions.

The process of small-scale policy experimentation followed by large-scale adoption is something of a bottom-up process, although it remains largely a formal, governmental approach. Often, a state-level policy experiment subsequently surfaces as a success at the national scale. It then becomes a top-down policy process as the federal government implements the (empirically validated) policy innovation and devolves it to states and localities. One example of this was health care reform during the 2000s. Originally a policy designed and deployed in Massachusetts in 2006, the model was modified by the federal government and implemented on a national basis in 2010, with variations tailored for and by individual states appearing across the country.

In recent memory, one of the most public manifestations of the traditional journey of the elevation of local policy experiments to the national stage have been State of the Union addresses by U.S. presidents. These speeches often have described successful state policy experiments reaching the national stage. After accumulating results sufficient to rigorously validate their designs and evaluate their outcomes, these local programs were deemed ready to scale. This vetting and evaluation provided a record of the policy's costs, coverage, impacts, and effectiveness. It was this evidence that provided empirical data that could shape a larger, national policy debate and policy modifications to the program to accommodate subnational variations.

In this construction, whether a state or locality is the original policy innovator or the subsequent policy adopter determines whether the process is bottom-up or top-down. And as policies cascade down from the federal to the state, regional, and local levels, the challenge of tailoring policies to local conditions (economic, institutional, social, and political) becomes significant and, on occasion, impossible. However, without the turn toward national-scale implementation, the result of localized policy experimentation is decidedly uneven.

Some places have services and develop capacities that other places do not. Regulations are relevant—that is, observed and/ or enforced—in some places and not others. When policies— access, opportunities, resources—are implemented incrementally across places, they produce inequalities. When they are also implemented incrementally over a period of time, those inequalities are compounded and become embedded. This uneven distribution of assets and capabilities underpins the growing critique of the fundamental failure of the incremental implementation strategies that dominate smart cities projects. Smart cities policies and programs promise access to new technologies that provide new opportunities and resources but without any clarity about the distribution across time or space of those resources.

How to move from testbed to scale is a core problem in the smart cities narrative. Because large-scale smart cities deployments depend on significant public investments in intelligent infrastructure and acquisition of smart cities systems and platforms, the public sector's disinterest in those investments is particularly problematic from an equity perspective. The absence of national policy investments essentially ensures that the smart cities project pursues an incremental deployment process that necessarily triggers concerns about the inherent inequalities that result from uneven investments. Urban innovation networks have emerged as a potential response, forming an alternative approach to implementation that (partially) substitutes for large-scale public-sector policy design and coordination.

POWER IN URBAN INNOVATION
NETWORKS: PICKING PRIORITIES

Urban innovation networks establish horizontal relationships among city governments to facilitate policy exchange among peers.[10] This exchange runs concurrent and in parallel with the vertical policy relationships running back and forth through national, subnational, and local governments. That is not to say that no power asymmetries operate in urban innovation networks, as there are in vertical hierarchies. For example, New York City or Paris has substantially more influence in a policy diffusion network than does Milwaukee or Toulouse. Large, rich, and politically influential places always have more power than smaller, less wealthy places—in these horizontal configurations as well as vertical ones. Urban innovation networks do not eliminate power dynamics, but they do destabilize the established practices of hierarchical policy transfer from federal governments to subnational jurisdictions. Simply put, cities are not looking to the federal or state government to propose or validate smart cities projects before deploying them. Instead, cities are turning their attention to other cities.[11]

In observing who is promoting smart cities through urban innovation networks, it becomes clear that the stakeholders involved reflect the complexity and underlying tension between the roles of the public and the private sector in operating cities and setting the agenda for cities. As private-, public-, and third-sector smart cities networks evolve, sets of privileged places— the *really* smart cities—also have emerged. These places are the recipients of the demonstration proje ct grants and resources that come through philanthropic investments, private-sector partnership, and federal government competitions and challenges.[12] In the absence of a broad commitment to infrastructure, these competitions and challenges chart a different path. They facilitate the implementation of smart cities technologies in select places in the hope that the innovations that occur through successful demonstration projects will compel future investment and national and international scaling.

This approach aligns with Justice Brandeis's statement about using subnational spaces as laboratories to test small-scale policy experiments. The difference is that these experiments are no longer seeded exclusively through governments. They are also seeded by actors from the private sector, both nonprofit and for-profit, with a variety of thematic interests and priorities determined not by voters but by shareholders or boards of directors. Knowing something about what these networks are, how they operate, and what they have accomplished is critical in the analysis of the smart cities project and the uneven innovation it is producing. Urban innovation networks, should they take hold, will represent a significant change in how subnational policy experimentation functions and how policy mobilities work in the United States and elsewhere. As an innovation process, these networks represent one of the most notable outcomes of the smart cities project.

Jamie Peck and Nik Theodore began the identification and analysis of the broader trend toward urban policy networks in their 2015 book, *Fast Policy*. In that book, they looked specifically at the spread of novel social policy models across cities in different countries. The specific policy cases they documented were participatory budgeting and conditional cash transfers. They looked closely at how conditional cash transfers moved from an experiment in Mexico to a large-scale policy experiment in New York City. Although Peck and Theodore concentrated on social policies rather than technology policies or urban innovation specifically, they identified an emerging trend that is essential for explaining the propagation of the smart cities narrative and the adoption of smart cities projects. Peck and Theodore also began the process of identifying the actors and institutions that were designing this networked approach to policy diffusion and establishing the priorities behind it.[13]

Urban innovation networks are instigated and often led by third-sector intermediaries—frequently, philanthropies or nongovernmental organizations—that are interested in urban innovation generally or in a specific theme or value associated with potential technology policy solutions operating at the city scale. The most prominent examples of these themes include resilience and sustainability. The proliferation of these networks is related to city-scale responses to global climate change, which are related to the slow and incomplete actions of national and international governments in response to that challenge. These networks have emerged as a multiscalar partnership model for experimentation and innovation organized around interventions that are available at the city scale, such as energy efficiency goals, urban resiliency programs, and ordinances and programs designed to shift policies and practices at city scale.[14] By engaging private, nonprofit, and philanthropic organizations, such networks supplement or substitute for the public sector's organizational capacity to engage complex policy challenges such as sustainability or resilience. One example, developed in 1993, is Local Governments for Sustainability's (ICLEI) Cities for Climate Protection (CCP) program. CCP required its city participants to voluntarily undertake a five-step process toward carbon emission reduction. In exchange, the program provided technical support and a platform for networking and knowledge sharing among member cities.[15]

These are voluntary horizontal networks of member cities that opt in to a given network based on an assessment by political leaders. In this sense, participation in urban innovation networks and consent to pursue the network's goals reflect an alignment of local political priorities with themes developed by intermediaries. However, the philanthropy or nongovernmental organization defining the network's thematic focus holds considerable power. First, the network leadership sets the agenda by selecting the theme of the network. Second, leaders select the members of the network. Third, they provide selected resources to cities in terms of funding and designated prime contractors for technical assistance. Finally, they set the rules for remaining in the network as well as the metrics for succeeding in it. The leadership in these networks has real power. That power results in a form of urban governance that operates outside the established model of decision making, financing, and priority setting for cities.

In other words, it is important to understand that these city networks, initiated by philanthropic or nongovernmental organizations, may shift the locus of power but not form some sort of egalitarian alternative to formal policy processes undertaken by state and local governments. Indeed, voluntary networks or thematic alliances are not new to economic development practice or in the organization of regional innovation systems. Industry clusters are only one private-sector example of voluntary networks serving as a forum for economic development policy mobilities. The difference, of course, is that industry cluster networks are composed of member firms rather than member cities. However, they are similar to urban innovation networks in how they operate to represent not only their members but also a theme that the network determines. In the case of industry clusters, the theme is often regional economic competitiveness as opposed to urban sustainability or resilience.

In previous analyses of such private-sector networks among small and medium-sized firms, Susan Christopherson and

I commented on how power is arranged and assigned in such networks:

> Networks of all kinds, including firm networks, are constructed around power relations. Networks encompass hierarchies of power or they wouldn't be networks. There would be no incentive for the more powerful members to remain in the network if they didn't disproportionately gain the benefits of network participation. Just as individuals "network" in order to promote their individual interests (rather than those of the network), so do firms. Networks can and frequently do take the form of hierarchies, with marginal benefit to the less powerful members.[16]

These urban innovation networks are complex in terms of priority setting and power dynamics, and they take a number of organizational forms. Generally, there are three main models (see Table 5.1). First, the Type 1 model is composed of member cities in a distributed network of municipal governments. In this case, a network member must be a city government to participate. Examples of the Type 1 model include the Bloomberg Innovation Delivery Teams and the Rockefeller Foundation's 100 Resilient Cities Program.[17] In these Type 1 cases, the lead philanthropy has two primary functions: to provide a city with increased capacity through direct investment in human capital to manage policies and programs aligned with a theme or priority, and to bring a "package" of private-sector partners to the network members in order to provide specialized technical assistance. Typically, network membership expands through iterative rounds of competitions organized through a request for proposals from the philanthropy or the consortium of philanthropies.

For example, the Rockefeller Foundation's 100 Resilient Cities initiative divided its selection of member cities into three

Characteristics

TABLE 5.1. A typology of urban innovation networks

	Structure	Selection criteria	Seeding capacity in cities	Access to designated providers	Showcasing demonstration projects	Policy mobility	Themes	Examples
Type 1	Philanthropic	Competitions	Yes	Yes	Yes	Yes	Mission driven	Rockefeller 100 Resilient Cities
Type 2	Distributed network	Opt-in w/ performance requirements	No	Maybe	Yes	Yes	Partnership driven	The Metrolab Network
Type 3	Research network	Opt-in	No	Yes	Yes	No (technology diffusion)	Project driven	Global Cities Team Challenge

competitive tranches over several years. Then three distinct cohorts of cities were brought into the network one at a time.

Once accepted as members in the network, cities received funding to support resilience work and access to the technical partners. These technical partners served as subcontractors for business, technology, and consulting services for the member cities. Some of the technical partners in the 100 Resilient Cities program included Siemens, PriceWaterhouseCoopers, Microsoft, Ernst and Young, and Cisco, as well as nongovernmental organizations such as the World Wildlife Fund, the Nature Conservancy, and Save the Children. Through the proliferation of best practices and a catalog of technical providers, Type 1 networks serve as one organizational framework through which policies, priorities, and signature demonstration projects catch the attention of city governments.

A second form of urban innovation network, the Type 2 model, connects multistakeholder partnerships within a city with parallel partnerships in other cities. These networks can be either project-specific partnerships organized for a designated purpose or more formally established partnerships that are envisioned as lasting through multiple projects and defined through a memorandum of understanding among partners. These city-level partnerships connect into a national or international community of partnerships that are designed to employ an incremental, scale-up approach to policy diffusion. These networks of partnerships add qualifying members to an established set of founding network partnerships. A key example of this model in North America is the MetroLab Network, which connects partnerships between research universities and the cities in which they are located with a network of city–university partnerships in other cities.

Type 2 networks act as facilitators and intermediaries. They do not provide resources directly to cities or their urban innovation partners. However, they do promote policy mobility through the partnership network by highlighting best practices and hosting a variety of workshops and convenings.

Still other urban innovation networks are organized around a competition or challenge model. The goal of these networks is to motivate individual cities to develop smart cities pilot projects. These Type 3 networks gather and highlight proposed pilot projects and select one or more for direct funding for implementation. Type 3 networks develop in two tiers: the cities that win funding for pilot projects, and the set of pilot projects proposed in the competition. In addition to funding the winning projects, Type 3 networks often, though not always, work to attract the interest of industries, philanthropies, or governments to fund the remaining projects and build awareness about urban innovation programs and projects.[18] In their initial stages, these networks have participants rather than members. The number of participants grows as the prominence of the network platform develops and as more applicants and winners opt in to showcase projects in both the design and implementation stages.

The National Institute of Standards and Technology's (NIST in the U.S. Department of Commerce) Global Cities Team Challenge (GCTC) is an example of a Type 3 urban innovation network. GCTC asks cities, institutions, and companies to submit demonstration projects to a platform intended to showcase ideas. GCTC also asks participants to join teams of public and private partners that are working on similar technical solutions; for example, urban sensing systems. GCTC then determines lead technology areas based on the projects collected, known as "action clusters" or "action super clusters." By hosting meetings and conferences, GCTC creates forums to facilitate "collisions" between private and public stakeholders. These "tech jams" are often a variation on a traditional trade show, with technology firms displaying their smart cities solutions and cities and research teams displaying demonstration projects for potential private-sector partners.

All three types of urban innovation networks establish priorities and set technology paths for their members and participants. These directions are set both implicitly and explicitly. Type 1 philanthropic networks set explicit priorities through the thematic areas that motivate their investments in technology and cities in the first instance. For example, We Work Cities, part of the Bloomberg Philanthropies' American Cities Initiative, made substantial investments in 100 U.S. cities to enhance the use of data in city policies, programs, and decision making. The project's 2017 $200 million budget was supplemented by an additional $42 million commitment in 2018.[19] Although initiated by New York City's former mayor Michael Bloomberg, We Work Cities invests in cities of various sizes outside New York, including small and midsized cities such as South Bend, Indiana, and New Orleans, Louisiana. The approach taken by We Work Cities is to provide cities with tools to manage and apply data to enhance operations, assist with technical training and skill building, and grow the internal capacity to use those data on an ongoing basis.

Similarly, the City Energy Project (CEP), another example of a Type 1 urban innovation network, focused its investment on municipal ordinances that promote energy efficiency and data transparency in building-level energy consumption. The City Energy Project was funded by three philanthropies in partnership, a consortium that includes the Doris Duke Foundation, the Kresge Foundation, and Bloomberg Philanthropies. CEP contracted with the Natural Resources Defense Council and the Institute for Market Transformation to operate the network and provide technical assistance to the partner cities as they pursued city-level legislation around energy efficiency goals.[20]

Within each partner city, CEP funded a position: a person to spearhead the effort to design an energy efficiency policy for that city and carry it through the legislative process. Like other Type 1 networks, CEP operated on a request-for-proposals model. CEP then selected member cities in two cohorts based on their, proposals, in which the cities opted in to the priorities explicated in the City Energy Project.

Type 2 and Type 3 urban innovation networks' priority setting in terms of preferred domains (public safety, mobility, energy efficiency) and preferred technology solutions (predictive data analytics, urban sensor systems) is somewhat subtler than the explicit goals of Type 1 networks. Type 2 and 3 priorities are evidenced in the selected spotlight cases that are used to demonstrate member or participant smart cities successes; for example, apps for crowdsourcing bicycle routes or environmental quality sensor deployments. Unlike Type 1 networks, in this process of priority setting, Type 2 and 3 networks do not explicitly state their interests and goals through a request for proposals around a definitive theme. Instead, initiatives such as the Global Cities Team Challenge and the MetroLab Network identify and showcase selected projects from member or participant cities and reveal priorities through what the networks highlight. These demonstration projects are often related to the priorities of philanthropic funders or corporate partners of the Type 2 or 3 networks themselves. In other words, the priorities of the funders of the Type 2 or Type 3 networks often drive the selection of highlighted projects and solutions. Thus, what network members and participants (and potential partners) see as selected and vetted successes, in the competitive environment laid out in chapter 4, is a highly curated collection of the projects that define a smart city—a collection curated in part by the interests of both private- and public-sector influencers operating behind an urban innovation network.

This process of priority setting, of course, is not unusual or unexpected. Funding drives priorities in other contexts as well. Type 1 urban innovation networks' endowments enable them to be explicit about their interests and avoid artificially adjusting their practices to consider the domain or technology interests of other funders or partners. This is not to say that they may not do so, merely that their motivations in this regard are not necessarily connected to forging a sustainable revenue model for their own operations. The Type 2 and 3 networks, however, face this challenge of sustainable, long-term funding for their partnerships, priorities, and networks.

URBAN INNOVATION NETWORKS AS POLICY MOBILITY INTERMEDIARIES

Urban innovation networks are another form of market intermediary seeking a revenue-generating space between established sectors and incumbent actors in the private and public sectors.[21] This is consistent with the emergence of labor market, supply chain, and innovation intermediaries across the new economy that have sprung up to fill the gaps that have opened among firms, governments, and other institutions. Like many intermediaries, urban innovation intermediaries manage relationships and information. The convenings, conferences, summits, and tech jams they arrange serve this purpose and generate funds from participants. In this way, urban innovation networks act as professional associations for those who are involved in the urban innovation industry and the smart cities project.

In the illustrative cases of city-to-city policy mobilities described in *Fast Policy*, particularly conditional cash transfers, an evaluation component was built into the policy experiment even as the process moved beyond traditional policy development practices. There are two key reasons for this. First, the advocates of the conditional cash transfers policy experiment intended to argue for the scaling up of the program should it be successful. They therefore needed evidence of that success. They designed metrics into the policy model from the beginning for the purposes of making the case for future policy expansion.

The second reason is that conditional cash transfer is a social policy program. The design and expansion of social policies—specifically, policies that address poverty alleviation and social mobility—are often subject to strict scrutiny by the governments that implement them. Social policies are frequently exposed to many rounds of recalibration for the means tests that determine eligibility and the specificities of the measurable effects. Further, the political discourse about social policies in the neoliberal context is often not about which poverty alleviation policy is most effective but about whether there should be antipoverty and social mobility policies at all. Thus, evidence is considered essential for policy diffusion.

No such high bar exists for technology policies. In contrast to the conditional cash transfers case, metrics and evaluation are almost entirely absent from the construction of policy diffusion practices in the smart cities project. There simply is no explicit or conscious intention to design the policy experiment for scalability in a traditional sense. In other words, diffusion is assumed rather than planned. As a consequence, there is no need for evidence of efficacy because there is no consideration of alternative solutions to the problem. In fact, no problem is identified in advance of the solution that is implemented. In fact, there is no real concern about making the case for public investments in smart cities data, objects, systems, or platforms. The smart cities project does not expect to encounter the hurdles faced by policies that address other social problems, such as poverty and social mobility. That is, the smart cities project is not designed to demonstrate broad and substantial benefits. The apparent absence of policy rigor, which is enabled through these new forms of policy mobility, allow smart cities to emerge as a policy project that is simply not designed to scale and, further, not designed to withstand standard assessments of benefits and costs.[22] Distributional equity is simply not measured, and it isn't expected.

Urban innovation networks represent a novel and important shift in policy design and development processes. However, they do not provide a substitute for public-sector financing or investments in cities. Likewise, they do not provide a substitute for professional and deliberate urban planning and policy work. And they were not intended to do so. In the absence of adequate investments in cities and the people who do the work of cities, urban innovation networks have been elevated to a role they were never constructed to fulfill. However, urban innovation networks are an alternative mechanism for organizing, framing, and sharing information about new policies with and among cities. In this way, they do look very much like the networks and intermediaries that build out other enabling industries.[23] Urban innovation networks function as a new type of intermediary, providing a service that once occurred within governments—specifically, information gathering and dissemination and the knowledge and relationship management necessary between different jurisdictions. Urban innovation networks are increasingly crowdsourcing and consolidating smart cities technical expertise using a distributed network approach.[24]

Still, the networks remain problematic. In part, the purpose of the networks and their functional limitations are not well understood by those either engaged in or observing them. The networks principally collect information about smart cities projects and programs rather than invest in smart cities data, objects, systems, and platforms. In some cases, Type 1 networks make investments in specified policies. But urban innovation intermediaries do not make smart cities; they provide capacities and services to smart cities actors, both private and public. The most robust urban innovation networks provide capacity to cities. The least robust extract information from members and participants to establish the value proposition of the network to its own funders. They seek to validate their existence as an intermediary providing access and influence.

So the value proposition of urban innovation networks is increasingly clear: it derives from the gathering and packaging of urban intelligence. A push to motivate members to implement smart cities projects, at any scale, is necessary to generate that intelligence. And the isolated testbed approach that emerges as that push is not designed for evaluation or replication. As a result, there are two significant policy problems with the smart cities testbed project approach that is promoted particularly by Type 2 and 3 networks. First, this approach produces a necessary unevenness within and across cities, which exacerbates existing inequalities. New services, ungraded infrastructure, and economic investments are landing unevenly across an already uneven landscape. Second, the testbed approach relegates cities and their communities and neighborhoods to experimental subjects. Without the ability to evaluate the outcomes of smart cities deployments, they are not policy experiments for people but, rather, technology experiments on people. The value of these projects is in their potential to provide better, enhanced, or expanded services for people. Without a plausible path to that potential in either the design or implementation of the project, it is merely an experiment that would not meet the strict standards set by any institutional review board.

The point, then, is that the emergence of urban innovation networks is not a solution to disengaged state and national governments. Further, the networks' incremental and episodic approach to necessary investments in people and places produces uncertainties and exacerbates interjurisdictional competition. These problems were only confirmed by the Rockefeller Foundation's 2019 announcement of its withdrawal from its 100 Resilient Cities program, which left member cities with resilience plans both adopted and in development, chief resilience officers on staff, and some cities with newly rebranded administrative offices such as the Atlanta's Mayor's Office of Resilience.[25]

Even with these problems of heightened competition, incremental intervention, and episodic engagement, urban innovation networks do fill a growing gap. In the absence of deliberate and rigorous policy design and experimentation by state and national governments, cities are increasingly engaged—despite their historic reliance on national and state governments—to design and evaluate new policies. These networks are substitutes for the technical expertise and professional community that systematic and continuous intergovernmental policy coordination once provided.

Much of the power of the smart cities project comes from the compelling narrative behind it. Smart cities bypass the history and complexities of urban policy and urban problems and reset the conversation about cities to begin with technology solutions rather than problem identification. The diffusion of that narrative has been critical for bringing a much broader set of interests to the conversation about the future of cities. Urban planners and city administrators, experts in public finance and local economic development, are now joined by a host of additional experts and stakeholders who are interested in how to rethink and redesign urban spaces. It appears that the diffusion of the smart cities narrative is equally as important as the mobility of smart cities policies in building a broader constituency that cares about cities. A conversation has begun among sectors and stakeholders across the economy—from energy to automobiles, to telecommunications, to software, to defense and security—about the city as a site of investment.

However, transferring technology into the public sector at the broad and inclusive scale claimed in the smart cities project is a substantial challenge. Even in the private sector, where much attention is paid to technology transfer and there are many models to choose from, the gap between design and implementation is so notoriously wide that insiders call the space between innovation and commercialization "the valley of death." In the private sector, a range of intermediaries work to bridge this gap. An extensive academic literature identifies these intermediaries and variations in how they operate in different places and at different times. It is perhaps time to place urban innovation networks into this body of work, to analyze the smart cities project as any other emerging industry and to train the lens of regional innovation systems on its assessment.

THE WORK OF SMART CITIES: EMBEDDING INNOVATION CAPACITY

Cities face many challenges in moving technological innovations into urban applications. Isolation is one of those challenges. After decades of devolution and privatization, coupled with the standard practice of contracting out rather than building internal capacity, cities generally have little latitude to strategize about smart cities from either a technological or a governance perspective. As a consequence, there is a tendency to accept solutions from vendors when presented rather than to identify specific, local problems and evaluate an array of potential technical solutions. One example is the rapid proliferation of numerous private schemes for dockless bicycle sharing and electric scooters across multiple cities simultaneously (see figures 5.1–5.5). Similarly, the rollout of street-side informational kiosks, typified by LinkNYC, is another. These examples highlight how little tailoring to local conditions occurs before widespread implementation of many smart cities objects and services.

There are notable exceptions. As the wave of new smart cities applications began to surface in 2010, Boston established the

FIGURE 5.1 Deployments of smart cities objects: variations on bicycle-sharing services. Contained folding bicycle service, Birmingham, England, 2013.

(*Source*: Benjamin Flowers)

FIGURE 5.2 Deployments of smart cities objects: variations on bicycle-sharing services. Bicycling rentals with fixed docking stations, Cluj-Napoca, Romania, 2017.

(*Source*: Benjamin Flowers)

FIGURE 5.3 Deployments of smart cities objects: variations on bicycle-sharing services. Toward multimodal mobility: bicycle rentals with fixed docking and adjacent to Union Station, Denver, Colorado, 2019.

(*Source*: Jose Felicino/Shutterstock)

FIGURE 5.4 Deployments of smart cities objects: variations on scooter-sharing services. Dockless scooters as mobile urban sensor systems. Grafting onto bicycle-sharing practices and infrastructure (bike lanes and business strategies). Scooters from competing companies on the sidewalk in Washington, D.C., 2018.

(*Source*: bakdc/Shutterstock)

FIGURE 5.5 Deployments of smart cities objects: variations on scooter-sharing services. Docked scooters as fixed urban sensor systems, Moscow, Russia, 2018.

(*Source*: Popovphoto/Shutterstock)

Mayor's Office of New Urban Mechanics to develop internal capacity around evaluating and adopting new tools and technologies. The Office of New Urban Mechanics consciously and consistently considers smart cities projects and programs within the broader context of urban policy and participatory planning. As a consequence, Boston tends to focus initiatives around specific issues identified by citizens and policy makers in the city rather than on the solutions presented by vendors. Outside the United States, Barcelona and Mexico City are often cited as examples of municipal governments that are making internal investments to develop their capacity to evaluate and tailor new technologies and fit them into a more comprehensive urban policy strategy.

For cities that lack either the resources or the inclination to replicate the investments of Boston or Barcelona, urban innovation networks do some of the work of smart cities. They provide a community of peers and experts. They provide a platform for knowledge exchange that crosses jurisdictional boundaries. The result is not a substitute for formal government—neither its authority and regulations nor its funding and resources—but a complement to it. Urban innovation networks provide a framework for cities to push national and state government toward a known and achievable set of operational standards. In other words, even with the caveats about the incomplete and partial work performed, urban innovation networks serve an increasingly important service as an intermediary, not as an alternative form of governance.

Similar to many new intermediary models, there are still gaps to fill and problems to solve in the design and functions of urban innovation networks. Chief among them is how to embed the missing validation and evaluation element into the practice of policy diffusion across cities. Although that absence of assessment is problematic, its addition to the model is entirely feasible.

Once it becomes clear that urban innovation networks are not the implementers of smart cities projects and programs or intelligent infrastructure but a platform for policy and program diffusion, then the policy vetting, validation, and evaluation function becomes a straightforward addition to that diffusion process. Such a change would confirm the commitment of urban innovation networks to scale smart cities to serve a wide constituency rather than to catalog demonstration projects in selected locations such as Toronto's waterfront or a designated testbed like Atlanta's North Avenue Smart Corridor (see figure 5.6).[26]

It is perhaps no surprise that rapid technological change requires more domain knowledge and more planning than do

FIGURE 5.6 Launch of the city of Atlanta's North Avenue Smart Corridor testbed project at The Ponce City Market. The ribbon-cutting ceremony included Mayor Kasim Reed and Atlanta's city leadership as well as the president of the Georgia Institute of Technology, a university research partner on the smart corridor project, Atlanta, Georgia, September 2017.

(*Image credit*: Raul Perez, Georgia Institute of Technology)

everyday operations. Substantial changes in the economy require changes in the institutions that facilitate and govern it. In the same way that industry has pursued lean production techniques, local governments have followed the these management models in an attempt to eliminate waste. Their goal, like that of their private-sector counterparts, was to achieve efficiency gains without sacrificing productivity or services. The challenge, of course, is the same in both contexts. In the public sector, as in the private sector, organizations that are too lean are unable to grow because they can neither adapt to a changing environment nor evaluate its effects on their operations. The organization simply cannot manage change. But unlike a firm, a local government has no choice. Adapting to changing conditions—economic, political, social, or environmental—is not optional for cities, whether the change is global warming or 5G networks. Sufficient internal capacity to understand, evaluate, and absorb change is simply necessary to operate a city.

Further, that capacity to adapt must be embedded rather than external. And this is at the heart of the conversation about urban and regional resilience: developing the capacity for cities and regions to act in the face of change.[27] Contracting out for capacity is not sufficient, for a reason. Cities need to build backward and forward interoperability into systems design. That requires institutional memory and a broad mandate beyond a project-specific brief. Interoperability is often overlooked by technology advocates. Governments, however, are constantly upgrading systems while maintaining current levels of services. Functional existing services and systems cannot be shut down because a potentially more effective or efficient technology arrives on the scene. Backward and forward interoperability are fundamental requirements of service integration in the public sector. Again, firms can stop manufacturing, but a city continues to govern and serve.

Fundamentally, people notice when no one picks up the trash. Cities are built to provide this continuity without interruption.

To that end, the emerging array of urban innovation networks has contributed substantially to raising awareness of the need for increasing capacity in cities. Cities have become so lean that "urban planning" has become a set of operations—for example, issuing building permits, facilitating public meetings, or administrating zoning hearings—rather than a deliberative process comprised of research and evaluation. Strategic and comprehensive planning for the future of cities is far less frequent and often engaged only when there is a legal requirement to do so. In order to increase the internal capacities required to adapt to changes, adopt new organizational and technological innovations, and legislate for smart cities, cities would need to invest in that long-term and deliberate planning that is so prominent in the academic discipline and so lacking in practice.

To a large extent, urban innovation networks have made investments that make a difference in jump-starting legislative action across the themes of sustainability and resilience. Broadly speaking, sustainability-focused urban innovation networks have successfully established that there are city-scale legislative responses to what are perceived to be global problems such as climate change. The challenge now is to see that model move beyond a thematic approach and into a more permanent and institutionalized practice of knowledge exchange and policy design, assessment, and evaluation; not as a substitute for increasing capacities in city government, but as a complement to the emerging work of smart cities.

6

SMART CITIES AS
PARTICIPATORY PLANNING

N addition to producing a new model of urban innovation intermediaries, the smart cities project holds the potential to expand civic participation by streamlining the process for engaging citizens in participatory planning. Early in the smart cities project, it became clear that new technology investments could provide a platform for regional economic development—specifically, firm creation, entrepreneurship, and growth. As a consequence, the case for smart cities investments has been primarily an economic one. However, a case also can be made for public investment in the smart cities project, given that technology upgrades to civic infrastructure could provide more access, more opportunity, and greater distributional equity. This is effectively the case made by those advocating for smart and inclusive urban innovation.

SMART CITIZENSHIP: UPGRADING
PARTICIPATORY PLANNING

The same technological tools that facilitate everything from e-commerce to just-in-time production have the ability to enhance and expand the ways in which citizens and residents relate to their governments and the decisions their governments make. This is true of not only cities but other communities as well. A whole academic subfield has developed around digital civics, focusing on the ways in which technologies can produce or provide platforms for enhanced community engagement.[1]

Of course, citizen participation is a cornerstone of democratic governance, and low levels of participation are problematic on many levels. In the digital civics conversation, there is an emphasis on what is meant or intended by community engagement and participation and, further, how citizenship and residency are defined. Often concepts such as *use, participation, membership, citizen*, and *resident* float around the civic technology discourse disembodied from the highly territorialized and legally delineated definitions of these concepts in the real-world governance of cities. Jurisdictions are not ambiguous, although what they functionally determine in terms of relative power and action does change over time. However, discussion about civic participation that operates within the smart cities project exists largely independent of the long conversation in urban and regional planning about community development, participatory planning, and the frameworks and practices that facilitate neighborhood and community planning in cities.

Citizen engagement in local government sits at the center of participatory planning practice. As noted in chapter 1, participatory planning developed largely as a response to large-scale technocratic urban renewal and regeneration projects in the mid-twentieth century. This sustained effort by both academics and planning practitioners produced three outcomes that are worth revisiting in the context of emerging models of "smart citizenship". First, participatory planning included a sustained analysis of the power dynamics operating within urban planning practices. Second, progressive planners proposed a set of institutional responses to confront those power dynamics by enabling organized responses by residents. Finally, academic planners produced a curriculum within urban and regional planning programs that trained practitioners to implement institutional responses and identify the power dynamics operating in city and regional governments.[2]

Participatory planning produced an analytical framework for planning practitioners to apply to decision making. But the effort went beyond critique; it also led to the design of models of institutionalized responses that could empower communities not merely to participate but to influence outcomes. The models were designed to be flexible so they could adapt to local contexts and reflect variations in administrative structures as well as in the character and goals of different places and communities. As a consequence, many U.S. cities have some form of neighborhood or community planning process that is recognized by the city for the purposes of consultation and dissemination of information.[3]

Among the most formal of these community planning systems are the neighborhood planning units (NPUs) in Atlanta. In 1974, then-Mayor Maynard Jackson established a system that designated 25 NPUs. These neighborhood organizations are self-governing and include both businesses and residents within the neighborhood. The NPUs were originally designed to review and assess zoning decisions, that included such things as zoning variances, liquor licenses, and festival permits, as well as issues with citywide implications such as changes to the city's comprehensive plan or fee structure. Because of this focus on land use planning, the NPUs primarily work with the city's planning department. A city planner is assigned to each NPU; the planner provides the NPU with information and conveys the NPU's decisions back to the planning department.

Similarly, in the 1990s, Minneapolis formalized its neighborhood planning process through the implementation of the Neighborhood Revitalization Program, which sought to create revitalization action plans for the communities within the city. Minneapolis took a more bottom-up than top-down approach to formalizing the community planning role for its 81 neighborhoods. Although Minneapolis recognizes 81 neighborhoods, the Neighborhood Revitalization Program process resulted in 67 neighborhood action plans, as some neighborhoods chose to work together. Over almost 30 years, the Neighborhood Revitalization Program process and the resulting revitalization plans have guided the city's investments in revenue obtained from tax-incrementing financing districts and have provided a geographic framework for statistical analysis.[4]

Although these organizations are well established in some cities, time has taken its toll on their efficacy and power. And because the model requires a degree of tailoring to local conditions, the organizations require a significant amount of time to design and maintain. The neighborhood planning model largely did not adapt to population expansions into the suburbs. As suburban communities expanded and formally incorporated as cities themselves, the concept of neighborhood planning units became increasingly diluted, both because people moved to places without traditions of neighborhood planning and because the model itself did not move with them. What emerged instead was a practice of neighborhood meetings that were often reactions to specific administrative actions rather than systematic engagement between a city and its neighborhoods. In other words, the community meeting became a way for cities to inform citizens of actions and decisions, not to institutionalize a dialogue about the future of the city or the neighborhood.

Particularly relevant to the smart cities project and digital civics is that the neighborhood planning model has not kept up with technology very well.[5] The monthly neighborhood planning meeting is no longer a primary means for information exchange within the community or between the community and the city. With the advent of neighborhood e-mail Listservs, community-specific online platforms, and neighborhood Web sites and blogs, the in-person community meeting has become almost antiquated. And the idea of the business conducted in those meetings—particularly the two-way information exchange between community members and city administration (police, fire, planning, schools)—has become reactive rather than routine. That is, people attend public neighborhood meetings in response to crises instead of as a matter of course. Residents attend when there is a school redistricting controversy or a proposal for a large subdivision. The everyday operational matters of the city, such as zoning variances, building permits, and business licenses, receive little attention. The result is that incremental changes are overlooked while big controversies appear sudden instead of being the culmination of a set of iterative changes made over time.

Effectively, the digital civics approach to community participation proposes a new model for participatory planning. Digital civics updates the neighborhood meeting concept with smart cities innovations, but it has yet to engage participatory planning as a practice. Interestingly, digital civics seems to take the city out of the participatory planning model. The new approach to civic engagement deterritorializes participatory planning, allowing for participation or membership to be defined by any community of interest rather than being defined by residency in a given jurisdiction or presence in a neighborhood.

Finally, digital civics attempts to build engagement and participation in alignment with the broader smart cities project rather than as a reaction to it.

Perhaps the most valuable contribution of digital civics to participatory planning is in how it moves technological innovations from behind-the-scenes analysis to the frontlines of community engagement. Planners have adapted to technological innovations and integrated them into their analysis, perhaps most successfully with geographic information systems, but have been slow to use technology tools for citizen engagement. Admirable as these modifications to the model are, they overlook the power and importance of the existing participatory planning model. As with much of the technology industry, digital civics fails to recognize the value of the incumbent system of engagement and participation. Neighborhood planning units were one reaction to the perceived technocratic excesses of city administrators in the 1960s and 1970s. Whether regarding urban renewal, the interstate highway systems, or superblock projects such as Boston's Government Center, the idea was that the asymmetrical power relationship between city planners and administrators and the neighborhoods was out of balance beyond what reasonably could be remedied by the four-year cycle at the ballot box.

During those decades, the scale of urban interventions had become too big, too invasive, too fast. To counter this power dynamic, progressive planners proposed that smaller-scale geographies could provide formal institutionalized structures for neighborhood-scale decision making. Where they were built into city governance, neighborhood planning processes went beyond voluntary advisory boards. The administrative authority to conduct the planning business of the jurisdiction remained with the city itself, but the neighborhood consultation process became mandatory; essential, though not binding. As a consequence, it became difficult for elected representatives to consistently over-look the opinions of their constituents once those opinions were on the record. This check on administrative power through citizen participation in decision making put pressure on elected officials not only during the election cycle but also in periods between elections. And in some places, it continues to do so.

In addition to their influence on decision making, neighbor-hood planning units serve as conduits for ongoing communi-cation and longer-term agenda setting. The meetings serve as spaces for city administrators to share information and test public opinion. Whether it is a localized police response to an uptick in crime or plans to invest in neighborhood "pocket parks," NPUs provide city administrators with a regularized and organized venue for sharing information with residents and for learning from them.

At a performative level, of course, a neighborhood planning meeting is a check mark on a process list. It enables city admin-istrators to claim they have consulted with the public in advance of an action. But on another level, neighborhood planning units have real power as an established platform for consultation and governance. The challenge for neighborhood planning systems going forward is interoperability between emergent and incum-bent systems of participatory planning. This is where the digital civics discussion within the smart cities project can work either with or in opposition to established frameworks of community development. The question is how to graft a technologically enhanced system of citizen empowerment onto effective and sys-tems of consultation that are already in place.

The inclusive innovation project involves designing a technology-enhanced model of participatory planning for smart citizenship, not simply civic participation. A first step is to recog-nize that there is a distinction between a citizen and a consumer.

And that distinction carries over to the question of civic engagement. Often, digital civics projects are designed to gather information from communities of users (residents, neighborhoods) in order to tailor smart cities solutions for the identified user needs and preferences. The goal is to provide community-informed or -inspired objects, systems, and platforms. In some cases, there is an effort to codesign these artifacts with communities. There is often an emphasis on a participatory design process, but that participation is fundamentally about producing solutions, not choosing among alternatives. The participatory design process in the smart cities context is, first, about gleaning information from communities of users and, second, about exchanging information with and among users. One example is the set of applications for crowdsourcing transportation routing for cars or bicycles.

Simply put, participatory design is not participatory planning. At one extreme, smart cities civic participation projects extract information from communities of users in the same way as any other product design process in the technology industry. These projects mine communities for information about individual characteristics and behaviors in order to tailor products and services. Political empowerment is neither a goal nor an outcome. At the other extreme, smart cities participation projects provide information to communities of users employing delivery systems that are specific to those communities—in the manner or medium of communication. In these cases, political empowerment is a possible secondary effect of reducing information asymmetries, but, again, is not the primary outcome.

It is for these reasons that digital civics and community engagement projects are a surprisingly comfortable fit in the broader smart cities project. These efforts do not destabilize existing power dynamics; neither do they challenge the new dynamics of the smart cities project. Because community participation is so underspecified, it is also nonthreatening. There is no clear relationship between digital civics and smart citizenship because there is no power analysis that contributes to or grafts onto institutional arrangements that empower citizens to influence or make real decisions.

The recommendation that emerges from this critique is clear: smart citizenship. Smart citizenship requires a recognition of, first, where citizen power already lies and, second, the design and implementation of technological tools that empower citizenship. A critique of power, similar to the one in this text, is necessary to maintain that focus on smart citizenship rather than civic participation. The goal is not to build a "bigger N" to design better-tailored technology tools. The project of gathering large amounts of data from communities of users to develop tools that deliver details about the composition and use of the urban built environment is not distinct from technocratic planning. It *is* technocratic planning.

The goal of smart citizenship is to support existing forms of active citizenship where communities already have an effective platform for participatory planning. In the places where those platforms do not exist, the goal is to help build them. One potential path is to design a generational rebooting of the neighborhood planning unit concept: an NPU 2.0.[6] That path requires a rethinking of what a technologically enhanced NPU 2.0 looks like in terms of changed functions and expanded mission. It also means recognizing and appreciating that many residents and citizens interact with their city and community through meetings, not smart phones. Although smart citizenship is, in part, about introducing a new generation of residents to the rights and responsibilities of civic engagement, it is also about broadening and enhancing accessibility for existing and established communities. Platforms for civic participation that rely solely on novel models of engagement ignore older communities, belying the bias in the technology toward consumers rather than citizens.

Finally, in order to enhance a neighborhood planning approach using smart citizenship, the model must expand its geographic reach to the places that were missed by the NPU 1.0 model: suburban and rural communities. For these communities, low densities, urban design, "thin" institutions, and isolation exacerbate the cost of information sharing and provide an inadequate revenue base for community planning. Smart cities technologies can significantly reduce the transportation and communication burdens for these jurisdictions. As a consequence, consistent citizen consultation, not only at election time but in the regular operations and priority setting for the community, is now possible. Further, the contrast between the Atlanta and Minneapolis approaches demonstrates multiple ways to define communities. Among the great administrative challenges for community planning has always been defining the boundaries of neighborhoods in a manner, and with a result, that is meaningful to the residents who live there.[7] What the Atlanta and Minneapolis cases show is that there are effective approaches from both the top down and the bottom up. In other words, it is possible that an NPU 2.0 approach enabled by smart citizenship could be applied to both large and small communities.

Technologies that are part of the smart cities project present the possibility of resolving two key barriers to citizen participation in public decision making: time and space. In past articulations of participatory planning, public meetings and citizen consultation dramatically slowed decision making and implementation. In this new iteration, new technologies allow for rapid engagement. This change in the time required for participatory planning means there could be more engagement at earlier stages in the policy design process. Indeed, that is what has occurred in recent years. It remains unclear how broad and representative that engagement can be in the future. This is where innovation has facilitated a shift in focus from *digital divide*, a concept that leans on lack of assets, to *digital inclusion*, a concept that assigns responsibility to cities and institutions to actively involve communities in decision making. Real participatory planning acknowledges that intelligence about the city is a two-way street. It is a dialogue about data and information about people and places. Neighborhood meetings are not an information delivery system but a forum for information exchange, policy analysis, and policy design. Smart cities technologies might make it possible to minimize the barriers and mitigate the work required to participate in and build forums and frameworks for smart citizenship.

CITIZENS ARE NOT CONSUMERS: PARTICIPATORY VS. PROPRIETARY PRACTICES OF DATA COLLECTION, OWNERSHIP, AND USE

There is more than a rhetorical tension between the roles of citizens and consumers in the smart cities project. Among the factors that will determine the future of the project is for whom it is designed. Technology firms design products and services for consumers; cities provide services to citizens—not some citizens but all citizens. Citizens are not customers. This is a surprisingly controversial statement. After decades of debate that recasts patients and students as clients, thinking about citizens as customers seems almost appropriate. However, the distinction between citizenship and consumption in the smart cities project is profoundly important. The rights and responsibilities of citizens and cities are different from the rights and roles of customers and companies.

Companies design for a target market of customers who demand and can afford a given product. Companies are not asked to provide equivalent services for an economically diverse citizenry that varies substantially in both its ability to pay and its willingness to do so. The distinction here is that the design of public services anticipates universal coverage within a given jurisdiction—or, at a minimum, a plausible rationale for the rollout of universal coverage. Citizens have rights to public services by virtue of their residency, not their ability to pay.

In part because many smart cities projects are not designed by experts in urban planning or policy, the programs confuse the question of targeted and universal program coverage. Often these projects overspecify the user community that is reached by a given technology deployment in order to demonstrate the applicability of the intervention to an underserved community. Although these efforts are often intended to tailor a technology or service to a disadvantaged or excluded community, they result in technology artifacts rather than public services. Many of the projects produced by programs such as Code for America or Data Science for Social Good result in programs that are not designed for scalability. In effect, both civic-driven and industry-driven smart cities projects fail to consider how public policies are designed. Public policies are not a fabric woven of piecemeal projects designed for communities of interest or practice distinguished from each other—in terms of needs, preferences, location, or demographics—by a so-called intelligent designer. Public services are designed for broad coverage. They are not intended to target markets but, rather, to provide services to citizens. Again, the identification of who is left out or left behind is one of the fundamental purposes of persistent program evaluation.

At the heart of the question of the appropriate design of smart cities projects is the issue of data and how citizens and consumers opt in in different ways to the urban services they use. As the market develops for smart cities objects, systems, and platforms, so do the standards and practices around the smart cities data that fuel these products and services and the standards governing the data produced by them. However, there is also a broader issue than that of standards and practices: the issue of data ownership. The smart cities project relies on urban data. The development and design of products and services depend on data about the behavior and characteristics of citizens and institutions in cities.

Economic geographers have argued that firm strategies reflect the specificities of the national regulatory regimes in which they are founded.[8] In the United States in particular, where many marquee technology companies such as Facebook, Google, Microsoft, and Amazon were founded and scaled up, the practices and standards around the collection of personal data (that is, data about the characteristics and behaviors of individuals) have followed an extractive model grounded in business strategies that were originally developed within the technology sector and driven by a need to develop a revenue stream. But receiving waste management services from your municipal government is not the same as opting in to a user agreement for a smart phone application. In the municipal context, the questions around data collected by cities for the purposes of providing services has never been an issue of information ownership; rather, it is one of appropriate use. The question of data ownership has not been an issue in a context in which governments use information to provide public services and maintain public records. The default assumptions behind data ownership have followed the path dependencies that were developed by the tech sector long before smart cities: whoever collects the data can use the data. Firms can sell or lease that information as well. There is no real acknowledgment that individual consumers may own the data derived about their characteristics and activities or control or influence the terms of use. The principle of "nothing about us without us" has not entered into the smart cities data discussion.

Instead, there have been episodic and conditional admissions in some industries that privacy and security concerns affect specific uses of individual consumer data. For example, limitations on the use of individual data have emerged in the financial services and health information contexts. Although people may not own the data collected on and about them, they are entitled to some level of protection from some potential uses (and abuses) of those data. In other words, the tradable uses of the data are regulated, but no one challenges the right of the company collecting the data to own it. Increasingly, there is a role for government in defining appropriate uses and acceptable levels of protection. In 2018, the first large-scale and direct regulatory challenge was raised about the idea that companies that collect data on individuals are solely entitled to determine the terms and conditions of use.

The European Union's general data protection legislation, known as the General Data Protection Regulation (GDPR), changed the situation for firms and organizations gathering data on individuals and developing revenue models from those data. The GDPR reflects a new regulatory regime that indicates a shift away from the voluntary industry governance of data controllers and processors through best practices of data extraction, collection, and use and toward governmental regulations applied directly to firms that are engaged in the collection and use of data on individuals.[9] The GDPR does not establish an individual property right to the data collected on an individual. It does, however, establish clear rights of access and use by third parties, described in the GDPR as "controllers and processers" of data.

It further establishes penalties for misuse and unsanctioned access. Among the types of unsanctioned use is the use of individual data without affirmative consent.[10]

For the smart cities project, this shift from voluntary industry governance of individual data to mandatory government regulation of firms presents an opportunity to reflect on and reconsider how cities should govern the data they hold on citizens and the data they collect. As noted earlier, the smart cities project largely evolved on a private-sector model in which data about the characteristics and activities of citizens are not treated as distinct from the data collected on customers in terms of processing or control. The guiding assumption in the development of the smart cities market is that monetizing *citizen data* can follow the same practices and standards as the firm strategies that were tested in the technology industries for monetizing *customer data*. And if that is perhaps too broad an assumption, at least the practices and standards in the health care and financial services industries could be applied, incorporating more robust privacy and security protections. However, business models would remain predicated on the assumption that a firm can use and process the data collected on consumers and citizens irrespective of that distinction for sale to third parties or for product development or marketing purposes. A blanket opt-in rather than opt-out customer user agreement still provides sufficient consent. The appropriate level of private use of individual data collected and processed by cities and in cities, however, is not so simple. Ultimately, the question of who owns publicly collected and processed data and who has transfer and use rights to those data is at the heart of the smart cities project. In many ways, it controls the revenue model and, thus, policy design. How cities answer that question might be the determining factor in how the smart cities project evolves for citizens or for consumers.

Real estate search portals illustrate the complexities of the issue.[11] Property tax records are public records that are collected and processed by localities. These records, which contain sales and ownership information, are often searchable online through a portal managed and maintained by a local government. In other words, individually identifiable public records on property ownership are available to anyone with the desire to look. Commercial real estate Internet search portals are built from these records and supplemented by industries, institutions, and individual contributions to item records, providing more detailed information on properties, school districts, neighborhoods, and the broader built environment. However, these real estate search portals do not include the names of property owners, whereas municipal property records do. This information is public, but it is not part of the service offered by those search portals. The data are not hidden; they simply sit with the city, not the company developing a commercial service from the information. These systems operate interdependently from each other despite the fact that the commercial service relies on public records.

The appropriate management of public data for private entrepreneurship is a constant challenge for local governments. To provide public services efficiently and comprehensively, localities collect data on people, property, institutions, and organizations and on their behaviors. These are generally referred to as public records: on property tax, car registrations, utility bills, jury duty service, code violations, and voter registration. The data are not collected or processed for purposes beyond those specified: the efficient operation of the city. Or, at least, that's the idea.

To the extent that citizens opt in to the data collection and processing activities of their local governments, they do so to facilitate the effective operations of those governments. The case of commercial real estate Internet search portals points to one type of practice that has emerged. As more and more technology companies have identified ways to commodify data about cities and the individuals who live in them, the firms have developed an array of accepted industry practices. The tendency to observe a boundary between the commercialization of personally identifiable individual information and the use of anonymized or aggregated versions of those data is one such practice.

However, the progressive privatization of the city—public services and public spaces—has set the stage for the commercial use of data collected and processed by local governments about the characteristics and behaviors of citizens and residents. Indeed, because private-sector subcontractors provide many public-sector services, an array of data sits with these third parties already, outside the city itself. And unless there are contractual arrangements specifying the ownership and use of those data or regulatory limitations to use of the information, private subcontractors have the opportunity to commodify citizen data for purposes for which no consent was requested and none was given.

This distinction between data collected and processed by local governments for public purposes and the acquisition of public data for private-sector product development is but one of the conceptual slippages in the smart cities project. Embedded in this distinction is the further difference between data collected and processed for research purposes or policy design and data collected for marketing and product development. This problem is not limited to the smart cities industry.[12] Recent discoveries of how individuals' data have been misused in other public contexts reveal the same conflation between consumer marketing and citizen participation. Some firms actively obfuscate these distinctions. Identifying themselves as data research intermediaries, such firms present data analytics as their core service, characterizing that work as research. The work that these firms perform, however, is defined by their clients, not the firms' capacities. Although data analytics can be used for research purposes, it is often used to offer various kinds of market intelligence ranging from the economic to the political. One well-known example is the now defunct Cambridge Analytics firm, which was caught up in the ethically suspect data use behind political campaigns in both the United States and the United Kingdom. This distinction between basic research and market intelligence is profoundly important in the smart cities context. It is also not that complicated.

Data analytics for consumers uses information on the characteristics and behaviors of individuals to design services and products and then target those products and services to potential customers. Marketing influences the design of the analytical process determining how data are collected, stored, analyzed, and monetized (sold and exchanged). Conversely, data analytics for citizens uses information about the characteristics and behaviors of individuals to design services and products for citizens, residents, and visitors. There is no marketing component embedded in such data collection, processing, or design.[13]

In the deployment of new public services, or in the process of expanding coverage of an existing service, there is often a need to build public awareness or promote citizen engagement. However, public awareness campaigns are not marketing strategies, and the slippage between these two processes is again facilitated by the misunderstanding that a citizen is a customer. There are examples of the importance of public awareness and citizen engagement campaigns in the context of technology and public service expansion. These cases illustrate why and how these efforts are distinct from marketing in the private sector. One such case is the deployment of 311 nonemergency-reporting systems in cities.[14] Dialing 311 links to a city service that is designed to expand and facilitate the ability of citizens to request (or report) a request for city services. The name of the service builds on the public's familiarity with 911 emergency services and 411 information services. However, 311 reports and requests can be made through city Web sites and mobile applications, not merely through phone calls. Many cities prefer that citizens make requests through mobile and Internet interfaces because such contact facilitates request tracking and subsequent analyses for performance assessment and planning purposes.

Deploying 311 as a traditional phone-based service and as a technology-enhanced service requires an effort to build citizen awareness. This is aligned with the sort of citizen education efforts that have long been best practice for the rollout of new services. It is certainly necessary to engage citizens in the design and review of a service to plan for enhancements and ascertain effectiveness. Further, it is useful for cities to estimate the scale of demand for the service and any increase in other city services as the result of enhanced reporting processes. A demand estimate is necessary to plan public budgets, staffing, and equipment. However, this is not—conceptually or analytically—the same thing as estimating the market for 311 services. The intended coverage of the service is all residents and visitors within the city. The goal is to moderate and ultimately eliminate any barriers to access or differential patterns of use. Research into the characteristics and behaviors of residents and visitors might be useful to determine how best to provide service coverage. The point here is to estimate demand for a new public service (311) and its effects on the demand for other public services, and to address any coverage gaps. In other words, the goal is not to target a specific market but, rather, to enable universal service coverage. Data facilitate efficient and equitable public service design and implementation.

DATA AS THE PRODUCT: REDEFINING RIGHTS TO INTANGIBLE ASSETS

One essential function of government is to define property rights and determine the legitimate (legal) methods of their exchange. In chapter 3, I argued that cities are of particular interest in the development and evolution of this emerging market because they are territories with known and predictable property rights. Cities are places with governance regimes and clear decision-making processes. How rights are allocated and enforced is not mysterious; those rights are on the public record. There is unambiguous precedent.

But in reality, cities have the power the change how property rights are assigned and exchanged. The assignment of rights is not static. Specifically, in the past, cities have responded to the commodification of intangible assets through legislation. New technologies lead to new products, processes, materials, and industry strategies, and those practices drive innovation in governance as well. Turning to history for analogs to better understand potential local responses to smart cities, one obvious illustration of innovative governance can be found: land use regulation and the emergence of zoning codes. The question, then, is whether this analog can serve as a precedent for how cities might respond to the smart cities project through a reconsideration of the allocation of property rights. There is potential for rethinking and reallocating the use rights to data obtained about the characteristics and behaviors of citizens at the scale of urban governance.

Land use regulations are arguably the most powerful policy tools in urban planning. Zoning could be considered as an example of innovation in local governance in response to technological change. This may seem counterintuitive, given that these land use laws first appeared in New York City more than a century ago and were upheld by the U.S. Supreme Court in Euclid v. Ambler in 1926.[15] However, the parallel to the fundamental rationale for city-scale regulation reaches back to ambiguities about who held the property rights to certain intangible assets. Again, this might seem counterintuitive. Land use regulation seems so tangible and territorialized in its current cartographic codifications. In reality, land use regulations are much more about *uses* than they are about *land*. And here is where the parallel to the collection and use of smart cities data becomes instructive.

Zoning regulations are often explained as mechanisms to minimize onerous land uses in dense environments where the externalities generated by one owner's use infringes on the uses of other land owners or the underlying value of the property they hold. For the smart cities project, then, it is useful to think of land use regulations as a regulatory analog based in a somewhat more nuanced understanding of infringement and a recognition that zoning can be viewed as defining an intangible asset—the right to the use of space—through its territorialization.

Land use controls vary widely across jurisdictions, both across countries and between cities. In places such as the United States, local governments have highly tailored land use regulations that are specific to each jurisdiction. Land use regulations achieve a very simple goal: they restrict the possible legitimate uses of any given property based on the characteristics and location of that property. That is, an owner cannot convert a given property to any use but is restricted to a set of allowable uses defined in the city's zoning code. In other words, localities allow the exercise of some property rights but not all possible property rights. Rights are restricted.

In the early twentieth century, as cities became denser and technological developments in architecture and engineering allowed property owners to build taller structures, new buildings began to loom over existing ones, cutting off access to light and air. As a result, existing property owners found that new buildings infringed on the value of their properties, extracting the value that the owners had not captured and commodified themselves. This is how the concept of air rights gradually emerged. The concept of property rights to the space above (and below) a given property is well established in common law; and, effectively, these are use rights to build above or below the two-dimensional plane of the land itself.

What was less clear in cities in the early twentieth century was who had the use rights to the space above a property not currently in use by the owner of the underlying property. Who could build in that empty space, and, once that right was established, could that right be traded? Could cities themselves sell the air rights to public property for private uses? Is there a property right to the empty space above a structure that is equivalent to the difference between the space occupied by the structure and the allowable, potential height the structure might have been built to occupy? Is there both a value to the potential to exercise air rights and the actual exercise of them? In other words, is there value to not exercising a use right to occupy air? In this context, the collection, use, and monetization of data seem almost tangible in comparison.

This example is intended to provide an analog to how property rights to the data collected on the characteristics and behaviors of citizens and residents are identified and assigned. This extension of property rights into the ground and the sky emerged from a long process of innovations in urban governance. It is now largely settled law. There is no need to assume that the use rights to those data lie with individuals who are capable of extracting the information either through fixed sensor systems deployed as a city service or through mobile services that operate under various kinds of commercial user agreements. In either case, it is neither obvious nor inevitable that property rights—and the terms of exchange and use—cannot be legislated differently by the governing jurisdictions from which the data are collected.

It need not be considered self-evident that the property and use rights to the data collected on and about citizens accrue to those capable of collecting the data rather than to those who generated the information. As data become monetized and traded, jurisdictions have the authority and obligation to appropriately regulate use of those data. If the city is the scale of action in the collection of data on individuals, it falls to cities—the local jurisdiction—to develop the regulatory regime. Given that cities regulate property rights, perhaps they are at the right scale for the regulation of data rights. Once the realization is made that *data are local, not global*, then so, too, will their regulation fall within the jurisdiction of the city.

As the smart cities conversation continues, so does the privatization conversation about cities and public infrastructure more generally. However, very little of the conversation about either the current level of public-sector privatization or the increasing levels of privatization of public infrastructure involves smart cities directly. The conversation about privatization and smart cities—to the extent that it exists as coherent emerges on two fronts: data and procurement.[16] The question of data access and ownership in the smart cities project is, therefore, especially important.

There is a long discourse in urban planning about the privatization of the city. This discourse is often particularly territorialized. It focuses on the privatization of public spaces such as city parks.[17] The declining public ownership of physical places has implications for what is considered legitimate use of perceived public spaces by the public, especially less enfranchised or disenfranchised communities such as children or the homeless. In spite of these highly problematic and systematic exclusions, cities have continued to experiment with the monetization of fixed assets. It appears that some cities have begun to see urban data as another asset with which they can develop alternative revenue streams. This experimentation is difficult to assess because it is deeply tied to how cities already contract with external providers for public services. Here lies the challenge. Smart cities data are generated and collected through the use of both spaces and services. The Sidewalk Labs development in Toronto is an example of the former, whereas the private contractors who provide bicycle-sharing services for cities are an example of the latter. In both cases, cities have a decision to make about not only the development partner or the service contractor but also the ownership and use of the data they collect and how that information is used. Cities are increasingly aware of this choice and its potential revenue implications. The question is whether citizens should be more aware of and engaged in these decisions and the trade-offs those decisions entail.

Note that unlike in the private sector, where firms generally seek to capture the services and products that present greater value, the tendency in the public sector is to allow those value-added services to migrate into the private sector. In this specific context, cities retain the platform but not the services. And this is where the next steps in the smart cities project become increasingly complicated. How will, and should, the public participate in the decision making that defines what is public and what is private in their own smart city?

The changes in technology that operationalized the previously unimagined uses of below- and above-ground property—effectively making land use regulations a three-dimensional rather than two-dimensional administrative project—seemed disruptive at the time. Governance responds to technological innovations and the strategies that industries and individuals develop with those new processes, products, and materials.

Purely technical solutions to urban challenges rarely measure up to the promises of their advocates. The diffusion of urban innovations—in policy and planning—requires adaptation to local contexts and communities. The core and periphery investment strategy adopted by the testbed and competition approaches creates uneven capacities across cities to design and absorb new technologies that are relevant to performance management and optimization. The creation of a core and periphery of places through the pattern of uneven investments in urban innovation has serious implications for the future spatial distribution of economic activities and the resulting *relative* resilience of regional economies.

Differential infrastructure and services mean that not only will (some) citizens select places based on smart city endowments, but so will firms. The uneven distribution of technologically embedded infrastructure affects the economic competitiveness of cities both inside and outside the core. Finally, peripheral cities are obligated to adopt the designs and models that are developed and tailored for leader cities, causing a convergence toward the needs, priorities, and circumstances of core cities that is reflected in the design of smart city solutions and strategies. The ad hoc implementation of such use cases and capacities produces a complex and uneven landscape that has the potential to reshape regional competition and shift the focus away from enhanced quality and coverage of public services and toward increased privatization.

7

SMART CITIES AS THE NEW
UNEVEN DEVELOPMENT

IN chapters 5 and 6, I began the process of proposing alternative approaches to the smart cities project. These proposals are predicated on the assertation that cities have the power to intervene in the smart cities project to shape the tactics and influence the goals the project seeks to achieve. New models of participatory planning are one way to shape some of those goals from the bottom up rather than the top down. Another potential intervention is to revisit the regulation of intangible assets—notably, data—using the tools that cities already have at their disposal. Although many cities are experimenting with making data widely available through open-data policies and data trusts, these efforts are a beginning rather than the end of a conversation about data regulation.[1] More deliberate regulation and greater participatory planning require recognition of the work that is needed to design and implement smart cities and to invest in that capacity.

Perhaps the most critical recommendation is to embed in cities themselves an increased capacity to take on the work that an expanded commitment to urban entrepreneurialism brings. If cities are to do more than manage services and, instead, serve as the platform for the design and development of new products and services, as well as act as a partner is those processes, then cities need the internal capacity to do that work. Urban innovation networks are one way to support this expanded role, but each city requires the ability to tailor these emerging services and products to its own needs and the characteristics of its communities. This is a somewhat obvious extension of the devolution that has characterized the neoliberal turn over recent decades. If national governments shift responsibilities and decision making to local governments, it stands to reason that cities would require increased capacity to perform those tasks. In this case, cities require the capacity to affirmatively regulate the smart cities project rather than retroactively respond to it.

An emphasis on technical innovation has obscured the need for innovations in urban governance and investments in local government. Cities have a great deal of power to regulate space. However, learning how to develop new tools and use those tools to regulate both virtual and physical space takes a sustained effort. In addition, there needs to be clarity about how cities want the smart cities project to unfold in their jurisdictions and how they want the benefits of those efforts to be distributed. In this chapter, I analyze how the existing processes of privatization and uneven development serve as the backdrop of the smart cities project and help to highlight where cities might act in designing a more equitable smart cities project.

It is difficult to overstate how much privatization complicates the smart cities project. However, it might be instructive to turn to the organization of work as an illustration of how the smart cities project is shifting the already porous boundaries between private and public spaces and services and the formal and informal labor markets. What the smart cities project does is accelerate privatization and expand labor flexibility. In doing so, the project, in its current form, produces a new form of uneven development.

In this chapter, I walk through those processes of privatization and flexibility to highlight these effects and draw attention to potential points of intervention.

ACCELERATING PRIVATIZATION: COMMODIFYING CITIES

The privatization of local services that is driven by outsourcing has been uneven and incomplete. It has also been episodic. Localities often outsource to vendors for a contract term and then bring that function back inside the city government in later years.[2] Efforts to change the coverage of public services and eligibility for specific services also have been part of the neoliberal project. However, some cities have not followed that pattern, instead expanding services and moving baselines by setting their own minimum wages, establishing municipal health insurance schemes, and providing enhanced public services to citizens.[3] Devolution laid the groundwork for further uneven innovation; it simply did not all move in one direction. Service contractions in some places are juxtaposed against service enhancements in others, creating a landscape of increasing inequalities.

The outsourcing of existing and established public services is not generally a focus in the smart cities conversation. In fact, rarely do advocates of smart cities engage in a discussion about government at all. Indeed, after forty years of minimizing the distinction between the public and the private, it may not be obvious to all stakeholders how privatization is driving the planning and implementation of smart cities. Although some cities outsource basic city services and others do not, almost all cities outsource a wide array of business services. These are the consulting and analysis services provided by well-known consulting firms such as Bain and Company, Deloitte, Ernst and Young, and the Boston Consulting Group. Unlike their counterparts in other industrialized countries, for strategic planning or project design and evaluation, U.S. cities and localities rarely bring in international nongovernmental public-sector specialists such as the Organisation for Economic Co-operation and Development or national or local specialists from the planning and policy research centers at universities. In other words, the planning for the future of cities has been outsourced to private consulting companies. And these firms, similar to the technology firms they work with, operate on a strategy of economies of scale. One size fits all; tailoring solutions to local contexts takes time and costs money.

Current outsourcing practices are one reason that the smart cities project has thus far been designed largely for customers and not citizens. But the ways in which smart cities data are collected by cities and in cities also makes a difference. This lack of clarity about who smart cities project and programs are designed for obscures how the rules that determine terms of ownership, use, and access to smart cities data are made and with what criteria. If smart cities were only about objects, systems, and platforms and not also about data, following this well-worn path of privatization still would be problematic from the perspective of the continued privatization of virtual and physical public spaces. However, the role of data makes this privatization project more than merely problematic. Data are both an end product of smart cities and an input into smart cities. Privatization of data, then, is also the privatization of the entire smart cities project. What complicates this data privatization question even more is how it affects the basic and fundamental design of public infrastructure.[4]

Reflection has lagged far behind the rapidly expanding ability to collect and process data about the individuals in the city. Some of the slippage between estimating and understanding citizens' demand for public services and marketing products and services to consumers is surely inadvert. It is simply a misunderstanding of the distinction between citizens and customers by those involved in technology development rather than those in public service. However, there are two other factors operating that are far less benign. Both factors derive from the processes of public-sector privatization, and these factors drive uneven innovation.

The first factor is public-sector privatization itself. The smart cities project did not develop in a neutral ideological context. Privatization, begun in earnest in the United States and the United Kingdom in the 1980s, changed how localities operate. Privatization changed which services cities provided to citizens and how they do so.[5] The neoliberal policies adopted at the national scale in both countries initiated processes of devolution and privatization that cascaded through state and local governments, affecting everything from social services to transportation infrastructure. Austerity has eroded the baseline level of public services in all but a few places.[6] The services that remain core functions of local governments—waste management, utilities, transit, public health, animal control—are frequently provided by private subcontractors rather than government employees. In some cases, the service providers are mission-driven nonprofit organizations. In the United States, since the 1990s, some of these providers have been faith-based organizations, particularly in child and family services. In other cases, the subcontractors are for-profit firms that balance the obligation to provide a public service with the need to produce a profit. These vendors, whether for-profit or nonprofit, collect information on citizens in the course of doing business.

Selling public services directly to citizens is a different privatization proposition altogether. It takes the city out of the business of provisioning selected public services and assessing their efficacy and distributional effects. Cities shape the governance of the administratively delineated geography that provides an experimental space for private-sector product design and market intelligence. That market intelligence then informs which services become publicly provisioned and which are offered privately. In this model, what determines the difference is not efficiency, equity, or consideration of universal coverage but the extent to which there is money to be made. Thus, uneven innovation leads to a whole new level of uneven development, a level at which the evolving services of the knowledge economy are captured by the private sector and where the market failures that emerge are left to the public sector to manage. Again, it is not a new story. What is new is the extent to which the public sector—specifically, cities—are subsidizing this private enterprise.

SUBSIDIZING UNEVEN INNOVATION

Recent years have seen a resurgence of interest in the concept of uneven and combined development, particularly in the field of international relations.[7] For economic geographers, this conversation has reanimated the research on uneven development that was popular in the 1970s and 1980s.[8] Both uneven development and uneven and combined development propose alternative explanations for the differences that can be observed between and among places as they experience various forms of capitalist development. Uneven and combined development further offers a commentary on the historical stages of development. In other words, although it is fairly clear why places that began on the path toward industrialization at different times remain at different stages in the process, it is less clear why different places do not follow the same linear progression through the development process. This is, of course, an important question for economic and political policy and substantially influences how nations manage their own governance as well as their interactions and interests with other governments. Hence, international relations scholars have turned to uneven and combined development as a potential explanatory framework.

For economic geographers, beyond a structural economic analysis, the importance of the concept of uneven and combined development is in its emphasis on the relational nature of differential levels of economic development between places. From colonialism to globalization, economic geography has been a relational enterprise. The explanations for the spatial distribution of economic activities between places are explanations for distributions across a differentiated landscape. From a policy perspective, the lack of a reliable pattern that produces economic progress in a predictable way is highly problematic. There is no formula. In addition, it is demonstrably not the case that the same level of public or private investments produces the same development outcomes across time and space. The development process, then, is both contingent and uncertain and, as we see so clearly at a wide variety of geographic scales, consequently uneven and inequitably distributed.

Urbanization, as a process within the panoply of development processes, triggers all these questions about levels of investment and the stages of development. Part of the prediction problem is simply complexity. The integrated urban systems we experience in everyday life are often not entirely decipherable. These systems exist in layers of both time and space. The layers of natural and engineered systems did not all come into being on the same day. They were not all implemented by the same actors. They are not all managed by the same entities. Cities are layered incumbent systems of economic, political, and social choices that have been made, retained, and abandoned over long periods.

The availability of technology solutions influences choices about both what is possible and what is preferred; not just their existence, but their relative value. And those choices reflect highly localized predilections as well as embedded path dependencies. We may not like the distribution of goods and services or the distribution of access and opportunity that these systems produce, but these systems do produce an allocation. Whether the systems reflect the most efficient or equitable possible choices is not only a different (though implicit) question lurking behind smart cities but also is the same question we have been asking about cities and economies for a long time. We are always making choices about how we organize the economy and the city to produce preferred outcomes. Who benefits (and who pays) for the distributional outcomes of the systems we choose and under what conditions tends to vary over time and space. And that variation tends to be significant economically and politically far more than technologically.

The core argument of this book is that the smart cities project was not—and is not—a technology project. It is a policy project. Consequently, it can be analyzed and understood through the lens of urban policy analysis and practice. That said, the smart cities project does present a complicated urban policy challenge. After forty years of deregulation, devolution, and privatization within cities, the smart cities project presents a renewed focus on urban infrastructure investment in a complex economic, political, and technical environment. Local governments have evolved in distinct ways in recent decades, which has resulted in significant variation among cities in terms of the regulation of land and labor markets as well as the characteristics of the built environment.[9] Different cities have pursued privatization in different ways, outsourcing some functions to private vendors while maintaining other functions within the city. These variations affect everything from police protection to park services. Further, the deregulation and privatization trends in national economies also have led to the rise of third-party intermediaries operating at the intersections between incumbent and emerging industries. This is the complex environment in which the smart cities project plots a path toward creating a market for smart cities objects, systems, platforms, and data and then subsequently serving it.

Fundamentally, smart cities are a policy problem, not a technology problem. The technology challenges are fairly straightforward issues of scalability and efficiency, and these are both heavily tied up with issues of cost. Simply put, the technology challenge is one of feasibility, not possibility. The policy challenge, however, is much more complex and uncertain. For those interested in cities, economies, and society, the policy questions are much more consequential.[10] These questions fall into two broad categories: (a) privatization and the smart cities project—who owns its infrastructure, data, systems, operations (noted earlier); and (b) funding for and distribution of the smart cities project— the revenue model and the construction of differentiated markets within the city: who pays, who benefits, and, ultimately, who has access and who does not.

In the conversation about economic development strategies and territorial innovation policies, the fundamental economic importance of cities is often lost. In the United States, metropolitan statistical areas (MSAs)—called *city-regions* in other countries—account for more that 90 percent of the country's gross domestic product. Conversely, the political power of cities is far outweighed by this economic influence in the United States at the national scale and often in state governments as well. Much of the literature on urban policies in the twentieth century focused on the limits to urban political power and the structures that limit the ability of cities to leverage investments and shape national policy.[11] There are many reasons for this, and an imbalance between economic and political power is not unique to the United States.[12] However, the legacy governance structures that provide disproportionate political power to places of low population at the expense of places of high population tends to be highly specific. In the United States, most of these imbalances flow from the geographic distribution of political representation that includes the Electoral College and gerrymandering.[13] In both cases, political geography sets the stage.[14]

This persistent mismatch between the economic and political power of cities affects their ability (and that of their citizens) to effectively influence the regulatory regimes that shape both public and private investment at the national and local levels. In other words, it is representation, not regulation, that limits the capacity of cities to engage the economic problems at the root of urban problems that are operating at the national and even the global scale.

This mismatch, of course, is not new. Nor are the many attempts to de-emphasize the economic importance of cities and regions to national economies and to the wider global economy ideologically neutral acts. To recognize urbanization economies is to acknowledge uneven development. For many policy makers, there is some ambivalence around this admission. The widespread embracing of Thomas Friedman's thesis that the world is flat was one indicator of the persuasive power of a counterargument to the value of urbanization economies.[15] The economic importance of cities lies in their ability to create and consolidate markets. These are primarily land and labor markets and the markets derived from them; for example, commercial real estate. However, cities are also at the heart of the process of financialization. And as financialization has become more important to the global economy, so, too, have cities.[16] This is one reason cities are the central scale defining the smart cities industry.

The flat world argument was an argument about economic and policy convergence.[17] However, it was not a serious asserta-tion about an undifferentiated landscape or the different stages of development; it was not actually an argument against uneven and combined development. Indeed, there is significant evidence that the convergences observed and anticipated in Freidman's analysis have subsequently proved uneven. The argument was intended to draw attention to the processes of globalization that seem to leap over the national boundaries that once limited technology diffu-sion and policy mobilities through barriers of culture, capacity, and governance. But what was less prominent in the flat world debate was the recognition that those leaps of investment over national boundaries often, if not always, landed in cities.[18]

The diffusion of global investments has both lent urban agglomerations privileged status and contributed to them, cre-ating more urbanization economies in more places.[19] Despite the absence of acknowledgment of agglomeration economies in many national policy-making forums, the alternative project in economic geography has continued to concentrate on the spatial implications of specific shifts in production systems and regula-tory regimes. Economic geography researchers also analyze the rise of some city-regions and the simultaneous decline of oth-ers. In this empirical project within economic geography, there is clear evidence of both urbanization economies and uneven development. Further, there is a sustained conversation about how innovation systems are themselves territorialized—how and why technology and cities seem so firmly intertwined.[20] This con-versation has continued largely in parallel with the smart cities project. It rarely intersects with it.

A focus on cities as a designated geography creates a significant challenge for traditional forms of innovation policy making and analysis. In traditional analyses of innovation policy, space is rarely considered a variable of interest, beyond its role in determining the scale of administration (state, national, local). The question of location is viewed primarily through a regulatory lens, as a question about which jurisdictions provide either an enabling or a prohibitive policy environment. For example, in the discussion about data localization, place matters because regulations either allow or inhibit the transfer of data over national boundaries. Space is important as a regulatory factor.

In contrast, economic geographers have viewed innovation policy differently. They argue that space matters because it influences the construction and operation of markets and the response of firms and institutions to the social and economic processes behind those constructions.[21] This is the second premise of this book: that the city is a site of subsidy and risk reduction for industries and firms generally and the tech sector specifically. Several decades of research on territorial innovation systems in economic geography and cognate disciplines have produced a substantial body of evidence that proximities matter for innovation processes.[22] The extensive analysis of industry clusters, agglomeration economies, and industrial districts demonstrated the importance of proximities for multiple industries over a substantial period. The related research on regional innovation systems, innovation neighborhoods, learning regions, and the innovative milieu demonstrated that proximities are even more important for high-technology industries and for enabling and evolving technologies. This body of research underpins the arguments made in chapter 3 about how important cities are for developing a market for smart cities objects, systems, platforms, and data regardless of how that market expands in the future into other contexts. So it is no surprise that the smart cities project has its own locational logic.

Of course, the emphasis on density, proximity, and urbanization economies leaves an obvious hole in the coverage of the smart cities project in terms of both physical and political geographies. What does the smart cities project offer for rural and low-density places? The smart cities project presents an overt and formal recognition of the role that urbanization economies play in technology development and diffusion. As such, not only does the smart cities project not resolve the uneven development between urban and rural places, but it builds more economically competitive cities.[23] By not addressing the economic value of cities relative to other places, the smart cities project makes claims of a broad public purpose without clarifying the value of that subsidy to a geographically diverse constituency. By ignoring scale as a meaningful category, the discourse seeks to evade the question of how to distribute the benefits and costs of economic growth that are enabled by technology investments in specific places. This evasion leaves distributional equity out of the design of the smart cities project.

Attempts to redefine the smart cities project as applicable to a broader category of smart communities have been driven largely by academic researchers and policy makers.[24] The goal is to broaden the constituency and expand access and opportunity for people who are left out and left behind as new technologies proliferate. Unfortunately, these efforts often fail to recognize that the lack of opportunities identified are the consequence of previous rounds of uneven development, not of project designs or policy failures in the smart cities project. Such inequality is a consequence of an economy problem. Technology diffusion as a process and technology markets as spaces primarily operate and are produced within urban agglomerations.[25] The effort to move the smart cities conversation away from cities and toward a more ambiguous, diffuse, and undefined geography is a political response to an economic problem.

The additional problem is that the smart communities discourse contributes to a re-emergence of an antiurban bias that has been magnified by the mismatch between representation and population. *Smart communities* sounds like a more inclusive term than *smart cities*, bringing under the umbrella of *smart* those places that have not been part of the technology conversation. But, in fact, the smart communities discourse is about something different from smart cities. It isn't about creating markets; it is about providing services. It is about deciding how basic technology and communication services are defined going forward and what level of public services will be expected and provided.

Whether the project is called *smart communities* or *smart cities*, it cannot reconcile entrenched urban and rural socioeconomic inequalities through the deployment of a 5G network.[26] There are technology deployments that exacerbate spatial inequality, but none that resolves it. For its part, the implementation of 5G technologies is on track to amplify inequalities both spatially and economically. According to the *New York Times*, "To get the benefits of 5G, users will have to buy new phones, while carriers will need to install new transmission equipment to offer the faster services."[27] Beyond the economic disparities produced by the required purchases, the spatial disparities between and within cities are already "baked into" the implementation strategies of leading firms.

AT&T's 5G network launched in Atlanta, Charlotte, Dallas, Houston, Indianapolis, Jacksonville, Louisville, Oklahoma City, New Orleans, Raleigh, San Antonio, and Waco. In the next six months, AT&T also plans to expand to Las Vegas, Los Angeles,

Nashville, Orlando, San Diego, San Francisco, and San Jose. In all cases, the network will only be present in "parts of" these cities.[28]

The distribution of the benefits of 5G are on track to be another example of uneven innovation. As the *New York Times* summarized the situation, "How fast will 5G be? The answer depends on where you live, which wireless services you use and when you decide to take the 5G plunge."[29]

The smart community's conversation is, as is the smart cities conversation, an object lesson in the concept of uneven development operating in practice. This is not to say that communities, as a broader category of people and places than cities, should not have access to these enabling technologies. It is, however, to say that this is essentially a political question about the distribution of public investment in people and places. The smart communities conversation is about whether the technologies that are concentrating in cities and regions will be distributed to places and people who are not in urban areas. The smart communities discourse does not recognize that the smart cities project is an industry-driven enterprise in market-making, as opposed to a civic project in enhanced public service delivery. The question of distributional equity is important. However, it is also important to understand how and why technology firms are choosing and using cities as the sites for designing and developing smart cities objects, systems, and platforms—why this technology project is positioned as specifically *urban* innovation.

In *Working Regions* (2013), I argued that the collocation of innovation and production was an increasingly essential characteristic in the knowledge economy. My observation was that for design-intensive and technology-driven industries, geographic distance between innovation and production was shrinking. These are dynamic processes, and this narrowing of distance did not apply then (and does not apply now) to all functions or all industries. But the narrowing of distance was evident in the connection between core design and innovation functions and prototype development and small-batch and niche manufacturing—for those products tailored to specific markets or subject to time constraints due to tastes or technology.

My argument in *Working Regions* was fundamentally about changes in the spatial organization of economic activities. It was an argument about which factors influence the concentration and dispersion of different elements of a production process, ranging from innovation through end product production. Turning toward the industry at hand, the question, then, is how innovation and production are spatially organized in the smart cities industry. That industry is both design intensive and technology driven. It also defines its own relevance as geographically specified—as *urban*. Further, the data that are generated by and in cities determine the design of smart cities products and services and the primary market for them.

The question then becomes, which factors govern the spatial organization of the smart cities industry? Does the production of smart cities objects, systems, and platforms necessarily concentrate in cities? Or does data mobility—geographically and legally—mean that the role of cities in the smart cities production process is, first, as the site of the data mine that determines design parameters and, second, as the product market? If this is the case, then the smart cities industry does not disrupt established production systems or the development of novel technologies. What is perhaps disruptive is how the industry has found a new site of simultaneous subsidy of both its products and its markets: *cities*. In economic development practice, cities are generally interested in subsidizing economic activities that bring jobs and revenues to its jurisdiction. If, indeed, there is no connectivity between the production processes in the industry and any specific city, then that proposition falls apart.

SUPPORTING WORK IN SMART CITIES WITH SMART CITIES

In previous chapters, I discussed how labor flexibility has increased as smart cities technologies have progressively turned the city into a platform for contingent work arrangements. Previous chapters have also noted the argument for increased capacity in local governments to design and manage the rollout of the urban technology project as it works through this whole array of experimental interventions and deployments. What remains unaddressed is how to theorize about the amplification of precarious work and how to understand and anticipate its likely impacts on scales beyond the traditional scope of the smart cities project—specifically, communities, households, and workers.

In her 2009 article discussing authenticity and the "urban village," Sharon Zukin pointed out that the celebrated neighborhood central to the work of Jane Jacobs would soon disappear,[30] because the urban village was a particular space on the American urban landscape that was contingent on an enabling economic structure.[31] In the coming decades, the processes of deindustrialization and globalization would destabilize the urban labor market and hollow out the working-class and middle-class jobs that formed the backbone of the urban village. The career ladders and social welfare system that produced steady employment, predictable paths of advancement, and affordable education, pensions, and heath care for the people who needed the neighborhoods that Robert Caro called "urban staging grounds" would erode and also be pulled back, resulting in a dual city occupied by the very rich and the working poor. In either case, the residents who remained either would not need or could not afford the neighborhoods of the urban staging ground.[32] In other words, the idealized communities of the Jane Jacobs era would be destroyed not only by urban renewal but also by the effects of industrial restructuring on the labor market.

Zukin's point was that it is important to understand both the economic structures that produce urban spaces and the processes that dictate how they are consumed. The work performed in cities matters because it constitutes that basic structure. However, the composition of the labor market and the organization of work often fall outside the core of urban-planning discussions. A focus on jobs—particularly the organization of work—tends to be far less popular in urban policy circles, in part because policy interventions in the labor market are almost always targeted at the supply side (education, training, school to work) rather than the demand side of the equation.[33] These policies rarely affect the organization of work; rather, they affect the capacities of the workers.

One unexpected result of the smart cities project is how significantly it has reorganized work in a relatively short period. The power of these new technologies, and the firm strategies enabled by them, to open up new forms of flexibility and informality has caught many commentators—and almost all regulators—off guard. Some cities have begun to react to these changes and experimented with regulations to slow them or force them to align with existing standards.[34] However, few have analyzed the implications of the broadening of precarious and contingent work arrangements and how the publicly subsidized smart cities platform facilitates it. That is, perhaps it is not merely a question of workplace regulation but one of platform regulation.

Notably, public support for regulation of the sharing economy has been uneven. The conveniences of ride sharing, house sharing, and scooters and bicycles have been popular with consumers, and even workers in the sharing economy are often willing to accept the negatives of flexibility given the positives they perceive. A recent study of Uber drivers in Washington, D.C., found that 50 percent of drivers would recommend the job to a friend even though 100 percent of drivers had trouble determining how much they were being paid by Uber for the work they performed as contractors for the company.[35]

Perhaps some context helps to explain these contradictions. Uber drivers are not the only precarious workers in the urban economy.[36] Housekeepers, home health aides, nannies, and childcare workers all endure the challenges of contingent work.[37] However, they are categorized as part of the "caring economy" rather than the sharing economy.[38] There is very little talk of their participation in the future of the smart city.

This is where another path might be possible. With a shift in analytical focus toward the city as a platform for work, there is a way to see how the urban technology project can provide for not only high-tech workers, or the sharing economy's service contractors, but also for workers across the economy. In particular, perhaps the project could provide for those who traverse the boundaries between the formal and informal labor markets and who work on contingent contracts. Throughout the book, I have discussed how the production of the smart cities platform is a publicly subsidized project. As such, there is a question about the return to the public for that investment. The sharing economy might be producing greater precariousness for some previously more formal occupations, but the dynamic and porous boundaries between formal and informal work and emerging forms of flexibility predate the smart cities boom.

To what extent can the smart cities platform improve the conditions of workers throughout the urban economy? In this context, the difference between a publicly provided 5G network and a privately provisioned network comes into focus. Perhaps there is a way to make the smart cities project support the informal and flexible work of workers in the modern city, not just the labor flexibility that the technology sector episodically creates (and destroys) for its own benefit. A public platform that provides services for everyone—whether home health aides, landscaping crews, or meal delivery drivers—presents a very different future for the city than does a privatized platform that is continually subsidized but not managed by the public sector.

8

CONCLUSIONS

The Local Is (Not) the Enemy

I N the summer 2018 issue of *Dwell* magazine, a popular periodical on design and architecture, an article entitled "Will Smart Cities Make Life Easier for Everyone?" quotes the director of MIT's Senseable Lab, Carlo Ratti. Ratti is a frequent speaker and published author on smart cities.[1] The article states, "applying digital technology to the built environment enables a city to respond to its citizens." Ratti also said, "We can imagine a city that adapts to human need, rather than the other way around— a living, tailored space that is molded to its inhabitants' needs, characters, and desires."[2] The article focuses particularly on the promise of devices enabled by the Internet of Things to improve cities for those with limited mobility or other challenges navigating the built environment. These technologies, of course, have the ability to make substantial improvements in the functionality of cities. However, those tangible improvements get lost in the rhetoric around "tailoring" cities for personal needs and creating "responsive" cities. Simply put, cities have a system for responding to their citizens: through the democratic process. That is how cities are tailored to the needs of their citizens—through a flexible, adaptive, and responsive democratic process. Preferences are conveyed through voting, not sensing.

Implementation of the smart cities project as described in previous chapters and in the press is an incremental process that is cast as a disruptive intervention. It will take time, and in that time, there is the opportunity to reflect on how cities and citizens can shape the smart cities project and how urban policy can respond to the technology experiments that are redrawing the boundaries between public and private interests and ownership. Technological adaptation is a feature in urban policy and planning; it is not new. It actually happens every day through individual choices and institutional decisions.

As discussed in chapter 3, the patterns of technology diffusion and industry change are often responses to emerging markets as well as the introduction of new materials, processes, or products that enable increased productivity, sustainability, or profitability, depending on the goals of the producer. In other words, new technologies enable optimization—in terms of efficiency or quality. But this optimization is predicated on the ability of institutions or firms to absorb new technologies, not simply to invent them. The growing role of cities in providing a platform for innovation creates new opportunities for firms but also for cities themselves.

For example, the expanding availability of public data enables civic and social innovators to develop new services or products, including software, sensors, and data and service subscriptions; to develop new processes for performance optimization to provision existing public services more efficiently; and to upgrade infrastructure and urban design investments to contribute to either new data or enhanced performance, or both. In other words, a possible outcome of investments in the smart cities platform is an agenda driven by civic innovation rather than one set through industry interests. The platform, like the city itself, can serve a social, political, and economic purpose.

Unfortunately, this has not yet proved to be the case. The public sector remains reticent to make significant infrastructure investments at the federal, state, or local level, particularly in the United States. The smart cities industry itself remains focused on the design, development, and deployment of an emerging class of cross-platform, service-integrated technology products to enhance service performance—particularly for citizens, workers, or cities, or for those with the ability to pay for that increased service performance. These are not actually infrastructure investments but, rather, tests of programs and products. And here lies the particular challenge for the smart cities project: who pays for it, and how will we determine who should pay for it? As discussed in chapter 7, the next step for smart cities might be not enhanced quality and coverage of public services but further public service privatization. This would drive the process further from an open innovation model, which could foster economic and social entrepreneurship, and closer to an antiquated and path-dependent closed innovation model replete with intellectual property limitations and proprietary platforms and services. Where and how science, technology, and innovation policies come to weigh in at the urban scale will determine a great deal about whether smart cities become a space of civic entrepreneurship and open innovation or merely a new terrain for uneven development.

As noted in chapter 2, debates about technology solutions to urban problems are not new. Cities have dealt with large-scale technological change before. In fact, balancing continuity and change is what cities do. The smart cities discourse, however, relies on an assumption of novelty. The hype and buzz around the smart cities project is, in part, predicated on a notion that the technologies and their potential value are unprecedented—immeasurably huge. The opportunity is so vast and its parameters so unknown that our current practices to evaluate, measure, assess, and make decisions about it are inadequate. The message to cities and to citizens from smart cities advocates is that you don't know what you're dealing with, but you don't want to get left behind.

It should perhaps be no surprise that a marriage between the technology industry and the real estate industry would result in a marketing effort consisting of well-established propaganda techniques. Even a cursory analysis demonstrates that four techniques occur regularly in the smart cities discourse: glittering generalities—vague phrases that promise much; bandwagon—everyone else is doing it; exigency—definite, immediate action is required; and free and bargain—you'll get something for free or at a bargain price.[3]

Notably, there are no real numbers in this context. In urban policy analysis, we are acclimated to managing uncertainties. We often use analytical techniques that deal in ranges, in qualitative evaluation, in relative values.[4] These techniques, which have been used for decades to make decisions in local governments, are almost entirely absent in the smart cities discourse. As noted in chapter 5, even where we assume that this business service capability would emerge to meet the demand—in the urban innovation networks—we see almost no turn toward evaluation as a service. There are handbooks or best practice guides but no sustained urban policy analysis capabilities.[5] These are not analytical guides but, rather, discussions of values: equity, community engagement, or quality. The guides present the goals, not a process for making the choices necessary to achieve those goals.

This is fundamentally the challenge that is at the intersection of smart cities and urban policy: they are operating on two different paradigms. Increasingly, the smart cities project defaults to a platform in which computers make decisions, whereas urban policy is predicated on a notion of people making choices. Individual choices are complicated and unpredictable. Decision trees are algorithms. In order to automate the city, it is necessary to aggregate and average individual choices into patterns and predictions. The "local" is the enemy because it is that variation that challenges the whole notion that it is possible to create an urban operating system.[6]

LEVERAGE LIES IN LOCAL VARIATION

Difference is power. Tailoring products and services—marketing models and data analysis techniques—to specific people and places is expensive and knowledge-intensive. That tailoring erodes economies of scale. The world does not provide one flat, undifferentiated global market. Rather, the world is made up of various locals, an array of distinct individual markets requiring modifications to accommodate differences in culture, institutions, preferences, norms, technologies, and governance. Developing the products and services for these localities requires empirical inputs from those places and people. The model requires real data, not merely idealized information. Static estimations are not enough. The product requires dynamic data. Data are the key input in smart cities objects, systems, and platforms. Here, then, we return to the industry's deeply territorialized priority: extracting data from cities and citizens.

To understand how smart cities objects and systems are being diffused across different places, analogs are useful. The advent of other significant innovations, such as the internal combustion engine, illustrate how the effects of new technologies on cities are not uniform but, rather, varied and uneven. Many cities accommodated to the explosion of private automobile ownership by engineering transportation systems that privileged the flow of private automobiles above all other forms of mobility for individuals (walking, bicycling) and groups (trains, streetcars). The pushback against prioritizing an urban form for *flow through* rather than *mobility in* began almost immediately in some places and was notably absent in others.

Today, however, the critique of urban design for a so-called car culture is firmly entrenched in the public discourse. Cities that were once synonymous with automobile-oriented urban sprawl, such as Atlanta, now have chief bicycle officers, dedicated bicycle and pedestrian infrastructure, and elaborate plans to do more for cyclists. For places that initially adopted the private automobile as an economic opportunity for residents and real estate interests, the externalities generated and the trade-offs produced eventually added up to a reconsideration of the benefits and a better understanding of the costs (see Figures 8.1 and 8.2).

FIGURE 8.1 Designing public infrastructure for smart, sustainable cities: a parking garage for bicycles owned by individuals, Munich, Germany, 2018.

(*Source*: Robert Jank/Dreamstime.com)

FIGURE 8.2 Designing public infrastructure for smart, sustainable cities: a secure, designated bicycle parking space in a historic district, Old Montreal, Canada, 2015.

(*Source*: Benjamin Flowers)

It is important to note that the ways in which cities responded to the proliferation of private automobiles varied. The result has been an uneven rather than uniform landscape with specific effects for people and firms. Some cities never turned over their policy priorities or their historic downtowns to automobiles. Many cities that initially allowed massive highways for through traffic to define the urban core eventually rolled back those decisions. Since the 1990s, so-called daylighting projects—removing highways in the urban core—have begun to gain popularity. The Cheonggye-cheon in Seoul, South Korea, is an iconic example of the removal of highways and urban redesign for mobility and livability within cities rather than passage through them (see Figure 8.3).

FIGURE 8.3 Redesigning smart cities: variations on urban regeneration projects to reclaim central-city spaces through linear parks and "daylighting projects" (freeway and railway redevelopment), The Cheonggyecheon, Seoul, South Korea, 2015.

(*Source*: Jennifer Clark)

In the United States, urban redesign interventions have been less physically ambitious (with a few notable exceptions, including Boston's Big Dig and Seattle's Alaska Way Viaduct). These projects involved reclaiming unused or derelict spaces for projects that integrate design and mobility and, to a growing degree, stimulate urban regeneration and the inevitable gentrification that follows (residential, commercial, and industrial). Examples of these projects include the High Line (see Figure 8.4) in New York City, the BeltLine in Atlanta, and planning for the Los Angeles River redevelopment in Los Angeles. Interventions such as these

FIGURE 8.4 Redesigning smart cities: variations on urban regeneration projects to reclaim central-city spaces through linear parks and "daylighting projects" (freeway and railway redevelopment), The High Line, New York City.

(*Source*: Sean Pavone/Shutterstock)

highlight the dynamic—and perhaps seemingly nonlinear—innovation processes that are driving urban development. In the same way that the processes of privatization involve cities contracting out services to private vendors and bringing public services back in house, the adoption and implementation of new technologies is episodic, uneven, and geographically varied within and across cities and regions. The deployment of smart cities objects, systems, and platforms is likely to follow similar dynamic patterns. Indeed, thus far that has proved to be the case.

In addition, aside from the physical interventions in the built environment, the policies that inform the operations and regulations of activities and actors in cities in response to technological change vary by time and space. Turning again to the example of the interface between the city and the automobile, the adoption of policies restricting the movement of individual cars within and across cities has quietly become commonplace. Congestion-pricing policies have reallocated the costs of the localized externalities generated by the car to the driver instead of the city. Congestion-pricing policies generally take one of two forms: by zones or by lanes. In both cases, the policy creates privileged spaces for cars to operate at a cost to the driver. That revenue is often (though not always) used to offset the costs of local infrastructure investments. London serves as the emblematic case of connecting congestion pricing to public infrastructure investments. In 2019, New York City was again poised to become the first U.S. city to adopt a congestion-pricing model after many years of consideration and policy debate.[7]

Although it has taken decades of incremental policy implementation to arrive at the point that congestion pricing is both broadly implemented and publicly accepted, it is, by definition, a policy that both uses and creates a differentiated landscape for cars and drivers. Fundamentally, that landscape appears with a new price tag that alters the calculus of the use and ownership for car owners and operators.

Perhaps it should not be surprising that when policies effectively shifting the costs of automobile externalities to drivers and owners rather than cities and regions becomes widespread, the wave of technologies contesting those externalities (congestion primary among them) emerges to propose rearrangements to the policy landscape and the built environment. The point, then, is to note that smart cities and the objects, systems, and platforms that the smart cities project seeks to deploy are operating *in* and *as a result of* incumbent systems of behaviors, policies, and strategies. The prominence of autonomous vehicles in the smart cities conversation should not be taken for granted, nor should the policy context.

The future of urban policy, on its current path, involves more investments in more diverse forms of urban mobility rather than in more individual automobiles. That is the alternative to autonomous vehicles. And that alternative urban future is driven by a series of urban policies, both programs and projects, that have reshaped the costs for consumers and reallocated the distribution of costs and risks between individual drivers and cities and their citizens. That is, cities and localities have the capacity to act and intervene in the ways in which costs and risks are distributed within their jurisdictions. The power of localities to reflect the preferences and values of their citizens is one of the original functions of cities. That capacity and the resulting geographic variation is what gives cities and regions so much power in what is otherwise often seen as an asymmetrical relationship between capital and space. Ultimately, places make the policies.

Just as citizens are not customers, cities are not companies. The rhetoric of privatization has permeated city halls and local governments so thoroughly that mayors and county commissioners routinely discuss strategies for monetizing public assets and diversifying revenue streams. The creative financing for public services and operations has moved from cost management and deferred maintenance to selling access to public assets and even the assets themselves, and increasingly data have become part of that equation.

City leaders often talk about sound fiscal management and Triple A bond ratings. To maintain these ratings, which minimize borrowing costs, cities pressure their police and firefighters into concession bargaining over wages and pensions in the hope of easing their obligations to these otherwise lauded first responders and producing a more investor-friendly balance sheet. Much could be said about the crises in local government financing. From Detroit to Liverpool, there is compelling physical evidence that financing mechanisms for local governments are inadequate at best and fundamentally broken at worst. Local leaders seem to fear raising taxes more than they fear downgrading from a bond-rating agency. As a consequence, localities increasingly use fines and fees to raise revenue from infractions committed by citizens and visitors. Some localities have stepped up their use of the police power to confiscate and impound the assets of those who fail to pay, thus generating a whole new revenue stream from seized property.

The path toward financial stability for cities is clearly based on an operational question. Investment is another matter. It should perhaps be no surprise, then, that when confronted with questions about long-term planning around sustainability and resilience that requires paradigm shifts and systems-wide changes, cities turn to outside investors, innovators, and leaders. This is where urban innovation networks have effectively challenged the privatization and outsourcing path dependencies that have so dominated urban administration since the 1980s. As noted in chapter 5, it is through seeding capacity within cities that urban innovation networks have highlighted the need for internal strategic planning competencies and technical expertise not just not about existing city functions but about future urban systems.

A theme throughout this book is that change is standard. Technology diffusion is not an exceptional state but a steady state of being. The speed and specificity of technological changes are difficult to anticipate, but the fact of technological transition is well understood. The question then is twofold. First, why are smart cities presented as an unexpected or exceptional change rather than a continuation of a dynamic process persistently in motion? Second, why have cities and communities been so seemingly unprepared to assess, analyze, adopt, and absorb technological changes that offer opportunities to provide needed and better services for citizens?

In this book, I have proposed a series of answers to the first question. These answers do not always lead to discrete policy recommendations. They are, unfortunately, more a critique of past practices and an analysis of the circumstances and path dependencies those practices have left on the landscape. Insofar as there is a core recommendation emanating from these specific arguments, it is that the absence of power analysis in the smart cities project is highly suspect. Power asymmetries operate whenever technological change is in motion. Technology offers the opportunity to rearrange power relationships between industry and government, individuals and institutions, cities and nations. Technology can change the rules of the game and the landscape on which the game is played. As a consequence, it is rarely recommended that technological change—particularly changes that are characterized as disruptive—be viewed as politically neutral.

A PROCESS FOR URBAN INNOVATION

What we know from decades of research in economic geography and its cognate disciplines is that there is power in regional variation: economic as well as political power. Throughout this book, I have underscored the novelty and importance of the emphasis on the urban in the smart cities discourse and the tension in the smart cities project over differences between places. Understanding the power of localization presents one site of action that is available to cities. Cities can force the smart cities industry to deal with their specificity simply by representing the interests of the cities' residents.[8]

Although a localized response to the power asymmetries in the smart cities project may seem conceptually complex, discrete policy recommendations have emerged from that analysis. It is possible for cities and local governments to be better prepared to respond to technological change. In the following section, I articulate policy recommendations that specifically address the question of how cities manage growth and change in a dynamic economic and technological environment.

First, investments in additional *embedded innovation capacity* within city government are necessary—more people and more expertise. Second, the obvious government reaction to the smart cities project is to expand *citizen rights to intangible assets*, specifically to data. Simply put, the response is to legislate. Cities should create urban policies that facilitate the capture of benefits from data and the increases in productivity that result from use of those data. Finally, new technologies provide an opportunity to increase the involvement of residents in the real-time governance of the city—to build on and *expand the participatory planning practices* that have been adopted unevenly in response to past waves of technocratic planning and infrastructure investments.

The smart cities project is complicated. It is intentionally complicated by a technology sector that has learned to obscure not only its motivations but its operations across many sectors over time. It is not as if the introduction of these enabling technologies has somehow been transparent and straightforward in other incumbent industries, such as manufacturing, medical devices, or financial services. What is different about the smart cities project is that these enabling technologies are diffusing into a space—administratively and territorially—that is governed by the public sector. Cities are responsible for the acts undertaken in their name. The choices cities make affect real people in real places in real time—people to whom cities are accountable.

So it is in this context that cities are increasingly asked to make choices about how to deploy and govern the smart cities project. In this book, I have outlined how the technology industry is creating the smart cities market and establishing demand for the data, objects, systems, and platforms the industry produces. I have also outlined how the smart cities industry is making the case for substantial amounts of public subsidy for this emerging industry while maintaining that regulation by the public sector is both impractical and unnecessary. Further, the smart cities project promotes the position that the evaluation and assessment of the tools and services it provides are also unnecessary. The ability of smart cities solutions to solve urban problems is presented as self-evident.

An emerging critique of the technology sector is that it promotes inequalities rather than mitigates them. Exposés about Silicon Valley's discriminatory human resources practices are outnumbered only by stories of predatory business practices. As noted throughout this book, economic geographers have long argued that firm strategies reflect the context from which they emerged. So, as technology firms turn their attention to cities, it should be understood that they are likely to employ the approaches and practices they know from the past rather than adapt to the ethics and standards of the public sector or specific communities.

The smart cities project provides a platform for economic development; it is not economic development by itself. And perhaps this is the key distinction moving forward. As cities and observers of the smart cities project become increasingly cognizant of the inequalities that are produced and magnified in the diffusion of new technologies, it might be the responsibility of the public sector to step up and intervene, not step back and allow the people and places to be cast as users and testbeds in an industry experiment rather than as citizens and communities in a city.

In her 1980 article, "What Would a Non-Sexist City Be Like?" Dolores Hayden asked readers to consider—to visualize—how to produce a city that did not reflect the institutionalized gendered norms that framed decisions about the design of and investments in our built environments (and the systems and services that operate it).[9] Similarly, Carlo Ratti asked us to visualize a city that is tailored to the needs of individuals. Hayden and Ratti are making different arguments, of course; Ratti is arguing for a technology solution, and Hayden is arguing for a shift in the patterns of social reproduction. Hayden's argument is simple: perhaps stop reproducing structural inequalities in *structures*. Hayden called for redesigning the American dream through an analysis of how we produce the built environment and why.[10] That is still the underlying issue. All too often, smart cities advocates are more interested in building (and experimenting) than in the systematic and sustained deconstruction of the old modes of production and the patterns of inequality they produce.[11]

In this book, I have posed a variation on Hayden's argument: stop reproducing uneven development patterns through technology solutions. Uneven innovation is a manifestation of an old problem: the sexist city, the racist city, the classist city, the city of unequal opportunities and unequal outcomes. I have also made two further points. First, cities are not the problem, but, second, cities may be the solution. Once the technology sector determined that cities were their preferred space of innovation, production, and consumption, cities gained the ability to manage and determine the smart cities project. Through the regulation of citizen rights to data, investments in the internal capacity within cities, the undertaking of strategic planning and policy analysis and evaluation, and the expansion of participatory planning, cities have an opportunity to shape the smart cities project. We may not see Hayden's nonsexist city emerge as a result, but we may see a future for cities that moves further away from an unequal past and toward a more equitable future.

EPILOGUE

The View from Inside the Urban Innovation Project

METHODOLOGY often takes a front seat in academic articles and a back seat in books. And so it is here. I was motivated to write this book because I found myself engaged in the work of smart cities. In the course of what became a five-year program of participant observation complemented by a series of research projects, I began to understand the complexities of the urban innovation project and the need to place it in a much broader context. I began speaking about smart cities in the same way as do many of my colleagues trained in urban planning, economic geography, and urban policy. I began by contesting this talk of "smart" and recoiling from what first presents as an implicit assumption that some cities—especially other, unspecified cities—are necessarily stupid. The problems with the smart cities discourse were just so glaringly obvious. The "smart" label implied agency. The smart cities conversation seemed to assume that low tech was somehow an intentional decision by local governments intent on being—and further, becoming—uncompetitive and unequal. The assignment to cities of a disproportionate level of agency and culpability after decades of disinvestment and antiregionalist policies seemed an unwelcome return to early debates about deindustrialization and the declining prospects for older, industrial regions.[1]

As an academic expert on cities and regional economies, innovation systems, and industrial clusters, my first reaction was to tell audiences that cities work. Cities succeed every single day in moving millions of people from home to work and back again. They provide a site and platform for production. They make money, aggregate money, allocate money, and move money more effectively and efficiently than any designed system ever has. We might not be able to build predictive models with specificity around the intricacies of all the interconnected systems that are operating every day to make these urban systems work in the contemporary city. We might not be able to accurately map or model these complex sociotechnical systems. Indeed, this has been the technical challenge that has irked computer scientists and urban modelers for almost fifty years now. However, it isn't clear that it is necessary to model the city. The city operates anyway. The city works.

All these outstanding questions have not stopped the smart cities project from capturing the attention of popular audiences and specialists. The smart cities concept promises access and opportunity through civic engagement and expanding public participation.[2] The concept promises, simultaneously, to generate new revenue via new markets and services and to save money through new efficiencies and systems optimization. Its advocates argue that smart cities are more efficient, more sustainable, more profitable, and more inclusive.

I have spent the better part of my professional career engaged with policy questions around technology diffusion projects. That is, I have analyzed how and in what ways emerging and enabling technologies alter the spatial distribution of economic activities as they influence the geography of production. For example, in previous research, I studied how photonics changed the optics industry—its production sites, markets, supply chains, and firm networks, and the allocation of competitive advantages across places.[3]

Universities played a role in that story. In the United States, as in many other advanced industrialized economies, universities are essential actors in precommercial research and development ecosystems. Universities conduct basic research that leads to many of the discoveries and eventual applications of new and emerging technologies. Therefore, universities are often part of the conversation about the development and application of innovations across sectors. Universities are widely recognized as sites of technology discovery and as intermediaries for technology transfer.[4]

In May 2015, my home university at that time (the Georgia Institute of Technology) joined an effort to put city–university partnerships at the center of the smart cities conversation (see figure epi.1). That effort, initiated and originally led by the

FIGURE EPI.1 The Georgia Institute of Technology's university–city partnership team at the launch of the city of Atlanta's North Avenue Smart Corridor project at The Ponce City Market, Atlanta, Georgia, September 2017.

(*Image credit*: Raul Perez, Georgia Institute of Technology)

White House Office of Science and Technology Policy (OSTP), convened city and university leaders around developing a research, design, and deployment strategy for smart cities projects. In this model, universities would serve as the laboratories for urban innovation research and cities would serve as the sites for deployment. The priorities of the cities would establish use cases that would shape design decisions. The network of city–university partnerships would serve as the diffusion strategy, with some cities and universities developing specializations within the network to create replicable programs that could be tailored to other cities in the network. In effect, the model was intended to promote and facilitate horizontal rather than vertical policy mobilities (see chapter 5).

The initial network gathering to establish the city–university partnerships, called the MetroLab Network, took place in a room I had been in before. I found myself, as a representative of my own technology-focused university, in a familiar room in the Eisenhower Executive Office Building in Washington, D.C. On two previous occasions, I sat in that room to represent my university in an initiative that was called the Advanced Manufacturing Partnership. This return to the same space caused me to reflect on the similarities in policy process across these seemingly different technology initiatives.

In the early 2010s, the Advanced Manufacturing Partnership was also an initiative of the Obama administration's Office of Science and Technology Policy. It, too, convened university and industry leadership around the design of policies and programs intended to upgrade the national innovation system in the United States. Its specific intention was to determine effective policy models to connect advanced research in universities more effectively with the nation's incumbent industrial system. In my book *Working Regions*, I detailed both aspects of that effort and the broader theoretical and policy questions about how and in what ways regional innovation systems operate, nested as they are in complex national economic contexts.[5]

So it was not lost on me, sitting in the same room on a second national technology diffusion project that viewed research universities as a critical partner, that this was the same innovation policy model, only a different industry. In this case, the industry was not advanced manufacturing but smart cities. The circumstances were strikingly similar. First, research universities were serving as a "neutral" broker in an emerging model of innovation policy. Second, the effort was intended to address a fragmented and incomplete institutional framework for the implementation and diffusion of technological changes. Third, legacy and incumbent systems mismatched with the pace and character of enabling technologies were creating entrenched path dependencies. Fourth, there was an uncertain role for the federal government as relationship broker or funder. Finally, there was a sense of urgency, a sense that continued economic competitiveness would be predicated on the design and implementation of these policies and the viability of the innovation ecosystems those policies were able to provide.

Another striking similarity between these two initiatives to invest in the nation's "intelligent infrastructure" was the absence (and possibly also ignorance of the existence) of domain experts in place-based economic development policies. Academics work in dense professional networks. Often, if not always, we know who else writes about the same topics and who researches the same questions. Over a thirty-year career, we tend to run into one another. What initially struck me in 2012 and 2014, as I sat in the room discussing the policies that would facilitate technology diffusion in advanced manufacturing, was how many people in the room were technology and industry experts—mechanical engineers, industrial systems specialists, or industrial chemists. The experts assembled knew how *to do* advanced manufacturing rather than how *to design policy* to support advanced manufacturing. At the time, I viewed this as unfortunate but also understandable for a number of reasons.

The first reason was that the Advanced Manufacturing Initiative was an initiative of the OSTP. It would stand to reason that the network known to these professionals might skew more heavily toward domain expertise in specific aspects of science and technology rather than innovation policy, manufacturing policy, or economic development. Although perhaps not ideal, it was not difficult to explain the relative dearth of economic development expertise brought to the advanced manufacturing project as simply a result of nonoverlapping professional networks.

The second reason was a policy gap among policy and academic professionals in areas such as advanced manufacturing. In 2012, when I was writing *Working Regions*, I was reminded that in the United States from about 1992 to 2008, the federal government and, to a lesser degree, even many state and local governments—simply stopped engaging manufacturing as an area in which policy innovation was of interest. To the extent that there were policies in place to explicitly support manufacturing, they were largely traditional economic development policies: firm-level subsidies and incentives aimed at recruitment, retention, and expansion.[6] Simply put, there was rarely a systems approach to policy and certainly no attempt to invest in policy innovations. These approaches were seen by academics largely as parochial. They were not explicitly geographic. The models were well known and their outcomes generally well documented. This lack of activity meant that there was little to study and little to implement. This lack of innovative policy activity over a fifteen-year period led to a lack of specialization among those who design and study policy.

It should be noted that this lack of interest and activity in the design of place-based innovation and industrial policy in the United States stands in sharp contrast to the work in the European Union and other industrialized countries during the same period. Especially in response to political disruptions such as Brexit and economic disruptions such as the 2008 global recession, policy makers in the European Union, United Kingdom, and other industrialized countries have turned to academic and policy experts to explain the place-specific ramifications of these economic transitions and propose explicitly place-based models to help manage those impacts.[7] That has not been the case in the United States. Instead, the policy focus at the national scale has shifted to incumbent industries and trade policy with little attention or analysis focused on place-based development strategies or variations in the local and regional impacts of national economic policies.[8]

It is perhaps surprising that in a conversation about production, there was little attention to place or the connections among urbanization economies, innovation, and growth.[9] It is important to recall that it was not a fringe argument in the 1980s and 1990s that advanced industrialized countries did not need manufacturing to maintain strong national economies. The argument was that in a flat world, lower-skill and lower-value activities inevitably would be outsourced. Further, this outsourcing was not perceived as a problem by many national economic policy makers. There would be winners and losers, but, on the whole, the winners would outnumber the losers. The policy problem was seen principally as a labor supply problem to be addressed by retraining, not a labor demand issue.

A decline in traditional manufacturing was not viewed as a significant problem for people or places. Even in cases where there appeared to be job losses or industrial decline, these effects would be temporary and soon remedied. Higher-value activities—again, the promise of technology—would replace what was lost. The *smart* high-tech economy—the "knowledge economy"—would replace the "dirty, dull, and dangerous" manufacturing economy. Innovation would create new opportunity. As a consequence of this consensus, we learned to stop counting jobs and start counting patents. We preferred to project the value of future knowledge rather than measure current conditions and what, in retrospect, were indications of a weak policy model for technology diffusion.

Innovation did indeed occur during this period, adding credence to the suggestion that an economy could run with minimal— or, perhaps more accurately, selective—production. The rise of Silicon Valley and the evolution of the software and computer industries seemed to be emblematic of the new industries and new, high-value production thesis. The rise of the tech services sectors also appeared to validate this laissez-faire approach to deindustrialization. This argument seemed to hold until, much faster than anticipated, the production of both software and computer equipment migrated overseas. Further, software and programming services—functions that were thought to be some-what embedded—also migrated overseas as skilled high-tech work was rapidly carved into routine processes and offshored.[10] That is, not only were there few policy experts talking about industrial restructuring as a process, but there were few who had the credibility to discuss the future of manufacturing.[11] And fewer people still were listening.

Finally, the third reason there were so few experts on man-ufacturing and innovation policy involved in policy making about advanced manufacturing was their affiliations. Many had moved into state governments or to university administration as the work in policy innovation atrophied. Few remained among the ranks of professors engaged in active, comparative, empirical research. Those in Washington, D.C., were often working in or with established think tanks debating the same questions, promoting the same arguments, and proposing the same policies that they had since 1992. Interestingly, in both the advanced manufacturing and smart cities initiatives initiated by OSTP in the 2010–2015 period, the network of Washington think tanks did not take center stage as part of the working groups or as technical advisers.

There has been some speculation about why the think-tank policy community was not tapped to lead these initiatives. One argument is that think tanks are perceived as too partisan and their views too entrenched for a conversation about policy innovation. It is perhaps also the case that think tanks have become increasingly revenue driven, seeking project funders and producing less original research. In other words, think tanks are advocates for policies rather than designers of policies. Finally, think tanks are not seen as institutional partners for evolving policy implementation. They present policies and, on occasion, also research policies, but they are not administrative entities with the authority or jurisdiction to implement policies. In a policy design environment that is largely stakeholder driven, the capacity to participate now defines who is identified as a partner.

And so, sitting in that same room in 2015 discussing city–university partnerships for the design and diffusion of smart cities technologies, I again observed that there were few people I knew professionally as domain experts on urban innovation and economic development. Only two other universities sent urban planners for a conversation about how cities and universities would partner to advance the smart cities project. So, much as with

OSTP's Future of Cities report, the early conversations about the MetroLab Network did not involve experts on cities.[12]

Several things became obvious in these early conversations. First, OSTP viewed urban research universities (especially technology-focused institutions) as the potential research and development departments of U.S. cities in a similar way that they saw universities as the research and development partners for America's manufacturing resurgence that was envisioned in the Advanced Manufacturing Partnership 1.0 and 2.0. This was in contrast to a historical role of "urban-serving universities" as a network of largely public teaching universities that had long partnered with cities on programs in social work, nursing, policing, teaching, and other community or public health and safety priorities. The MetroLab Network was, instead, a partnership about technology and research, not teaching and service.

Second, OSTP expected cities and universities to create working alliances in advance of resourcing the project. In other words, rather than use funding opportunities as the incentive for developing partnerships, OSTP used the opportunity to define future funding priorities as the incentive for participation. This is similar to the approach used with the Advanced Manufacturing Partnership. Third, OSTP's smart cities initiative stemmed from the recognition that a public-sector network was required to take on the smart cities challenge—one that was operating independently from the private-sector networks and consortia that were actively making markets and setting proprietary standards in the smart cities industry.

In this sense, then, the efforts to create city–university partnerships and public-sector networks to engage and facilitate the smart cities project were designed to develop intermediaries and institutions that were capable of managing urban innovation. Anticipating the policy decisions that would be required to make the necessary investments to implement intelligent infrastructure, the federal government looked to its long-standing partners in the (implicit) national innovation system: research universities. And although the local and regional partners were identified in 2015, the federal role in the smart cities project as funder, policy designer, policy evaluator, standards setter, and conveners has since stalled. As a consequence, the smart cities project has proceeded as an industry-driven initiative that has been implemented unevenly, incrementally, and episodically in various cities, with various technologies, at various times. A broad view of the smart cities project is thus very difficult to develop. Consequently, most books and articles about smart cities analyze case studies of cities or projects rather than contextualizing the smart cities project itself within the long arc of urban and regional development policy changes.

So it behooves us to return to what we do know about cities. What makes cities are people—the choices they make, the places they go, the things they buy, and where they live and work.[13] The built environment shapes those choices, and urban systems facilitate or aggravate both moving across and living in cities. But at their core, cities are complex political, economic, and social systems. Cities are defined by the choices people make, not the decisions defined by algorithms and executed by machines. The challenge of smart cities is not one of technology alone. The question then becomes—beyond a grasp of the underlying technologies—how do we make choices about technology and what it means, and what it can do for cities?

What are the prerequisites for studying smart cities? Does the mastery of smart cities require knowledge of cities themselves? Stated another way, could you effectively study biotechnology without mastering organic chemistry or biology? Could you study astrophysics without an understanding of physics and mathematics? These questions are animating the emergence of urban science and urban innovation programs at the graduate and undergraduate levels as academics within the disciplines traditionally concerned with cities struggle to analyze where the smart cities project fits into the existing curriculum. Rather than follow the path laid out by the introduction of geographical information systems and spatial analysis—which was to develop internal capacity within the discipline—many urban planning programs are sharing the smart cities curriculum with (if not ceding it to) engineering and computer science.

I began teaching university courses about how to study cities in 2004 at Cornell University. The first course I taught was an introduction to urban fieldwork that was tailored to undergraduate urban studies students. The course was intended to prepare students for careers that required understanding the actors and processes that shape the urban environment. Since then, I have taught many other courses on urban policy and urban and regional economic development. In my experience, every year, these courses change at the margins, if not in their core content. They change because cities themselves are dynamic—what cities do, and why, and how, changes over time and, thus, so does the study of cities. Now in my second decade of teaching these courses, I see them through the lens of the evolution of the field itself. Cities have never stood still. There is no reason that the curriculum about them should either.

I have been constantly reminded of the evolving nature of both the discipline and the practice through the two core books I use in my urban policy analysis teaching: *Basic Methods of Policy Analysis and Planning* and *Fast Policy*.[14] Both books emphasize the speed at which policy analysis and policy diffusion occur and the role of institutions and analysts in speeding policy change—and their corresponding responsibilities for slowing it down—to be more deliberate, assess alternatives, and make informed determinations about what works and what doesn't and for whom. In other words, smart cities experts need to understand efficiency, equity, distribution, and impact in addition to technology. Fundamentally, smart cities are about being smart, not just being high tech.

Historically, social science fields that focused on cities were subfields of much larger disciplines—economics, political science, geography, history. After decades of deindustrialization and disinvestment in cities, these subfields are not always the most popular or publicized. However, urban planning—to varying degrees—is the exception to the subfield rule. Within urban planning, the consensus has long been that urban planning is a discipline of its own. Its disciplinary boundaries run parallel to architecture, in that there is a core curriculum, a professional master's degree, professional certifications, and a clear professional practice. One is trained as an urban planner to work in urban planning. In other words, urban planning rarely has been identified as an interdisciplinary project and often has resisted the claims of other disciplines to knowledge about the planning and analysis of cities.

However, the smart cities project has emerged as an explicitly interdisciplinary project. Its home is fluid rather than fixed. A number of disciplines that include digital media, civil engineering, and computer science already have weighed in on the smart cities project and its promise and problems. What has been far less often discussed is the power of the smart cities project. This book is about the power of the smart cities project to reshape the urban policy environment through both the technologies made available and the choices made by cities in response to those opportunities.[15] In the book, I describe how and why uneven development of the past has reproduced an uneven innovation future for cities. And I proposed how to redirect the smart cities project toward a more sustainable and equitable path by using the power of cities, the power of place, to set the rules and define the priorities of the smart cities project. The task now is to get to it.

NOTES

1. UNEVEN INNOVATION: THE EVOLUTION OF THE URBAN TECHNOLOGY PROJECT

1. Jane Jacobs, *The Death and Life of Great American Cities* (New York: Vintage, 1961); Robert A. Caro, *The Power Broker: Robert Moses and the Fall of New York* (New York: Vintage, 1975).
2. Robert Goodman, *After the Planners* (New York: Simon & Schuster, 1972); Alan A. Altshuler, *The Urban Transportation System: Politics and Policy Innovation* (Cambridge, MA: MIT Press, 1981).
3. Ann Markusen, "Fuzzy Concepts, Scanty Evidence, Policy Distance: The Case for Rigour and Policy Relevance in Critical Regional Studies," *Regional Studies* 33, no. 9 (December 1999): 869.
4. Rob Kitchin, "Making Sense of Smart Cities: Addressing Present Shortcomings," *Cambridge Journal of Regions, Economy and Society* 8, no. 1 (March 2015): 131–36, https://doi.org/10.1093/cjres/rsu027.
5. Simon Marvin, Andrés Luque-Ayala, and Colin McFarlane, eds., *Smart Urbanism: Utopian Vision or False Dawn?* (New York: Routledge; London: Taylor & Francis, 2016); Andrew Karvonen, Federico Cugurullo, and Federico Caprotti, eds., *Inside Smart Cities: Place, Politics and Urban Innovation* (New York: Routledge, 2019); Ben Green, *The Smart Enough City: Putting Technology in Its Place to Reclaim Our Urban Future* (Cambridge, MA: MIT Press, 2019).
6. Pierre Clavel, *The Progressive City: Planning and Participation, 1969–1984* (New Brunswick, NJ: Rutgers University Press,1986); J. K. Gibson-Graham, Jenny Cameron, and Stephen Healy, *Take Back the Economy* (Minneapolis: University of Minnesota Press, 2013).

7. John Forester, "Planning in the Face of Power," *Journal of the American Planning Association* 48, no. 1 (Winter 1982): 67–80, https://doi.org /10.1080/01944368208976167.

8. Craig M. Dalton and Jim Thatcher, "What Does a Critical Data Studies Look Like, and Why Do We Care?" *Society & Space*, May 12, 2014, http://societyandspace.org/2014/05/12/what-does-a-critical-data -studies-look-like-and-why-do-we-care-craig-dalton-and-jim -thatcher/; Craig M. Dalton, Linnet Taylor, and Jim Thatcher, "Critical Data Studies: A Dialog on Data and Space," *Big Data & Society* 3, no. 1 (January 5, 2016), https://doi.org/10.1177/2053951716648346.

9. Neil Smith, *Uneven Development: Nature, Capital, and the Production of Space* (New York: Blackwell, 1984), 4.

10. Jamie Peck, "Labor, Zapped/Growth, Restored? Three Moments of Neoliberal Restructuring in the American Labor Market," *Journal of Economic Geography* 2, no. 2 (April 2002): 179–220, https://doi.org /10.1093/jeg/2.2.179; Joan Fitzgerald, *Moving Up in the New Economy* (Ithaca, NY: Cornell University Press, 2006); Jamie Peck, *Work-Place: The Social Regulation of Labor Market* (New York: Guilford Press, 1996).

11. Jamie Peck and Nikolas Theodore, *Fast Policy: Experimental Statecraft at the Thresholds of Neoliberalism* (Minneapolis: University of Minnesota Press, 2015).

12. David Bailey, Helena Lenihan, and Alex De Ruyter, "A Cautionary Tale of Two 'Tigers': Industrial Policy 'Lessons' from Ireland and Hungary?" *Local Economy* 31, no. 8 (December 1, 2016): 873–91, https:// doi.org/10.1177/0269094216677779; Peter Dicken, *Global Shift: Mapping the Changing Contours of the World Economy*, 7th ed. (New York: Guilford Press, 2015).

13. Margaret Pugh O'Mara, *Cities of Knowledge: Cold War Science and the Search for the Next Silicon Valley* (Princeton, NJ: Princeton University Press, 2005); Jennifer Clark, "Siting 'Scientific Spaces' in the US: The Push and Pull of Regional Development Strategies and National Inno- vation Policies," *Environment and Planning C: Government and Policy* 32, no. 5 (October 2014): 880–95, https://doi.org/10.1068/c1271r.

14. Jennifer Clark, *Working Regions: Reconnecting Innovation and Production in the Knowledge Economy* (London: Routledge, 2013).

15. Gordon Clark, *Unions and Communities Under Siege: American Com- munities and the Crisis of Organized Labor* (Cambridge: Cambridge

University Press, 1989); Edward J. Malecki, "Jockeying for Position: What It Means and Why It Matters to Regional Development Policy When Places Compete," *Regional Studies* 38, no. 9 (December 2004): 1101–20; Gillian Bristow, "Everyone's a 'Winner': Problematising the Discourse of Regional Competitiveness," *Journal of Economic Geography* 5, no. 3 (2005): 285–304.

16. Bennett Harrison, *Lean and Mean: The Changing Landscape of Corporate Power in the Age of Flexibility* (New York: Basic Books, 1994); John Kenneth Galbraith, *The New Industrial State*, 3rd ed. (New York: Penguin, 1967).

17. Elizabeth Dwoskin, "Google Reaped Millions in Tax Breaks as It Secretly Expanded Its Real Estate Footprint across the U.S.," *Washington Post*, February 15, 2019, https://www.washingtonpost.com/business/economy/google-reaped-millions-of-tax-breaks-as-it-secretly-expanded-its-real-estate-footprint-across-the-us/2019/02/15/7912e10e-3136-11e9-813a-0ab2f17e305b_story.html; Patricia Cohen, "In Amazon Fight, Progressives Showed What They Want: A New Economic Agenda," Business, *New York Times*, February 17, 2019, https://www.nytimes.com/2019/02/16/business/amazon-economy-taxes.html; Chris McGreal, "Is Bezos Holding Seattle Hostage? The Cost of Being Amazon's Home," Cities, *Guardian*, July 4, 2018, http://www.theguardian.com/cities/2018/jul/04/is-bezos-holding-seattle-hostage-the-cost-of-being-amazons-home; Greg LeRoy and Maryann Feldman, "Cities Need to Stop Selling out to Big Tech Companies. There's a Better Way," Cities, *Guardian*, July 3, 2018, http://www.theguardian.com/cities/2018/jul/03/cities-need-to-stop-selling-out-to-big-tech-companies-theres-a-better-way; Greg LeRoy, "Public Auction, Private Dealings: Will Amazon's HQ2 Veer to Secrecy Create a Missed Opportunity for Inclusive, Accountable Development?" Good Jobs First, April 2018, https://www.goodjobsfirst.org/hide/public-auction-private-dealings-will-amazons-hq2-veer-secrecy-create-missed-opportunity; Dominic Rushe, "US Cities and States Give Big Tech $9.3bn in Subsidies in Five Years," Cities, *Guardian*, July 2, 2018, http://www.theguardian.com/cities/2018/jul/02/us-cities-and-states-give-big-tech-93bn-in-subsidies-in-five-years-tax-breaks; Dominic Rushe, "'It's a Huge Subsidy': The $4.8bn Gamble to Lure Foxconn to America," Cities, *Guardian*, July 2, 2018, http://www.theguardian.com/cities/2018/jul/02/its-a-huge-subsidy-the-48bn-gamble-to-lure-foxconn-to-america.

18. Jennifer Clark, John Harrison, and Ernest Miguelez, "Connecting Cities, Revitalizing Regions: The Centrality of Cities to Regional Development," *Regional Studies* 52, no. 8 (August 3, 2018): 1025–28, https://doi.org/10.1080/00343404.2018.1453691.

19. Gerald Frug, *City Making: Building Communities without Building Walls* (Princeton, NJ: Princeton University Press, 2001); Peter Dreier, John H. Mollenkopf, and Todd Swanstrom, *Place Matters: Metropolitics for the Twentyfirst Century*, 3rd ed. (Lawrence: University Press of Kansas, 2014); Gerald Frug, *City Bound: How States Stifle Urban Innovation* (Ithaca, NY: Cornell University Press, 2013).

20. Eric Gordon and Adriana de Souza e Silva, *Net Locality: Why Location Matters in a Networked World* (Chichester, UK: Wiley-Blackwell, 2011).

21. Dalton, Taylor, and Thatcher, "Critical Data Studies"; Jim Thatcher, "You Are Where You Go, the Commodification of Daily Life Through 'Location,'" *Environment and Planning A* 49, no. 12 (December 2017): 2702–17, https://doi.org/10.1177/0308518X17730580.

22. Yanni A. Loukissas, *All Data Are Local: Thinking Critically in a Data-Driven Society* (Cambridge, MA: MIT Press, 2019).

23. Taylor Shelton, Matthew Zook, and Alan Wiig, "The 'Actually Existing Smart City,'" *Cambridge Journal of Regions, Economy and Society* 8, no. 1 (October 27, 2014): 13–25, https://doi.org/10.1093/cjres/rsu026; Julian Agyeman and Duncan McLaren, "Apps Don't Make a City Smart," Opinions, *Boston Globe*, August 14, 2016, https://www.bostonglobe.com/ideas/2016/08/13/apps-don-make-city-smart/YrEuTHcHAFA rq5piutinrN/story.html; Robert Hollands, "Will the Real Smart City Please Stand up? Intelligent, Progressive or Entrepreneurial?," *City* 12, no. 3 (2008): 303–20.

24. Clark, *Working Regions*.

25. Rachel Weber, "Extracting Value from the City: Neoliberalism and Urban Redevelopment," *Antipode* 34, no. 3 (July 1, 2002): 519–40, https://doi.org/10.1111/1467-8330.00253.

26. Jamie Peck, "Labor and Agglomeration: Control and Flexibility in Local Labor Markets," *Economic Geography* 68, no. 4 (October 1992): 325–47; Katherine Stone, *From Widgets to Digits: Employment Regulation for the Changing Workplace* (New York: Cambridge University Press, 2004).

27. Alex Rosenblat, *Uberland: How Algorithms Are Rewriting the Rules of Work* (Oakland, CA: University of California Press, 2018), 207.

28. Anthony M. Townsend, *Smart Cities: Big Data, Civic Hackers, and the Quest for a New Utopia* (New York: W. W. Norton, 2013); John Friedmann and Clyde Weaver, *Territory and Function: The Evolution of Regional Planning* (London: E. Arnold, 1979).

29. Thomas Lodato, Emma French, and Jennifer Clark, "Open Government Data in the Smart City: Interoperability, Urban Knowledge, and Linking Legacy Systems," *Journal of Urban Affairs*, October 16, 2018, https://doi.org/10.1080/07352166.2018.1511798; Thatcher, "You Are Where You Go."

30. Marco Oved, "Google's Sidewalk Labs Plans Massive Expansion to Waterfront Vision," *Thestar.Com*, February 14, 2019, https://www.thestar.com/news/gta/2019/02/14/googles-sidewalk-labs-plans-massive-expansion-to-waterfront-vision.html.

31. ESRC, "Why GDPR Matters for Research," *ESRC Blog* (blog), May 25, 2018, https://blog.esrc.ac.uk/2018/05/25/why-gdpr-matters-for-research/; State of California, "Consumer Right to Privacy Act (CaCPA)," 17–0039 Cal. Civ. Code § 1798.100 § (2018); Daisuke Wakabayashi, "California Passes Sweeping Law to Protect Online Privacy," Technology, *New York Times*, July 30, 2018, https://www.nytimes.com/2018/06/28/technology/california-online-privacy-law.html.

32. Gordon and Silva, *Net Locality*.

33. Dalton, Taylor, and Thatcher, "Critical Data Studies"; Thatcher, "You Are Where You Go"; Philip Ashton, Rachel Weber, and Matthew Zook, "The Cloud, the Crowd, and the City: How New Data Practices Reconfigure Urban Governance" *Big Data & Society* 4, no. 1 (June 2017), https://doi.org/10.1177/2053951717706718.

34. Saskia Sassen, *The Global City: New York, London, Tokyo* (Princeton, NJ: Princeton University Press, 2001); Manuel Castells and Peter Hall, *Technopoles of the World: The Making of Twenty-First-Century Industrial Complexes* (London: Routledge, 1994); Allen Scott and Edward Soja, *The City: Los Angeles and Urban Theory at the End of the Twentieth Century* (Oakland, CA: University of California Press, 1996).

35. Ash Amin and Nigel Thrift, *Seeing Like a City*, (Cambridge, UK: Polity, 2016).

36. Edward J. Malecki, *Technology and Economic Development: The Dynamics of Local, Regional and National Competitiveness*, 2nd ed. (Essex, UK: Longman, 1997); Edward L. Glaeser, *Triumph of the City: How Our*

Greatest Invention Makes Us Richer, Smarter, Greener, Healthier, and Happier (New York: Penguin, 2011).

37. Henri Lefebvre, *The Production of Space* (Malden, MA: Blackwell, 2011).
38. Karvonen, Cugurullo, and Caprotti, *Inside Smart Cities.*
39. Fred Block, "Problems with the Concept of Capitalism in the Social Sciences," *Environment and Planning A: Economy and Space* 51, no. 5: 1166–77, https://doi.org/10.1177/0308518X19838866.
40. Doreen Massey, "In What Sense a Regional Problem?," *Regional Studies* 13, no. 2 (1979): 233–43, https://doi.org/10.1080/09595237900185191.
41. Brett Goldstein and Lauren Dyson, eds., *Beyond Transparency: Open Data and the Future of Civic Innovation* (San Francisco: Code for America Press, 2013); Michael Batty, *The New Science of Cities*, repr. ed. (Cambridge, MA: MIT Press, 2017); Nicholas De Monchaux, *Local Code: 3,659 Proposals about Data, Design & the Nature of Cities* (New York: Princeton Architectural Press, 2016); Stephen Goldsmith and Susan Crawford, *The Responsive City: Engaging Communities Through Data-Smart Governance* (San Francisco: Jossey-Bass, 2014).
42. Eric Neumayer and Richard Perkins, "Uneven Geographies of Organizational Practice: Explaining the Cross-National Transfer and Diffusion of ISO 9000," *Economic Geography* 81, no. 3 (2005): 237–59, https://doi.org/10.1111/j.1944-8287.2005.tb00269.x.

2. SMART CITIES AS SOLUTIONS

1. Wanda Lau, "Q+A: What Is a Smart City? Three Experts Explain," *Architect*, January 14, 2019, https://www.architectmagazine.com/technology/q-a-what-is-a-smart-city-three-experts-explain_o.
2. Lau, "Q+A: What Is a Smart City?"
3. Norman Krumholz, "Equitable Approaches to Local Economic Development," *Policy Studies Journal* 27, no. 1 (1999): 83–95, https://doi.org/10.1111/j.1541-0072.1999.tb01955.x.
4. Carl V. Patton, David S. Sawicki, and Jennifer Clark, *Basic Methods of Policy Analysis and Planning*, 3rd ed. (New York: Routledge, 2013).
5. Krumholz, "Equitable Approaches to Local Economic Development"; Neil Brenner and Nik Theodore, "Cities and the Geographies of 'Actually Existing Neoliberalism,'" *Antipode* 34, no. 3 (June 2002): 349–79, https://doi.org/10.1111/1467-8330.00246.

6. Eugene McCann, "Urban Policy Mobilities and Global Circuits of Knowledge: Toward a Research Agenda," *Annals of the Association of American Geographers* 101, no. 1 (2011): 107–30; Silvia Crivello, "Urban Policy Mobilities: The Case of Turin as a Smart City," *European Planning Studies* 23, no. 5 (May 4, 2015): 909–21, https://doi.org/10.1080 /09654313.2014.891568; Russell Prince, "Policy Transfer, Consultants and the Geographies of Governance," *Progress in Human Geography* 36, no. 2 (April 1, 2012): 188–203, https://doi.org/10.1177/0309132511417659.

7. Robert Goodspeed, "Smart Cities: Moving beyond Urban Cybernetics to Tackle Wicked Problems," *Cambridge Journal of Regions, Economy and Society* 8, no. 1 (March 1, 2015): 79–92, https://doi.org/10.1093/cjres /rsu013.

8. Richard Fry, "Millennials Expected to Outnumber Boomers in 2019" (Washington, DC: Pew Research Center, March 1, 2018), http://www .pewresearch.org/fact-tank/2018/03/01/millennials-overtake-baby -boomers/.

9. Kia Kokalitcheva, "Uber and Lyft Race Google to Become the All-in-One Transit App," *Axios*, February 27, 2019, https://www.axios.com /the-race-to-become-the-all-in-one-transport-app-1726ef49-cd28 -4ef2-b5cb-69b9ab458a11.html.

10. Robert Goodman, *After the Planners* (New York: Simon & Schuster, 1972).

11. Lynne B. Sagalyn, "Public/Private Development: Lessons from History, Research, and Practice," *Journal of the American Planning Association* 73, no. 1 (March 31, 2007): 7–22, https://doi.org/10.1080/01944360708976133; Lynne B. Sagalyn, "Negotiating for Public Benefits: The Bargaining Calculus of Public–Private Development," *Urban Studies* 34, no. 12 (December 1997): 1955–70, https://doi.org/10.1080/0042098975169; Pierre Clavel and Robert Kraushaar, "On Being Unreasonable: Progressive Planning in Sheffield and Chicago," *International Planning Studies* 3, no. 2 (June 1998): 143–62, https://doi.org/10.1080/13563479808721706; Mildred E. Warner, "Private Finance for Public Goods: Social Impact Bonds," *Journal of Economic Policy Reform* 16, no. 4 (December 2013): 303–19, https://doi.org/10.1080/17487870.2013.835727; Matthew Goldstein and Patricia Cohen, "Public–Private Projects Where the Public Pays and Pays," DealBook, *New York Times*, June 6, 2017, https://www.nytimes .com/2017/06/06/business/dealbook/trump-infrastructure-plan-privatized -taxpayers.html.

12. Rob Kitchin, "Making Sense of Smart Cities: Addressing Present Shortcomings," *Cambridge Journal of Regions, Economy and Society* 8, no. 1 (March 2015): 131–36, https://doi.org/10.1093/cjres/rsu027; Amy Glasmeier and Susan Christopherson, "Thinking about Smart Cities," *Cambridge Journal of Regions, Economy and Society* 8, no. 1 (March 2015): 3–12, https://doi.org/10.1093/cjres/rsu034.

13. Marco Oved and Paul Hunter, "Privacy Expert Steps down from Advisory Role with Sidewalk Labs," *Toronto Star*, October 20, 2018, https://www.thestar.com/news/gta/2018/10/20/privacy-expert-steps-down-from-advisory-role-with-sidewalk-labs.html.

14. John Forester, "Planning in the Face of Power," *Journal of the American Planning Association* 48, no. 1 (Winter 1982): 67–80, https://doi.org/10.1080/01944368208976167.

15. Kerner Commission, *Report of the National Advisory Commission on Civil Disorders* (Washington, DC: National Advisory Commission on Civil Disorders, 1968).

16. Kenneth T. Jackson, *Crabgrass Frontier: The Suburbanization of the United States* (New York: Oxford University Press, 1985); Peter Hall, *Cities of Tomorrow: An Intellectual History of Urban Planning and Design Since 1880*, 4th ed. (Hoboken, NJ: Wiley-Blackwell, 2014).

17. Peter Dreier, John H. Mollenkopf, and Todd Swanstrom, *Place Matters: Metropolitics for the Twentyfirst Century*, 3rd ed., Studies in Government and Public Policy (Lawrence, KS: University Press of Kansas, 2014); William W. Goldsmith, "Who Cares about the Inner City?," *Journal of the American Planning Association* 63, no. 1 (Winter 1997): 154.

18. William Hollingsworth Whyte, *City: Rediscovering the Center* (New York: Doubleday, 1988); Joel Garreau, *Edge City: Life on the New Frontier* (New York: Anchor Books, 1992).

19. John Kenneth Galbraith, *Age of Uncertainty*, illustr. ed. (London: Houghton, 1977).

20. Galbraith, *Age of Uncertainty*, 303.

21. David L. Imbroscio, "Shaming the Inside Game: A Critique of the Liberal Expansionist Approach to Addressing Urban Problems," *Urban Affairs Review* 42, no. 2 (2006): 224–48, https://doi.org/10.1177/1078087406291444.

22. Edward G. Goetz, "Fair Share or Status Quo? The Twin Cities Livable Communities Act," *Journal of Planning Education and Research* 20, no. 1

(September 1, 2000): 37–51, https://doi.org/10.1177/0739456001128992582; Edward G. Goetz, Karen Chapple, and Barbara Lukermann, "Enabling Exclusion: The Retreat from Regional Fair Share Housing in the Implementation of the Minnesota Land Use Planning Act," *Journal of Planning Education and Research* 22, no. 3 (March 1, 2003): 213–25, https://doi.org/10.1177/0739456x02250304; David Rusk, *Inside Game/Outside Game: Winning Strategies for Saving Urban America* (Washington, DC: Brookings Institution, 1999); Myron Orfield, *Metropolitics: A Regional Agenda for Community and Stability* (Washington, DC: Brookings Institution Press, 1997); Dreier, Mollenkopf, and Swanstrom, *Place Matters*.

23. Edward G. Goetz, *Shelter Burden: Local Politics and Progressive Housing Policy* (Philadelphia: Temple University Press, 1993).

24. Jennifer Clark and Susan Christopherson, "Integrating Investment and Equity: A Critical Regionalist Agenda for a Progressive Regionalism," *Journal of Planning Education and Research* 28, no. 3 (2009): 341–54, https://doi.org/10.1177/0739456X08327371.

25. Doreen Massey, "In What Sense a Regional Problem?" *Regional Studies* 13, no. 2 (1979): 233–43.

26. Massey, "In What Sense a Regional Problem?", 243.

27. Alberta M. Sbragia, *Debt Wish: Entrepreneurial Cities, U.S. Federalism, and Economic Development* (Pittsburgh: University of Pittsburgh Press, 1996); Rachel Weber, "Extracting Value from the City: Neoliberalism and Urban Redevelopment," *Antipode* 34, no. 3 (July 1, 2002): 519–40, https://doi.org/10.1111/1467-8330.00253.

28. Linda Lobao et al., "The Shrinking State? Understanding the Assault on the Public Sector," *Cambridge Journal of Regions, Economy and Society* 11, no. 3 (October 29, 2018): 389–408, https://doi.org/10.1093/cjres/rsy026.

29. Lilly Irani, "Hackathons and the Making of Entrepreneurial Citizenship," *Science, Technology & Human Values* 40, no. 5: 799–824, https://doi.org/10.1177/0162243915578486; Thomas Lodato and Carl DiSalvo, "Issue-Oriented Hackathons as Material Participation," *New Media & Society* 18, no. 4 (April 1, 2016): 539–57, https://doi.org/10.1177/1461444816629467.

30. Thomas Lodato, Emma French, and Jennifer Clark, "Open Government Data in the Smart City: Interoperability, Urban Knowledge, and Linking Legacy Systems," *Journal of Urban Affairs*, October 16, 2018, https://doi.org/10.1080/07352166.2018.1511798.

31. John P. Holdren et al., *Technology and the Future of Cities* (Washington, DC: Executive Office of the President, President's Council of Advisors on Science and Technology, February 2016).

32. Susan Fainstein and Ann Markusen, "The Urban Policy Challenge: Integrating across Social and Economic Development Policy," in *Race, Poverty, and American Cities*, ed. John Boger and Judith Wegner (Chapel Hill: University of North Carolina Press, 1996); Gerald Frug, *City Making: Building Communities without Building Walls* (Princeton, NJ: Princeton University Press, 2001).

33. Alisa Valderrama and Larry Levine, *Financing Stormwater Retrofits in Philadelphia and Beyond* (New York: Natural Resources Defense Council, February 2012).

3. SMART CITIES AS EMERGING MARKETS

1. Gordon Clark et al., eds., *The New Oxford Handbook of Economic Geography* (Oxford: Oxford University Press, 2018).

2. Susan Christopherson and Jennifer Clark, *Remaking Regional Economies: Power, Labor, and Firm Strategies in the Knowledge Economy* (New York: Routledge, 2007).

3. Peter Dicken, *Global Shift: Mapping the Changing Contours of the World Economy*, 7th ed. (New York: Guilford, 2015).

4. Ava Kofman, "Google's Sidewalk Labs Plans to Package and Sell Location Data on Millions of Cellphones," *Intercept*, January 28, 2019, https://theintercept.com/2019/01/28/google-alphabet-sidewalk-labs-replica-cellphone-data/; Marco Oved and Paul Hunter, "Privacy Expert Steps down from Advisory Role with Sidewalk Labs," *Toronto Star*, October 20, 2018, https://www.thestar.com/news/gta/2018/10/20/privacy-expert-steps-down-from-advisory-role-with-sidewalk-labs.html.

5. Christopherson and Clark, *Remaking Regional Economies*.

6. Jennifer Clark, *Working Regions: Reconnecting Innovation and Production in the Knowledge Economy* (London: Routledge, 2013).

7. Alan Wiig, "IBM's Smart City as Techno-Utopian Policy Mobility," *City* 19, no. 2–3 (May 4, 2015): 258–73, https://doi.org/10.1080/13604813.2015.1016275; Sotirios Paroutis, Mark Bennett, and Loizos Heracleous, "A Strategic View on Smart City Technology: The Case of IBM

Smarter Cities during a Recession," *Technological Forecasting and Social Change* 89 (November 2014): 262–72, https://doi.org/10.1016/j .techfore.2013.08.041; Amy Glasmeier and Susan Christopherson, "Thinking About Smart Cities," *Cambridge Journal of Regions, Economy and Society* 8, no. 1 (March 2015): 3–12, https://doi.org/10.1093/cjres /rsu034; Taylor Shelton and Jennifer Clark, "Technocratic Values and Uneven Development in the 'Smart City,'" *Metropolitics*, May 10 (2016), http://www.metropolitiques.eu/Technocratic-Values-and-Uneven .html.

8. Anthony M. Townsend, *Smart Cities: Big Data, Civic Hackers, and the Quest for a New Utopia* (New York: Norton, 2013).

9. Harold Wolman and Gerry Stoker, "Understanding Local Economic Development in a Comparative Context," *Economic Development Quarterly* 6, no. 4 (November 1992): 406–17, https://doi.org/10.1177 /089124249200600407; Pierre Clavel and Robert Kraushaar, "On Being Unreasonable: Progressive Planning in Sheffield and Chicago," *International Planning Studies* 3, no. 2 (June 1998): 143–62, https://doi .org/10.1080/13563479808721706.

10. William W. Goldsmith, "Enterprise Zones: If They Work, We're in Trouble," *International Journal of Urban and Regional Research* 6, no. 3 (September 1, 1982): 435–42, https://doi.org/10.1111/j.1468-2427.1982 .tb00392.x.

11. Michael Porter, *The Competitive Advantage of Nations* (New York: Free Press, 1990); Michael Porter, "The Competitive Advantage of the Inner City," *Harvard Business Review* 73, no. 3 (May–June 1995): 55–71.

12. Jane S. Pollard, "From Industrial District to 'Urban Village'? Manufacturing, Money and Consumption in Birmingham's Jewellery Quarter," *Urban Studies* 41, no. 1 (2004): 173–93. https://doi.org/10.1080 /0042098032000155731; Ann Markusen, "A Consumption Base Theory of Development: An Application to the Rural Cultural Economy," *Agricultural and Resource Economics Review* 36, no. 1 (2007).9–23, https:// doi.org/10.1017/S1068280500009412.

13. Richard Florida, *The Rise of the Creative Class: And How It's Transforming Work, Leisure, Community, and Everyday Life* (New York: Basic Books, 2002); William Julius Wilson, *The Truly Disadvantaged: The Inner City, the Underclass, and Public Policy*, repr. ed. (Chicago: University of Chicago Press, 1990).

14. David Harvey, "The Right to the City," *New Left Review* 53 (September /October 2008): 23–40, https://newleftreview.org/issues/II53/articles /david-harvey-the-right-to-the-city.

15. In 2017, the Smart Cities and Inclusive Innovation research team at Georgia Tech designed a six-stage stylized typology of university-based smart cities research as a model for explaining to stakeholders the extent to which smart cities applications crossed scales and markets. This discussion is an expansion on that typology.

16. Jennifer Clark, "Remodeling Capitalism: A Return to Scale," *Environment and Planning A: Economy and Space* 51, no.5: 1178–80, https://doi .org/10.1177/0308518X19851320.

17. Alan Blinder and Nicole Perlroth, "A Cyberattack Hobbles Atlanta, and Security Experts Shudder," U.S., *New York Times*, March 29, 2018, https://www.nytimes.com/2018/03/27/us/cyberattack-atlanta-ransomware .html; Thomas Lodato, Emma French, and Jennifer Clark, "Open Government Data in the Smart City: Interoperability, Urban Knowledge, and Linking Legacy Systems," *Journal of Urban Affairs*, 2018, https://doi.org/10.1080/07352166.2018.1511798.

18. Taewoo Nam and Theresa A. Pardo, "Conceptualizing Smart City with Dimensions of Technology, People, and Institutions," in *Proceedings of the 12th Annual International Digital Government Research Conference: Digital Government Innovation in Challenging Times*, Dg.o ʾ11 (New York: Association for Computing Machinery, 2011), 282–91, https://doi .org/10.1145/2037556.2037602; Linnet Taylor et al., "Customers, Users or Citizens? Inclusion, Spatial Data and Governance in the Smart City," SSRN Scholarly Paper (Rochester, NY: Social Science Research Network, June 9, 2016), http://papers.ssrn.com/abstract=2792565; Taylor Shelton, Matthew Zook, and Alan Wiig, "The 'Actually Existing Smart City,'" *Cambridge Journal of Regions, Economy and Society* 8, no. 1 (October 27, 2014): 13–25, https://doi.org/10.1093/cjres/rsu026; William J. Craig, Trevor M. Harris, and Daniel Weiner, eds., *Community Participation and Geographic Information Systems* (London: Taylor & Francis, 2002); Angela M. Evans and Adriana Campos, "Open Government Initiatives: Challenges of Citizen Participation," *Journal of Policy Analysis and Management* 32, no. 1 (2013): 172–203; Renee Sieber, "Public Participation Geographic Information Systems: A Literature Review and Framework," *Annals of the Association of American*

Geographers 96, no. 3 (September 2006): 491–507, https://doi.org/10.1111 /j.1467-8306.2006.00702.x; Craig M. Dalton, Linnet Taylor, and Jim Thatcher, "Critical Data Studies: A Dialog on Data and Space," *Big Data & Society* 3, no. 1 (January 5, 2016): 205395171664834, https://doi .org/10.1177/2053951716648346; Rob Kitchin, *The Data Revolution: Big Data, Open Data, Data Infrastructures and Their Consequences* (Thousand Oaks, CA: SAGE, 2014).

19. "Smart City Challenge: Lessons for Building Cities of the Future" (Washington, DC: US Department of Transportation, 2017), https:// www.transportation.gov/sites/dot.gov/files/docs/Smart%20City %20Challenge%20Lessons%20Learned.pdf.

20. Don Clark, "5G Is Coming This Year. Here's What You Need to Know," Technology, *New York Times*, January 1, 2019, https://www.nytimes .com/2018/12/31/technology/personaltech/5g-what-you-need-to-know .html.

21. "Guide to the General Data Protection Regulation (GDPR)," May 25, 2018, https://ico.org.uk/for-organisations/guide-to-the-general-data -protection-regulation-gdpr/.

22. Mildred Warner and Robert Hebdon, "Local Government Restructuring: Privatization and Its Alternatives," *Journal of Policy Analysis and Management* 20, no. 2 (2001): 315–36, https://doi.org/10.1002/pam.2027.

23. Jennifer Clark and Supraja Sudharsan, "Firm Strategies and Path Dependencies: An Emerging Economic Geography of Industrial Data," *Regional Studies*, July 3, 2019., https://doi.org/10.1080/00343404 .2019.1619926.

24. Jim Thatcher, "You Are Where You Go, the Commodification of Daily Life Through 'Location,'" *Environment and Planning A* 49, no. 12 (December 2017): 2702–17, https://doi.org/10.1177/0308518X17730580.

25. "The World's Most Valuable Resource Is No Longer Oil, but Data," *Economist*, May 6, 2017, https://www.economist.com/leaders/2017/05/06 /the-worlds-most-valuable-resource-is-no-longer-oil-but-data.

26. Harriet Bulkeley, Pauline M, McGuirk, and Robyn Dowling, "Making a Smart City for the Smart Grid? The Urban Material Politics of Actualising Smart Electricity Networks," *Environment and Planning A: Economy and Space* 48, no. 9 (September 2016): 1709–26, https://doi.org /10.1177/0308518X16648152; Matthew A. Zook, "Grounded Capital: Venture Financing and the Geography of the Internet Industry, 1994–2000,"

Journal of Economic Geography 2, no. 2 (April 1, 2002): 151–77, https://doi .org/10.1093/jeg/2.2.151.

27. Clark and Sudharsan, "Firm Strategies and Path Dependencies."

28. George C. Homsy and Mildred E. Warner, "Cities and Sustainability: Polycentric Action and Multilevel Governance," *Urban Affairs Review* 51, no. 1 (January 1, 2015): 46–73, https://doi.org/10.1177 /1078087414530545.

29. Lodato, French, and Clark, "Open Government Data in the Smart City"; Thatcher, "You Are Where You Go."

4. SMART CITIES AS THE NEW URBAN ENTREPRENEURSHIP

1. Charles M. Tiebout, "A Pure Theory of Local Expenditures," *Journal of Political Economy* 64, no. 5 (1956): 416; Eric S. Sheppard, Trevor J. Barnes, and Claire Pavlik, *The Capitalist Space Economy: Geographical Analysis after Ricardo, Marx and Sraffa* (London: Unwin Hyman, 1990).

2. Emily Badger, "Why Cities Can't Stop Poaching from One Another," The Upshot,*New York Times*, June 8, 2018, https://www.nytimes.com /2018/06/08/upshot/why-cities-cant-stop-poaching-from-one -another.html; David Streitfeld and Claire Ballentine, "Seattle Officials Repeal Tax That Upset Amazon," Technology, *New York Times*, June 12, 2018, https://www.nytimes.com/2018/06/12/technology/seattle-tax-amazon .html; Nick Wingfield, "Amazon Chooses 20 Finalists for Second Headquarters," Technology, *New York Times*, January 19, 2018, https://www .nytimes.com/2018/01/18/technology/amazon-finalists-headquarters .html.

3. David Harvey, "From Managerialism to Entrepreneurialism: The Transformation of Urban Governance in Late Capitalism," *Geographiska Annaler* 71, series b (1989): 3–17; Bernard J. Frieden and Lynne B. Sagalyn, *Downtown, Inc.: How America Rebuilds Cities* (Cambridge, MA: MIT Press, 1991); Lynne B. Sagalyn, *Times Square Roulette: Remaking the City Icon* (Cambridge, MA: MIT Press, 2001).

4. Ian R. Cook and Kevin Ward, "Trans-Urban Networks of Learning, Mega Events and Policy Tourism: The Case of Manchester's Commonwealth and Olympic Games Projects," *Urban Studies* 48, no. 12 (September 2011): 2519–35, https://doi.org/10.1177/0042098011411941.

5. Gillian Bristow, "Everyone's a 'Winner': Problematising the Discourse of Regional Competitiveness," *Journal of Economic Geography* 5, no. 3 (2005): 285–304; Edward J. Malecki, "Jockeying for Position: What It Means and Why It Matters to Regional Development Policy When Places Compete," *Regional Studies* 38, no. 9 (December 2004): 1101–20; Jennifer Clark and Susan Christopherson, "Integrating Investment and Equity: A Critical Regionalist Agenda for a Progressive Regionalism," *Journal of Planning Education and Research* 28, no. 3 (2009): 341, https://doi.org/10.1177/0739456X08327371.

6. Joan Fitzgerald and Nancey Green Leigh, *Economic Revitalization: Cases and Strategies for City and Suburb* (Thousand Oaks, CA: SAGE, 2002); Andy Pike, Andrés Rodríguez-Pose, and John Tomaney, *Local and Regional Development* (New York: Routledge, 2006), http://www.loc.gov/catdir/enhancements/fy0654/2006005421-d.html.

7. Jamie Peck and Kevin Ward, *City of Revolution: Restructuring Manchester* (Manchester, UK: Manchester University Press, 2002); Rachel Weber, *From Boom to Bubble: How Finance Built the New Chicago* (Chicago: University of Chicago Press, 2015).

8. Susan Fainstein, *The City Builders: Property Development in New York and London, 1980–2000*, rev. ed. (Lawrence: University Press of Kansas, 2001); Bernard J. Frieden and Lynne B. Sagalyn, *Downtown, Inc.: How America Rebuilds Cities* (Cambridge, MA: MIT Press, 1991).

9. Carey Durkin Treado, "Pittsburgh's Evolving Steel Legacy and the Steel Technology Cluster," *Cambridge Journal of Regions, Economy and Society* 3, no. 1 (2010): 105–20, https://doi.org/10.1093/cjres/rsp027.

10. Michael Storper et al., *The Rise and Fall of Urban Economies: Lessons from San Francisco and Los Angeles*, (Stanford, CA: Stanford Business Books, 2016); Richard Walker, *Pictures of a Gone City: Tech and the Dark Side of Prosperity in the San Francisco Bay Area*, Spectre (Oakland, CA: PM Press, 2018).

11. Harald Bathelt, Anders Malmberg, and Peter Maskell, "Clusters and Knowledge: Local Buzz, Global Pipelines and the Process of Knowledge Creation," *Progress in Human Geography* 28, no. 1 (2004): 31–56, https://doi.org/10.1191/0309132504ph469oa; Michael Storper and Anthony J. Venables, "Buzz: Face-to-Face Contact and the Urban Economy," *Journal of Economic Geography* 4, no. 4 (2004): 351–70, https://doi.org/10.1093/jnlecg/lbh027.

12. Richard Florida, *The Rise of the Creative Class: And How It's Trans-forming Work, Leisure, Community, and Everyday Life* (New York: Basic Books, 2002).

13. Fitzgerald and Leigh, *Economic Revitalization*; Benjamin Sitton Flowers, *Skyscraper: The Politics and Power of Building New York City in the Twentieth Century* (Philadelphia: University of Pennsylvania Press, 2009); Cook and Ward, "Trans-Urban Networks of Learning, Mega Events and Policy Tourism"; Benjamin Sitton Flowers, *Sport and Architecture*, (London: Routledge, 2017).

14. Paul E. Peterson, *City Limits* (Chicago: University of Chicago Press, 1981).

15. Harvey, "From Managerialism to Entrepreneurialism."

16. Emily Badger, "Tech Envisions the Ultimate Start-Up: An Entire City," The Upshot, *New York Times*, February 24, 2018, https://www .nytimes.com/2018/02/24/upshot/tech-envisions-the-ultimate-start -up-an-entire-city.html; Farhad Manjoo, "How Tech Companies Conquered America's Cities," Technology, *New York Times*, June 21, 2018, https://www.nytimes.com/2018/06/20/technology/tech-companies -conquered-cities.html.

17. Mari Sibley, "AT&T, San Jose Sew Up Model Small Cell Deal," *Light Reading*, March 14, 2018, https://www.lightreading.com/smart-cities /atandt-san-jose-sew-up-model-small-cell-deal/d/d-id/743032; Melissa Gregg, "Available in Selected Metros Only: Rural Melancholy and the Promise of Online Connectivity," *Cultural Studies Review* 16, no. 1 (2010): 155–69, https://doi.org/10.5130/csr.v16i1.1450.

18. Ben Green, *The Smart Enough City: Putting Technology in Its Place to Reclaim Our Urban Future* (Cambridge, MA: MIT Press, 2019); Stephen Goldsmith and Susan Crawford, *The Responsive City: Engaging Communities Through Data-Smart Governance* (San Francisco: Jossey-Bass, 2014).

19. Greg Schrock, Marc Doussard, and Laura Wolf-Powers, "The Maker Economy in Action: Entrepreneurship and Supportive Ecosystems in Chicago, New York and Portland," Research Monograph Funded by the Ewing Marion Kauffman Foundation's Program on Metropolitan Entrepreneurship, 2017, https://static1.squarespace.com/static/5812d937 be6594b79f6b7c82/t/58177ff3197aea6c5f212446/1477935092051/The+Maker +Economy+in+Action+--+Final+Report.pdf.

20. Benjamin Schneider, "From the Ruins of a Retail Meltdown, Post-Industrial Playgrounds Emerge," *CityLab*, November 16, 2017, https://www.citylab.com/life/2017/11/sears-warehouses-find-new-life-as-post-industrial-playgrounds/545936/.

21. Cecilia Kang, "Pittsburgh Welcomed Uber's Driverless Car Experiment. Not Anymore." Technology, *New York Times*, May 21, 2017, https://www.nytimes.com/2017/05/21/technology/pittsburgh-ubers-driverless-car-experiment.html; Alison Griswold, "Uber Asked a Lot of Pittsburgh for Its Self-Driving Cars, and Offered Back Very Little," *Quartz*, December 29, 2016, https://qz.com/874548/uber-asked-a-lot-of-pittsburgh-for-its-self-driving-cars-and-offered-back-very-little/.

22. Green, *The Smart Enough City*.

23. Peer Hull Kristensen and Jonathan Zeitlin, *Local Players in Global Games: The Strategic Constitution of a Multinational Corporation* (Oxford: Oxford University Press, 2005); Susan Christopherson and Jennifer Clark, *Remaking Regional Economies: Power, Labor, and Firm Strategies in the Knowledge Economy* (New York: Routledge, 2007).

24. Susan Christopherson, "Market Rules and Territorial Outcomes: The Case of the United States," *International Journal of Urban and Regional Research* 17, no. 2 (June 1993):274–88, https://doi.org/10.1111/j.1468-2427.1993.tb00481.x; Susan Christopherson, "Why Do National Labor Market Practices Continue to Diverge in the Global Economy? The 'Missing Link' of Investment Rules," *Economic Geography* 78, no. 1 (January 2002): 1–20, https://doi.org/10.1111/j.1944-8287.2002.tb00173.x.

25. Walter Isard et al., *Methods of Interregional and Regional Analysis* (Aldershot, UK: Ashgate, 1998).

26. Richard E. Klosterman et al., *Planning Support Methods: Urban and Regional Analysis and Projection* (Lanham, MD: Rowman & Littlefield, 2018).

27. Michael Batty, *The New Science of Cities*, repr. ed. (Cambridge, MA: MIT Press, 2017).

28. The U.S. National Science Foundation has made substantial investments in cyber physical systems research, including shifting the administration of smart cities research into a division led by specialists in this domain rather than by social scientists who specialize in cities. The National Institute of Standards and Technology in the Department of Commerce has followed suit, casting smart cities research as primarily

a set of technical questions that fall within cyber physical systems research.

29. Richard S. Bolan, "Rationality Revisited: An Alternative Perspective on Reason in Management and Planning," *Journal of Management History* 5, no. 2 (1999): 68–86, https://doi.org/10.1108/13552529910260082; Richard S. Bolan, "The Practitioner as Theorist: The Phenomenology of the Professional Episode," *Journal of the American Planning Association* 46, no. 3 (July 1980): 261–74, https://doi.org/10.1080/01944368008977042; Craig M. Dalton, Linnet Taylor, and Jim Thatcher, "Critical Data Studies: A Dialog on Data and Space," *Big Data & Society* 3, no. 1 (January 5, 2016), https://doi.org/10.1177/2053951716648346.

30. John Forester, "Critical Theory and Planning Practice," *Journal of the American Planning Association* 46, no. 3 (July 1980): 275–86, https://doi.org/10.1080/01944368008977043.

31. John P. Holdren et al., *Technology and the Future of Cities* (Washington, DC: Executive Office of the President, President's Council of Advisors on Science and Technology, February 2016), 2.

32. Holdren et al., *Technology and the Future of Cities*, 8.

33. Feargus O'Sullivan, "In London, Uber Fights for Its License— The Atlantic," *City Lab: The Atlantic*, 2018, https://www.citylab.com /amp/article/562322/?utm_source=twb&__twitter_impression=true; Heather Somerville, "Seattle Passes Law Letting Uber, Lyft Drivers Unionize," *Reuters*, December 15, 2015, https://www.reuters.com /article/us-washington-uber/seattle-passes-law-letting-uber-lyft -drivers-unionize-idUSKBN0TX2NO20151215; Adam Satariano, "Uber Claims to Have Changed. A London Judge Will Decide." Technology, *New York Times*, June 25, 2018, https://www.nytimes.com/2018/06/24 /technology/uber-london-appeal.html; Dan Levine, "Uber Drivers Granted Class Action Status in Lawsuit over Employment," *Reuters*, September 1, 2015, https://www.reuters.com/article/us-uber-tech-drivers -lawsuit/u-s-judge-gives-uber-drivers-class-action-status-idUSKCN0 R14O920150901.

34. Kang, "Pittsburgh Welcomed Uber's Driverless Car Experiment. Not Anymore."; Griswold, "Uber Asked a Lot of Pittsburgh for Its Self-Driving Cars, and Offered Back Very Little."

35. OECD, *SME and Entrepreneurship Policy in Canada*, (Paris: OECD Publishing, 2017), https://doi.org/10.1787/9789264273467-en.

36. Paul Quintas, David Wield, and Doreen Massey, "Academic-Industry Links and Innovation: Questioning the Science Park Model," *Technovation* 12, no. 3 (April 1992): 161–75, https://doi.org/10.1016/0166-4972(92)90033-E.

37. Julie T. Miao, "Parallelism and Evolution in Transnational Policy Transfer Networks: The Case of Sino-Singapore Suzhou Industrial Park (SIP)," *Regional Studies* 52, no. 9 (January 24, 2018): 1191–1200, https://doi.org/10.1080/00343404.2017.1418979; Jennifer Clark, "Siting 'Scientific Spaces' in the US: The Push and Pull of Regional Development Strategies and National Innovation Policies," *Environment and Planning C: Government and Policy* 32, no. 5 (October 2014): 880–95, https://doi.org/10.1068/c1271r.

38. Yasuyuki Motoyama, *Global Companies, Local Innovations: Why the Engineering Aspects of Innovation Making Require Co-Location* (Aldershot, UK: Ashgate, 2012).

39. Jennifer Clark, Hsin I. Huang, and John P. Walsh, "A Typology of Innovation Districts: What It Means for Regional Resilience," *Cambridge Journal of Regions, Economies, and Society* 3, no. 1 (2010): 121–37, https://doi.org/10.1093/cjres/rsp034; Andrea Morrison, "Gatekeepers of Knowledge within Industrial Districts: Who They Are, How They Interact," *Regional Studies* 42, no. 6 (2008): 817–35, https://doi.org/10.1080/00343400701654178; Greg Giuffrida, Jennifer Clark, and Stephen Cross, "Putting Innovation in Place: Georgia Tech's Innovation Neighborhood of 'Tech Square'" Proceedings of the 10th European Conference on Innovation and Entrepreneurship, Genoa, Italy September 2015, 214–222 (Atlanta, Georgia, September 2015), http://www.gatech.edu/sites/default/files/documents/ECIE-2015-Giuffrida-Clark-Cross.pdf.

40. Bruce Katz and Julie Wagner, "The Rise of Innovation Districts: A New Geography of Innovation in America" (Washington, DC: Brookings Institution, 2014).

41. Schrock, Doussard, and Wolf-Powers, "The Maker Economy in Action"; Laura Wolf-Powers et al., "The Maker Movement and Urban Economic Development," *Journal of the American Planning Association* 83, no. 4 (October 2, 2017): 365–76, https://doi.org/10.1080/01944363.2017.1360787; Mark Hatch, *The Maker Movement Manifesto: Rules for Innovation in the New World of Crafters, Hackers, and Tinkerers* (New York: McGraw-Hill, 2013).

42. Jamie Peck, *Work-Place: The Social Regulation of Labor Markets* (New York: Guilford Press, 1996).

43. Francoise Carre, Virginia duRivage, and Chris Tilly, "Representing the Part-Time and Contingent Workforce: Challenges for Unions and Public Policy," in *Restoring the Promise of American Labor Law*, ed. Sheldon Friedman et al. (Ithaca, NY: ILR Press, 1994), 314–23; Chris Benner, *Work in the New Economy: Flexible Labor Markets in Silicon Valley* (Oxford, UK: Blackwell, 2002); Katherine Stone, *From Widgets to Digits: Employment Regulation for the Changing Workplace* (New York: Cambridge University Press, 2004).

44. Katherine Stone, "The New Psychological Contract: Implications of the Changing Workplace for Labor and Employment Law," *UCLA Law Review* 48 (2001): 540–49.

45. Ruth Milkman and Ed Ott, eds., *New Labor in New York: Precarious Workers and the Future of the Labor Movement* (Ithaca, NY: ILR Press, 2014).

46. Thomas Lodato and Jennifer Clark, "Flexible Work, Flexible Work Spaces: The Emergence of the Coworking Industry in US Cities." October 31, 2016, Georgia Tech's Center for Urban Innovation Blog, https://gtcui.wordpress.com/2016/10/31/flexible-work-flexible-work -spaces-the-emergence-of-the-coworking-industry-in-us-cities/.

47. Martin Carnoy, Manuel Castells, and Chris Benner, "Labour Markets and Employment Practices in the Age of Flexibility: A Case Study of Silicon Valley," *International Labour Review* 136, no. 1 (Spring 1997): 27; Christopherson and Clark, *Remaking Regional Economies*.

5. SMART CITIES AS URBAN
INNOVATION NETWORKS

1. Ron A. Boschma and Koen Frenken, "Why Is Economic Geography Not an Evolutionary Science? Towards an Evolutionary Economic Geography," *Journal of Economic Geography* 6, no. 3 (June 1, 2006): 273–302, https://doi.org/10.1093/jeg/lbi022; Danny MacKinnon et al., "Evolution in Economic Geography: Institutions, Political Economy, and Adaptation," *Economic Geography* 85, no. 2 (2009): 129–50, https:// doi.org/10.1111/j.1944-8287.2009.01017.x; Jennifer Clark, *Working Regions: Reconnecting Innovation and Production in the Knowledge Economy*

(London: Routledge, 2013).; Ron Martin and Peter Sunley, "Towards a Developmental Turn in Evolutionary Economic Geography?," in *Evolutionary Economic Geography: Theoretical and Empirical Progress*, ed. Dieter F. Kogler (New York: Routledge, 2016).

2. Henry Etzkowitz and L. A. Leydesdorff, *Universities and the Global Knowledge Economy: A Triple Helix of University-Industry-Government Relations* (London: Pinter, 1997).

3. Christopher Flavelle, "Rockefeller to Wind Down Biggest Private Climate Resilience Push," *Bloomberg News*, April 1, 2019, https://www.bloomberg.com/news/articles/2019-04-01/rockefeller-announces-end-of-major-climate-resilience-initiative.

4. Emily Badger, "Tech Envisions the Ultimate Start-Up: An Entire City," The Upshot, *New York Times*, February 24, 2018, https://www.nytimes.com/2018/02/24/upshot/tech-envisions-the-ultimate-start-up-an-entire-city.html

5. Jamie Peck and Nik Theodore, "Mobilizing Policy: Models, Methods, and Mutations," *Geoforum* 41, no. 2 (March 2010): 169–74, https://doi.org/10.1016/j.geoforum.2010.01.002.

6. Jennifer Clark, "Coordinating a Conscious Geography: The Role of Research Centers in Multi-Scalar Innovation Policy and Economic Development in the US and Canada," *Journal of Technology Transfer* 35, no. 5 (2010): 460–74, https://doi.org/10.1007/s10961-009-9137-z.

7. Jennifer Clark, "Resilient Regions and Open Innovation: The Evolution of Smart Cities and Civic Entrepreneurship," in *Creating Resilient Economies: Entrepreneurship, Growth and Development in Uncertain Times*, ed. Tim Vorley and Nick Williams (Northampton, MA: Edward Elgar, 2017), 109–22, http://www.e-elgar.com/shop/creating-resilient-economies.

8. New State Ice Co. v. Liebmann, 285 U.S. 262 (March 21, 1932).

9. Royce A. Singleton Jr., and Bruce C. Straits, *Approaches to Social Research*, 5th ed. (New York: Oxford University Press, 2010); Carl V. Patton, David S. Sawicki, and Jennifer Clark, *Basic Methods of Policy Analysis and Planning*, 3rd ed. New York: Routledge, 2013).

10. Susan Christopherson, Michael Kitson, and Jonathan Michie, "Innovation, Networks and Knowledge Exchange," *Cambridge Journal of Regions, Economy and Society* 1, no. 2 (2008): 165–73, https://doi.org/10.1093/cjres/rsn015.

11. Pierre Clavel, *Activists in City Hall: The Progressive Response to the Reagan Era in Boston and Chicago* (Ithaca, NY: Cornell University Press, 2010); Bloomberg Philanthropies, "City Hall Innovation Team Playbook: The Innovation Delivery Approach to Develop and Deliver Bold Innovation" (New York: Bloomberg Philanthropies, March 2015), https://www .bbhub.io/dotorg/sites/2/2014/08/Innovation-Team-Playbook_2015 .pdf; Alexander Burns, "Bloomberg's Next Anti-Washington Move: $200 Million Program for Mayors," Politics, *New York Times*, June 25, 2017, https://www.nytimes.com/2017/06/25/us/politics/michael-bloomberg -mayors-trump.html.

12. Taylor Shelton and Jennifer Clark, "Technocratic Values and Uneven Development in the 'Smart City,'" *Metropolitics*, May 10 (2016), http:// www.metropolitiques.eu/Technocratic-Values-and-Uneven.html; Rockefeller Foundation, "Challenge Eligibility and Criteria," 100 Resilient Cities, 2018, http://www.100resilientcities.org/challenge-eligibility -criteria/; Michael R. Bloomberg and Anne Hidalgo, "Why Cities Will Be Vital Players at Paris Climate Talks," *Huff Post* (blog), June 30, 2015, https://www.huffingtonpost.com/michael-bloomberg /paris-climate-talks-bloomberg_b_7683246.html; "Mike Bloomberg Names Los Angeles, Portland, San Diego, and San Jose as Winners in Bloomberg American Cities Climate Challenge," Bloomberg Philanthropies, accessed July 1, 2019, https://www.bloomberg.org/press /releases/mike-bloomberg-names-los-angeles-portland-san-diego -san-jose-winners-bloomberg-american-cities-climate-challenge/.

13. Jamie Peck and Nikolas Theodore, *Fast Policy: Experimental Statecraft at the Thresholds of Neoliberalism* (Minneapolis: University of Minnesota Press, 2015).

14. Clark, "Resilient Regions and Open Innovation"; Jennifer Clark, "Policy Through Practice: Local Communities, Self-Organization, and Policy," in *The New Oxford Handbook of Economic Geography*, ed. Gordon L. Clark, Maryann P. Feldman, Meric S. Gertler, and Dariusz Wojcik, 2nd ed. (Oxford: Oxford University Press, 2018).

15. Harriet Bulkeley and Michele M. Betsill, "Rethinking Sustainable Cities: Multilevel Governance and the 'Urban' Politics of Climate Change," *Environmental Politics* 14, no. 1 (February 1, 2005): 42–63, https://doi.org/10.1080/0964401042000310178; Michele M. Betsill and

Harriet Bulkeley, "Transnational Networks and Global Environmental Governance: The Cities for Climate Protection Program," *International Studies Quarterly* 48, no. 2 (June 1, 2004): 471–93, https://doi.org/10.1111/j.0020-8833.2004.00310.x.

16. Susan Christopherson and Jennifer Clark, *Remaking Regional Economies: Power, Labor, and Firm Strategies in the Knowledge Economy* (New York: Routledge, 2007), 7.

17. Harriet Bulkeley and Michele M. Betsill, "Revisiting the Urban Politics of Climate Change," *Environmental Politics* 22, no. 1 (2013): 136–54, https://doi.org/10.1080/09644016.2013.755797; Rockefeller Foundation, "What Is 100 Resilient Cities?," 100 Resilient Cities, 2018, http://www.100resilientcities.org/about-us/; Mike Herd and Murithi Mutiga, "100 Resilient Cities Announces Hundredth Member, but 'Work Is Only Just Beginning,'" Cities, *Guardian*, May 25, 2016, https://www.theguardian.com/cities/2016/may/25/rockefeller-100-resilient-cities-washington-lagos-manchester-belfast; Burns, "Bloomberg's Next Anti-Washington Move"; Bloomberg Philanthropies, "City Hall Innovation Team Playbook"; Ruth Puttick, Peter Baeck, and Philip Colligan, "I-Teams: The Teams and Funds Making Innovation Happen in Governments Around the World" (Nesta & Bloomberg Philanthropies, June 2014), https://www.bbhub.io/dotorg/sites/2/2014/06/Nesta_2014_Report_final_webcombined.pdf; Noah Kirsch, "Michael Bloomberg Takes on Trump, Pledges $42 Million to U.S. Cities," *Forbes*, May 23, 2018, https://www.forbes.com/sites/noahkirsch/2018/05/23/michael-bloomberg-takes-on-trump-pledges-42-million-to-us-cities/; Rebecca Carriero, "Mike Bloomberg's Annual Letter on Philanthropy," Bloomberg Philanthropies, May 23, 2018, https://www.bloomberg.org/press/releases/mike-bloombergs-annual-letter-philanthropy-says-mayors-data-antidote-washingtons-divisive-assault-facts/.

18. This is the case with the Georgia Smart Communities Challenge, an initiative of the Georgia Institute of Technology in partnership with regional organizations and local governments. It is also, to some extent, the approach taken by the 2016 U.S. Department of Transportation's Smart Cities Challenge, which was awarded to Columbus, Ohio.

19. Carriero, "Mike Bloomberg's Annual Letter on Philanthropy"; Kirsch, "Michael Bloomberg Takes on Trump, Pledges $42 Million to U.S. Cities."

20. Kirsch, "Michael Bloomberg Takes on Trump, Pledges $42 Million to U.S. Cities"; Burns, "Bloomberg's Next Anti-Washington Move."

21. Jennifer Clark, "Manufacturing by Design: The Rise of Regional Intermediaries and the Reemergence of Collective Action," *Cambridge Journal of Regions, Economy and Society* 7, no. 3 (2014): 433–48, https://doi.org/10.1093/cjres/rsu017.

22. Patton, Sawicki, and Clark, *Basic Methods of Policy Analysis and Planning.*

23. Franz Todtling and Michaela Trippl, "Knowledge Links in High-Technology Industries: Markets, Networks or Milieu? The Case of the Vienna Biotechnology Cluster," *International Journal of Entrepreneurship and Innovation Management* 7, no. 2–5 (2007): 345–65; Franz Todtling, "Regional Networks of High-Technology Firms—The Case of the Greater Boston Region," *Technovation* 14, no. 5 (1994): 323; Jennifer Clark, "Hidden in Plain Sight: The North American Optics and Photonics Industry," in *The Handbook of Manufacturing Industries in the Global Economy*, ed. John Bryson, Jennifer Clark, and Vida Vanchan (Northampton, MA: Edward Elgar, 2015); Nichola J. Lowe and Laura Wolf-Powers, "Who Works in a Working Region? Inclusive Innovation in the New Manufacturing Economy," *Regional Studies* 52, no. 6 (June 3, 2018): 828–39, https://doi.org/10.1080/00343404.2016.1263386.

24. Clark, *Working Regions.*

25. Flavelle, "Rockefeller to Wind Down Biggest Private Climate Resilience Push."

26. Jennifer Clark, "Designing the Smart City: A Programmatic Approach to Inclusive Innovation in Atlanta," *Atlanta Studies*, September 19, 2017, https://doi.org/10.18737/atls20170919.

27. Rolf Pendall, Kathryn A. Foster, and Margaret Cowell, "Resilience and Regions: Building Understanding of the Metaphor," *Cambridge Journal of Regions, Economy and Society* 3, no. 1 (March 1, 2010): 71–84, https://doi.org/10.1093/cjres/rsp028; Jennifer Clark, Hsin-I. Huang, and John P. Walsh, "A Typology of 'Innovation Districts': What It Means for Regional Resilience," *Cambridge Journal of Regions, Economy and Society* 3, no. 1 (March 1, 2010): 121–37, https://doi.org/10.1093/cjres/rsp034.

6. SMART CITIES AS PARTICIPATORY PLANNING

1. Peter Johnson and Pamela Robinson, "Civic Hackathons: Innovation, Procurement, or Civic Engagement?," *Review of Policy Research* 31, no. 4 (July 1, 2014): 349–57, https://doi.org/10.1111/ropr.12074; Brett Goldstein and Lauren Dyson, eds., *Beyond Transparency: Open Data and the Future of Civic Innovation* (San Francisco: Code for America Press, 2013); Christopher A. Le Dantec, *Designing Publics, Design Thinking, Design Theory* (Cambridge, MA: MIT Press, 2016); Thomas Lodato, Emma French, and Jennifer Clark, "Open Government Data in the Smart City: Interoperability, Urban Knowledge, and Linking Legacy Systems," *Journal of Urban Affairs*, October 16, 2018, https://doi.org/10.1080/07352166.2018.1511798.

2. Jennifer Clark and Susan Christopherson, "Integrating Investment and Equity: A Critical Regionalist Agenda for a Progressive Regionalism," *Journal of Planning Education and Research* 28, no. 3 (2009): 341–54, https://doi.org/10.1177/0739456X08327371; John Forester, "Bridging Interests and Community: Advocacy Planning and the Challenges of Deliberative Democracy," *Journal of the American Planning Association* 60, no. 2 (Spring 1994): 153; Pierre Clavel, "The Evolution of Advocacy Planning," *Journal of the American Planning Association* 60, no. 2 (Spring 1994): 146–49, https://doi.org/10.1080/01944369408975564.

3. Susan E. Clarke, "Neighborhood Policy Options: The Reagan Agenda," *Journal of the American Planning Association* 50, no. 4 (Autumn 1984): 493–501, https://doi.org/10.1080/01944368408976782.

4. Nate Gotlieb, "Neighborhood Groups Surprised by NRP Reallocation," Civic Beat, *Southwest Journal*, February 27, 2017, http://www.southwestjournal.com/news/civic-beat/2017/02/minneapolis-nrp-phase-ii-reallocation/.

5. Maria Manta Conroy and Jennifer Evans-Cowley, "E-Participation in Planning: An Analysis of Cities Adopting On-Line Citizen Participation Tools," *Environment and Planning C: Government and Policy* 24, no. 3 (June 2006): 371–84, https://doi.org/10.1068/c1k.

6. During a discussion in Boston in March 2018 that was facilitated by the Engagement Lab at Emerson College (The Right to the Smart City Symposium), a group of us developed the concept of a technology

upgrade to the neighborhood planning unit system, exemplified by the Atlanta system, as a possible framework for merging participatory planning and the digital civics and civic innovation work that often seemed to operate independent of it. The final report from that symposium, "Right to the Smart City: Designing for Public Value and Civic Participation," included a series of recommendations. In addition, in spring 2019, the Center for Civic Innovation in Atlanta launched a participatory design process to ascertain the viability of a variation on this concept.

7. Taylor Shelton and Ate Poorthuis, "The Nature of Neighborhoods: Using Big Data to Rethink the Geographies of Atlanta's Neighborhood Planning Unit System," October 25, 2018, https://doi.org/10.17605/OSF.IO/P9W2B.

8. Peer Hull Kristensen and Jonathan Zeitlin, *Local Players in Global Games: The Strategic Constitution of a Multinational Corporation* (Oxford: Oxford University Press, 2005); Susan Christopherson, "Market Rules and Territorial Outcomes: The Case of the United States," *International Journal of Urban and Regional Research* 17, no. 2 (June 1993): 274–88, https://doi.org/10.1111/j.1468-2427.1993.tb00481.x.

9. See *Guide to the General Data Protection Regulation (GDPR)*: "The GDPR applies to 'controllers' and 'processors'. A controller determines the purposes and means of processing personal data. A processor is responsible for processing personal data on behalf of a controller" (https://ico.org.uk/media/for-organisations/guide-to-data-protection/guide-to-the-general-data-protection-regulation-gdpr-1-0.pdf, p. 8).

10. Affirmative consent for specific uses of data collected on individuals is a long-standing requirement in social science research and governs the collection of data on individual characteristics in most, in not all, formal research settings (e.g., universities) under a formal structure called *institutional review boards*, or IRBs.

11. Economics & Statistics Administration, "Open Data Impact: How Zillow Uses Open Data to Level the Playing Field for Consumers," Economic & Statistics Administration, U.S. Department of Commerce, October 27, 2015, http://www.esa.doc.gov/under-secretary-blog/open-data-impact-how-zillow-uses-open-data-level-playing-field-consumers.

12. Economic and Social Research Council (ESRC), "Why GDPR Matters for Research," *ESRC Blog* (blog), May 25, 2018, https://blog .esrc.ac.uk/2018/05/25/why-gdpr-matters-for-research/.

13. This may change as cities seek alternative revenue models and commodify public assets. Increasingly, some cities are viewing data as a public asset to sell or license, much as they would public space.

14. Dietmar Offenhuber, "Infrastructure Legibility—A Comparative Analysis of Open311-Based Citizen Feedback Systems," *Cambridge Journal of Regions, Economy and Society* 8, no. 1 (March 1, 2015): 93–112, https://doi .org/10.1093/cjres/rsu001.

15. Village of Euclid, Ohio v. Ambler Realty Co., 272 U.S. 365 (1926).

16. Ugo Rossi, "The Variegated Economics and the Potential Politics of the Smart City," *Territory, Politics, Governance* 4, no. 3 (May 12, 2015): 337–53, https://doi.org/10.1080/21622671.2015.1036913.

17. James Defilippis, "From a Public Re-Creation to Private Recreation: The Transformation of Public Space in South Street Seaport," *Journal of Urban Affairs* 19, no. 4 (1997): 405; Matthew Goldstein and Patricia Cohen, "Public–Private Projects Where the Public Pays and Pays," DealBook, *New York Times*, June 6, 2017, https://www.nytimes .com/2017/06/06/business/dealbook/trump-infrastructure-plan -privatized-taxpayers.html; Matt A. V. Chaban, "Unwelcome Mat Is Out at Some of New York's Privately Owned Public Spaces," *New York Times*, September 7, 2015, http://www.nytimes.com/2015/09/08 /nyregion/unwelcome-mat-is-out-at-some-of-new-yorks-privately -owned-public-spaces.html; Jason R. Hackworth, *The Neoliberal City: Governance, Ideology, and Development in American Urbanism* (Ithaca, NY: Cornell University Press, 2007), http://www.loc.gov/catdir/toc /ecip0617/2006023306.html; Andrew E. G. Jonas, "The Formation of American Local Governments: Private Values in Public Institutions," *Journal of Regional Science* 35, no. 3 (August 1995): 517; Rachel Weber, "Extracting Value from the City: Neoliberalism and Urban Redevelopment," *Antipode* 34, no. 3 (July 1, 2002): 519–40, https://doi.org /10.1111/1467-8330.00253; Norman I. Fainstein and Susan S. Fainstein, "Economic Restructuring and the Politics of Land Use Planning in New York City," *Journal of the American Planning Association* 53, no. 2 (Spring 1987): 237–48, https://doi.org/10.1080/01944368708976658.

7. SMART CITIES AS THE NEW UNEVEN DEVELOPMENT

1. Peter Conradie and Sunil Choenni, "On the Barriers for Local Government Releasing Open Data," *Government Information Quarterly* 31, suppl. 1 (2014): S10–S17, https://doi.org/10.1016/j.giq.2014.01.003; Center for Open Data Enterprise, "Launching the U.S. Open Data Toolkit: Putting Government Data to Work," *Medium* (blog), July 24, 2018, https://medium.com/@odenterprise/launching-the-u-s-open-data-toolkit-putting-government-data-to-work-43207ba63af2; David Hand, "Open Data Is a Force for Good, but Not without Risks," *Guardian*, July 10, 2012, https://www.theguardian.com/society/2012/jul/10/open-data-force-for-good-risks; Erik Lakomaa and Jan Kallberg, "Open Data as a Foundation for Innovation: The Enabling Effect of Free Public Sector Information for Entrepreneurs," *IEEE Access* 1 (2013): 558–63, http://ieeexplore.ieee.org/stamp/stamp.jsp?tp=&arnumber=6584732&isnumber=633654; Brett Goldstein and Lauren Dyson, eds., *Beyond Transparency: Open Data and the Future of Civic Innovation* (San Francisco: Code for America Press, 2013).

2. Amir Hefetz and Mildred E. Warner, "Beyond the Market versus Planning Dichotomy: Understanding Privatisation and Its Reverse in US Cities," *Local Government Studies* 33, no. 4 (August 1, 2007): 555–72, https://doi.org/10.1080/03003930701417585; Amir Hefetz, Mildred E, Warner, and Eran Vigoda-Gadot, "Privatization and Intermunicipal Contracting: The US Local Government Experience 1992–2007," *Environment and Planning C: Government and Policy* 30, no. 4 (2012): 675–92, https://doi.org/10.1068/c11166.

3. Jennifer Clark, "Policy Through Practice: Local Communities, Self-Organization, and Policy," in *The New Oxford Handbook of Economic Geography*, 2nd ed., ed. Gordon L. Clark, Maryann P. Feldman, Meric S. Gertler, and Dariusz Wojcik (Oxford: Oxford University Press, 2018).

4. Rob Kitchin, "The Real-Time City? Big Data and Smart Urbanism," *GeoJournal* 79, no. 1 (February 1, 2014): 1–14, https://doi.org/10.1007/s10708-013-9516-8; Kristin Musulin, "What Mary Meeker's 2018 Trends Report Signals for Smart Cities," *Smart Cities Dive*, 2018,

https://www.smartcitiesdive.com/news/mary-meeker-2018-trends
-report-smart-cities/525038/; Karima Kourtit, Peter Nijkamp, and John
Steenbruggen, "The Significance of Digital Data Systems for Smart City
Policy," in "Digital Support Tools for Smart Cities," ed. Peter Nijkamp,
Roger Stough, Karima Kourtit, special issue, *Socio-Economic Planning
Sciences*, 58, no. suppl. C (June 1, 2017): 13–21, https://doi.org/10.1016/j
.seps.2016.10.001; Anthony M. Townsend, *Smart Cities: Big Data, Civic
Hackers, and the Quest for a New Utopia* (New York: Norton, 2013).

5. Peter S. Goodman, "In Britain, Austerity Is Changing Everything,"
World, *New York Times*, May 28, 2018, https://www.nytimes.com
/2018/05/28/world/europe/uk-austerity-poverty.html.

6. Melissa Gregg, "Hack for Good: Speculative Labour, App Development and the Burden of Austerity," *Fibreculture Journal*, no. 25 (2015):
185–202, https://doi.org/10.15307/fcj.25.186.2015.

7. Michael Dunford and Weidong Liu, "Uneven and Combined Development," *Regional Studies* 51, no. 1 (January 2, 2017): 69–85, https://
doi.org/10.1080/00343404.2016.1262946.

8. Doreen Massey, *Spatial Divisions of Labour: Social Structures and the
Geography of Production* (London: Macmillan, 1984).

9. Clark, "Policy Through Practice."

10. Emily Badger, "Tech Envisions the Ultimate Start-Up: An Entire
City," The Upshot, *New York Times*, February 24, 2018, https://www
.nytimes.com/2018/02/24/upshot/tech-envisions-the-ultimate-start
-up-an-entire-city.html.

11. Myron Orfield, *Metropolitics: A Regional Agenda for Community and
Stability* (Washington, DC: Brookings Institution Press, 1997); Susan
E. Clarke and Gary L. Gaile, *Work of Cities* (Minneapolis: University of
Minnesota Press, 1998); Gerald Frug, *City Making: Building Communi-
ties without Building Walls* (Princeton, NJ: Princeton University Press,
2001); Manuel Pastor, *Regions That Work: How Cities and Suburbs Can
Grow Together*. Globalization and Community, Vol. 6 (Minneapolis:
University of Minnesota Press, 2000).

12. Simona Iammarino, Andres Rodríguez-Pose, and Michael Storper,
"Regional Inequality in Europe: Evidence, Theory and Policy Implications" (London: Centre for Economic Policy Research, 2018), https://
cepr.org/active/publications/discussion_papers/dp.php?dpno=12841.

13. Michael Wines, "Drive against Gerrymandering Finds New Life in Ballot Initiatives," U.S., *New York Times*, July 23, 2018, https://www.nytimes.com/2018/07/23/us/gerrymandering-states.html.

14. Emily Badger, "Are Rural Voters the 'Real' Voters? Wisconsin Republicans Seem to Think So," The Upshot, *New York Times*, December 6, 2018, https://www.nytimes.com/2018/12/06/upshot/wisconsin-republicans -rural-urban-voters.html.

15. Susan Christopherson, H. Garretsen, and R. Martin, "The World Is Not Flat: Putting Globalization in Its Place," *Cambridge Journal of Regions, Economy and Society* 1, no. 3 (November 1, 2008): 343–49, https://doi .org/10.1093/cjres/rsn023.

16. Rachel Weber, *From Boom to Bubble: How Finance Built the New Chicago* (Chicago: University of Chicago Press, 2015).

17. Harry Charles Katz and Owen Darbishire, *Converging Divergences: Worldwide Changes in Employment Systems* (Ithaca, NY: Cornell University Press, 1999).

18. Saskia Sassen, *The Global City: New York, London, Tokyo* (Princeton, NJ: Princeton University Press, 2001); Peter Taylor and Ben Derudder, *World City Network: A Global Urban Analysis*, 2nd ed. (Abingdon, UK: Routledge, 2015).

19. Michael Storper, *The Regional World: Territorial Development in a Global Economy* (New York: Guilford Press, 1997); Allen Scott, *Regions and the World Economy: The Coming Shape of Global Production, Competition, and Political Order* (Oxford: Oxford University Press, 1998).

20. Jennifer Clark, "Siting 'Scientific Spaces' in the US: The Push and Pull of Regional Development Strategies and National Innovation Policies," *Environment and Planning C: Government and Policy* 32, no. 5 (October 2014): 880–95, https://doi.org/10.1068/c1271r.

21. Susan Christopherson and Jennifer Clark, *Remaking Regional Economies: Power, Labor, and Firm Strategies in the Knowledge Economy* (New York: Routledge, 2007).

22. Ron A. Boschma, "Proximity and Innovation: A Critical Assessment," *Regional Studies* 39, no. 1 (2005): 61–74, https://doi.org/10.1080 /0034340052000320887.

23. Stefano de Falco, Margarita Angelidou, and Jean-Paul D. Addie, "From the 'Smart City' to the 'Smart Metropolis'? Building Resilience in the Urban Periphery," *European Urban and Regional Studies* 26, no. 2 (April 2019): -5–23, https://doi.org/10.1177/0969776418783813;

Andre Perry, "Opinion | Who Gets Left Out of the Urban Tech Boom?," Opinion, *New York Times*, July 21, 2018, https://www.nytimes.com /2018/07/19/opinion/amazon-hq2-google-pittsburgh-jobs.html.

24. The Smart and Connected Communities program within the National Science Foundation restructured its funding calls in 2018 to remove the explicit focus on cities:

> Communities in the United States . . . and around the world are entering a new era of transformation in which residents and their surrounding environments are increasingly connected through rapidly-changing intelligent technologies. This transformation offers great promise for improved wellbeing and prosperity, but poses significant challenges at the complex intersection of technology and society. The goal of the NSF Smart and Connected Communities (S&CC) program solicitation is to accelerate the creation of the scientific and engineering foundations that will enable smart and connected communities to bring about new levels of economic opportunity and growth, safety and security, health and wellness, and overall quality of life. This goal will be achieved through integrative research projects that pair advances in technological and social dimensions with meaningful community engagement. For the purposes of this solicitation, communities are defined as having geographically-delineated boundaries—such as towns, cities, counties, neighborhoods, community districts, rural areas, and tribal regions—consisting of various populations, with the structure and ability to engage in meaningful ways with proposed research activities. A "smart and connected community" is, in turn, a community that synergistically integrates intelligent technologies with the natural and built environments, including infrastructure, to improve the social, economic, and environmental well-being of those who live, work, or travel within it. Smart and Connected Communities (S&CC), (U.S. National Science Foundation, 2018), https://www.nsf.gov/funding/pgm_summ .jsp?pims_id=505364.

25. Clark, "Siting 'Scientific Spaces' in the US."
26. Eduardo Porter, "Why Big Cities Thrive, and Smaller Ones Are Being Left Behind," Economy, *New York Times*, October 10, 2017, https:// www.nytimes.com/2017/10/10/business/economy/big-cities.html.

27. Allan Holmes, "5G Cell Service Is Coming. Who Decides Where It Goes?," Technology, *New York Times*, March 2, 2018, https://www.nytimes.com/2018/03/02/technology/5g-cellular-service.html.

28. Jacob Kastrenakes, "AT&T's 5G Network Goes Live in 12 Cities—but You Can't Use It Yet," *The Verge*, December 18, 2018, https://www.theverge.com/2018/12/18/18146246/att-5g-us-launch-hotspot-service-plan-price.

29. Holmes, "5G Cell Service Is Coming. Who Decides Where It Goes?"

30. Sharon Zukin, "Changing Landscapes of Power: Opulence and the Urge for Authenticity," *International Journal of Urban and Regional Research* 33, no. 2 (June 2009): 543–53, https://doi.org/10.1111/j.1468-2427.2009.00867.x.

31. Sharon Zukin, *Naked City: The Death and Life of Authentic Urban Places*, repr. ed. (Oxford: Oxford University Press, 2011).

32. John H. Mollenkopf and Manuel Castells, *Dual City: Restructuring New York* (New York: Russell Sage Foundation, 1991); Matthew P. Drennan, *The Information Economy and American Cities* (Baltimore, MD: Johns Hopkins University Press, 2002); Robert A. Caro, *The Power Broker: Robert Moses and the Fall of New York* (New York: Vintage, 1975).

33. Jennifer Clark and David Bailey, "Labour, Work and Regional Resilience," *Regional Studies* 52, no. 6 (June 3, 2018): 741–44, https://doi.org/10.1080/00343404.2018.1448621.

34. Georgios Zervas, Davide Proserpio, and John W. Byers, "The Impact of the Sharing Economy on the Hotel Industry: Evidence from Airbnb's Entry into the Texas Market," in *Proceedings of the Sixteenth ACM Conference on Economics and Computation*, EC '15 (New York: Association for Computing Machinery, 2015), 637, https://doi.org/10.1145/2764468.2764524; Emily Badger, "What's the Right Number of Taxis (or Uber or Lyft Cars) in a City?," The Upshot, *New York Times*, August 10, 2018, https://www.nytimes.com/2018/08/10/upshot/uber-lyft-taxi-ideal-number-per-city.html; Janet Burns, "New York Gives Uber Drivers Unemployment Rights in Blow to Nonemployee Model," *Forbes*, July 20, 2018, https://www.forbes.com/sites/janetwburns/2018/07/20/new-york-gives-uber-drivers-unemployment-rights-in-blow-to-non-employee-model/; Emma G. Fitzsimmons, "New York City Caps Uber and Lyft Vehicles in a Crackdown," New York, *New York Times*, August 9, 2018, https://www.nytimes.com/2018/08/08/nyregion/uber-vote-city-council-cap.html; Mike O'Brien, "A New Law

Is Letting Uber Drivers Unionize," *The Nation*, July 1, 2016, https://www.thenation.com/article/a-new-law-is-letting-uber-drivers-unionize/; Heather Somerville, "Seattle Passes Law Letting Uber, Lyft Drivers Unionize," *Reuters*, December 15, 2015, https://www.reuters.com/article/us-washington-uber/seattle-passes-law-letting-uber-lyft-drivers-unionize-idUSKBN0TX2NO20151215; Noam Scheiber, "Labor Dept. Says Workers at a Gig Company Are Contractors," Economy, *New York Times*, April 29, 2019, https://www.nytimes.com/2019/04/29/business/economy/gig-economy-workers-contractors.html.

35. "The Uber Workplace in DC" (Washington, DC: Kalmanovitz Initiative for Labor and the Working Poor, Georgetown University, April 2019), https://lwp.georgetown.edu/wp-content/uploads/Uber-Workplace.pdf.

36. Kendra Strauss, "Precarious Work and Winner-Take-All Economies," in *The New Oxford Handbook of Economic Geography*, ed. Gordon L. Clark et al. (Oxford: Oxford University Press, 2018), 1–11.

37. Eduardo Porter, "Tech Is Splitting the U.S. Work Force in Two," Business, *New York Times*, March 12, 2019, https://www.nytimes.com/2019/02/04/business/economy/productivity-inequality-wages.html.

38. J. K. Gibson-Graham, Jenny Cameron, and Stephen Healy, *Take Back the Economy* (Minneapolis: University of Minnesota Press, 2013).

8. CONCLUSIONS:
THE LOCAL IS (NOT) THE ENEMY

1. Carlo Ratti and Matthew Claudel, *The City of Tomorrow: Sensors, Networks, Hackers, and the Future of Urban Life* (New Haven, CT: Yale University Press, 2016).

2. Kelly Vencill Sanchez, "Will Smart Cities Make Life Easier for Everyone?," *Dwell* (July 20, 2018), https://www.dwell.com/article/smart-city-technology-mit-sensable-cities-lab-6b26d0a3.

3. Many political science books itemize common propaganda techniques. Here I am relying on a mimeographed list of 13 common propaganda techniques from my sixth-grade teacher, Mrs. Williams.

4. Carl V. Patton, David S. Sawicki, and Jennifer Clark, *Basic Methods of Policy Analysis and Planning*, 3rd ed. (New York: Routledge, 2013).

5. See, for example, the Metrolab Network's human services guide, "First, Do No Harm: Ethical Guidelines for Applying Predictive Tools Within Human Services," Data Science and Human Services Lab (Washington, DC, 2017), https://metrolabnetwork.org/wp-content/uploads/2017/09/Ethical-Guidelines-for-Applying-Predictive-Tools-within-Human-Services_Sept-2017.pdf.

6. Trevor J. Barnes and Matthew W. Wilson, "Big Data, Social Physics, and Spatial Analysis: The Early Years," *Big Data & Society* 1, no. 1 (July 10, 2014), https://doi.org/10.1177/2053951714535365; Trevor J. Barnes, "Retheorizing Economic Geography: From the Quantitative Revolution to the 'Cultural Turn,'" *Annals of the Association of American Geographers* 91, no. 3 (September 2001): 546–65, https://doi.org/10.1111/0004-5608.00258.

7. Winnie Hu, "Congestion Pricing Falters in New York, Again," New York, *New York Times*, April 1, 2018, https://www.nytimes.com/2018/03/31/nyregion/congestion-pricing-new-york.html; Winnie Hu, "Over $10 to Drive in Manhattan? What We Know about the Congestion Pricing Plan," New York, *New York Times*, March 28, 2019, https://www.nytimes.com/2019/03/26/nyregion/what-is-congestion-pricing.html; Aarian Marshall, "The Age of Congestion Pricing May Finally Be upon Us," *Wired*, March 1, 2019, https://www.wired.com/story/age-of-congestion-pricing-nyc/.

8. Emily Badger, "Blue Cities Want to Make Their Own Rules. Red States Won't Let Them.," The Upshot, *New York Times*, July 6, 2017, https://www.nytimes.com/2017/07/06/upshot/blue-cities-want-to-make-their-own-rules-red-states-wont-let-them.html.

9. Dolores Hayden, "What Would a Non-Sexist City Be Like? Speculations on Housing, Urban Design, and Human Work," *Signs: Journal of Women in Culture and Society* 5, no. S3 (1980): S170–S187.

10. Dolores Hayden, *Redesigning the American Dream: The Future of Housing, Work, and Family Life* (New York: Norton, 1984).

11. Ratti and Claudel, *The City of Tomorrow*; Rima Auof, "'China Is One of the Best Places for Experimenting' with Urban Technology Says Carlo Ratti," de zeen, April 25, 2019, https://www.dezeen.com/2019/04/25/carlo-ratti-interview-china-smart-cities-urban-technology-shenzhen-biennale/.

EPILOGUE: THE VIEW FROM INSIDE THE
URBAN INNOVATION PROJECT

1. Dolores Hayden, *Redesigning the American Dream: The Future of Housing, Work, and Family Life* (New York: Norton, 1984).
2. Jennifer Clark, "Resilient Regions and Open Innovation: The Evolution of Smart Cities and Civic Entrepreneurship," in *Creating Resilient Economies: Entrepreneurship, Growth and Development in Uncertain Times*, ed. Tim Vorley and Nick Williams (Northampton, MA: Edward Elgar, 2017), 109–22, http://www.e-elgar.com/shop/creating-resilient-economies.
3. Susan Christopherson and Jennifer Clark, "Power in Firm Networks: What It Means for Regional Innovation Systems," *Regional Studies* 41, no. 9 (2007) 1223–36, https://doi.org/10.1080/00343400701543330; Susan Christopherson and Jennifer Clark, *Remaking Regional Economies: Power, Labor, and Firm Strategies in the Knowledge Economy* (New York: Routledge, 2007); Jennifer Clark, *Working Regions: Reconnecting Innovation and Production in the Knowledge Economy* (London: Routledge, 2013).
4. Maryann P. Feldman, "Where Science Comes to Life: University Bioscience, Commercial Spin-Offs, and Regional Economic Development," *Journal of Comparative Policy Analysis* 2, no. 3 (2000): 345–61, https://doi.org/10.1080/1387698000841265I; Harley F. Etienne, *Pushing Back the Gates: Neighborhood Perspectives on University-Driven Revitalization in West Philadelphia* (Philadelphia: Temple University Press, 2012); John Harrison and Ivan Turok, "Universities, Knowledge and Regional Development," *Regional Studies* 51, no. 7 (July 3, 2017): 977–81, https://doi.org/10.1080/00343404.2017.1328189.
5. Clark, *Working Regions*.
6. Joan Fitzgerald and Nancey Green Leigh, *Economic Revitalization: Cases and Strategies for City and Suburb* (Thousand Oaks, CA: SAGE, 2002); Andy Pike, Andrés Rodríguez-Pose, and John Tomaney, *Local and Regional Development* (New York: Routledge, 2006), http://www.loc.gov/catdir/enhancements/fy0654/2006005421-d.html.
7. Jennifer Clark and David Bailey, "Labour, Work and Regional Resilience," *Regional Studies* 52, no. 6 (June 3, 2018): 741–44, https://doi.org/10.1080/00343404.2018.1448621; Ivan Turok et al., "Global Reversal,

Regional Revival?," *Regional Studies* 51, no. 1 (January 2, 2017): 1–8, https://doi.org/10.1080/00343404.2016.1255720; David Bailey, Christos Pitelis, and Philip R. Tomlinson, "A Place-Based Developmental Regional Industrial Strategy for Sustainable Capture of Co-Created Value," *Cambridge Journal of Economics* 42, no. 6 (November 2018): 1521–42, https://doi.org/10.1093/cje/bey019.

8. Fred Block, "A Strategy for Rebuilding the Manufacturing Sector in the United States" (The Century Foundation, September 20, 2017), https://s3-us-west-2.amazonaws.com/production.tcf.org/app/uploads /2017/09/20104210/a-strategy-for-rebuilding-the-manufacturing-sector -in-the-united-states.pdf; Jennifer Clark and Marc Doussard, "Devolution, Disinvestment and Uneven Development: US Industrial Policy and Evolution of the National Network for Manufacturing Innovation," *Cambridge Journal of Regions, Economies, and Society* 12, no. 2 (July 2019): 251–70, https://doi.org/10.1093/cjres/rsz009.

9. Jennifer Clark, John Harrison, and Ernest Miguelez, "Connecting Cities, Revitalizing Regions: The Centrality of Cities to Regional Development," *Regional Studies* 52, no. 8 (August 3, 2018): 1025–28, https://doi.org/10.1080/00343404.2018.1453691.

10. Jamie Peck, *Offshore: Exploring the Worlds of Global Outsourcing* (Oxford: Oxford University Press, 2017).

11. Bennett Harrison, *Lean and Mean: The Changing Landscape of Corporate Power in the Age of Flexibility* (New York: Basic Books, 1994).

12. John P. Holdren et al., *Technology and the Future of Cities* (Washington, DC: Executive Office of the President, President's Council of Advisors on Science and Technology, February 2016).

13. Jane Jacobs, *The Death and Life of Great American Cities* (New York: Vintage, 1961).

14. Carl V. Patton, David S. Sawicki, and Jennifer Clark, *Basic Methods of Policy Analysis and Planning*, 3rd ed. (Upper Saddle River, NJ: Routledge, 2013); Jamie Peck and Nik Theodore, *Fast Policy: Experimental Statecraft at the Thresholds of Neoliberalism* (Minneapolis: University of Minnesota Press, 2015).

15. Susan Christopherson, "On Being Outside 'the Project,'" *Antipode* 21, no. 2 (1989): 83–89, https://doi.org/10.1111/j.1467-8330.1989.tb00181.x.

BIBLIOGRAPHY

Agyeman, Julian, and Duncan McLaren. 2016. "Apps Don't Make a City Smart." Opinions, *Boston Globe*. August 14, 2016. https://www.bostonglobe .com/ideas/2016/08/13/apps-don-make-city-smart/YrEuTHcHAFA rq5piutınrN/story.html.

Altshuler, Alan A. 1981. *The Urban Transportation System: Politics and Policy Innovation*. Cambridge, MA: MIT Press.

Amin, Ash, and Nigel Thrift. 2016. *Seeing Like a City*. Cambridge, UK: Polity.

Ashton, Philip, Rachel Weber, and Matthew Zook. 2017. "The Cloud, the Crowd, and the City: How New Data Practices Reconfigure Urban Governance?" *Big Data & Society* 4, no. 1 (June). https://doi.org/10.1177 /2053951717706718.

Auof, Rima. 2019. "'China Is One of the Best Places for Experimenting' with Urban Technology Says Carlo Ratti." de zeen (April 25). https://www .dezeen.com/2019/04/25/carlo-ratti-interview-china-smart-cities-urban -technology-shenzhen-biennale/.

Badger, Emily. 2017. "Blue Cities Want to Make Their Own Rules. Red States Won't Let Them." The Upshot, *New York Times*, July 6, 2017. https://www .nytimes.com/2017/07/06/upshot/blue-cities-want-to-make-their-own -rules-red-states-wont-let-them.html.

———. 2018a. "Are Rural Voters the 'Real' Voters? Wisconsin Republicans Seem to Think So." The Upshot, *New York Times*, December 6, 2018. https://www.nytimes.com/2018/12/06/upshot/wisconsin-republicans -rural-urban-voters.html.

———. 2018b. "Tech Envisions the Ultimate Start-Up: An Entire City." The Upshot, *New York Times*, February 24, 2018. https://www.nytimes.com/2018/02/24/upshot/tech-envisions-the-ultimate-start-up-an-entire-city.html.

———. 2018c. "What's the Right Number of Taxis (or Uber or Lyft Cars) in a City?" The Upshot, *New York Times*, August 10, 2018. https://www.nytimes.com/2018/08/10/upshot/uber-lyft-taxi-ideal-number-per-city.html.

———. 2018d. "Why Cities Can't Stop Poaching from One Another." The Upshot, *New York Times*, June 8, 2018. https://www.nytimes.com/2018/06/08/upshot/why-cities-cant-stop-poaching-from-one-another.html.

Bailey, David, Helena Lenihan, and Alex De Ruyter. 2016. "A Cautionary Tale of Two 'Tigers': Industrial Policy 'Lessons' from Ireland and Hungary?" *Local Economy* 31, no. 8 (December 1): 873–91. https://doi.org/10.1177/0269094216677779.

Bailey, David, Christos Pitelis, and Philip R. Tomlinson. 2018. "A Place-Based Developmental Regional Industrial Strategy for Sustainable Capture of Co-Created Value." *Cambridge Journal of Economics* 42, no. 6 (November): 1521–42. https://doi.org/10.1093/cje/bey019.

Barnes, Trevor J. 2001. "Retheorizing Economic Geography: From the Quantitative Revolution to the 'Cultural Turn.'" *Annals of the Association of American Geographers* 91, no. 3 (September): 546–65. https://doi.org/10.1111/0004-5608.00258..

Barnes, Trevor J., and Matthew W, Wilson. 2014. "Big Data, Social Physics, and Spatial Analysis: The Early Years." *Big Data & Society* 1, no. 1 (July 10). https://doi.org/10.1177/2053951714535365.

Bathelt, Harald, Anders Malmberg, and Peter Maskell. 2004. "Clusters and Knowledge: Local Buzz, Global Pipelines and the Process of Knowledge Creation." *Progress in Human Geography* 28, no. 1: 31–56, https://doi.org/10.1191/0309132504ph469oa.

Batty, Michael. 2017. *The New Science of Cities*. Reprint, Cambridge, MA: MIT Press, 2017.

Benner, Chris. 2002. *Work in the New Economy: Flexible Labor Markets in Silicon Valley.* Oxford, UK: Blackwell.

Betsill, Michele M., and Harriet Bulkeley. 2004. "Transnational Networks and Global Environmental Governance: The Cities for Climate Protection

Program." *International Studies Quarterly* 48, no. 2 (June 1): 471–93. https://doi.org/10.1111/j.0020-8833.2004.00310.x.

Binz, Christian, Bernhard Truffer, and Lars Coenen. 2014. "Why Space Matters in Technological Innovation Systems—Mapping Global Knowledge Dynamics of Membrane Bioreactor Technology." *Research Policy* 43, no. 1: 138–55. https://doi.org/10.1016/j.respol.2013.07.002.

Blinder, Alan, and Nicole Perlroth. 2018. "A Cyberattack Hobbles Atlanta, and Security Experts Shudder." U.S., *New York Times*, March 29, 2018. https://www.nytimes.com/2018/03/27/us/cyberattack-atlanta-ransomware.html.

Block, Fred. 2017. "A Strategy for Rebuilding the Manufacturing Sector in the United States." The Century Foundation, September 20, 2017. https://s3-us-west-2.amazonaws.com/production.tcf.org/app/uploads/2017/09/20104210/a-strategy-for-rebuilding-the-manufacturing-sector-in-the-united-states.pdf.

——. 2019. "Problems with the Concept of Capitalism in the Social Sciences." *Environment and Planning A: Economy and Space* 51, no. 5: 1166–77. https://doi.org/10.1177/0308518X19838866.

Bloomberg, Michael R., and Anne Hidalgo. 2015. "Why Cities Will Be Vital Players at Paris Climate Talks." *Huff Post* (blog), June 30, 2015. https://www.huffingtonpost.com/michael-bloomberg/paris-climate-talks-bloomberg_b_7683246.html.

Bloomberg Philanthropies. 2015. "City Hall Innovation Team Handbook: The Innovation Delivery Approach to Develop and Deliver Bold Innovation." New York: Bloomberg Philanthropies, March. https://www.bbhub.io/dotorg/sites/2/2014/08/Innovation-Team-Playbook_2015.pdf.

——. 2018. "Mike Bloomberg Names Los Angeles, Portland, San Diego, and San Jose as Winners in Bloomberg American Cities Climate Challenge." October 17, 2018. https://www.bloomberg.org/press/releases/mike-bloomberg-names-los-angeles-portland-san-diego-san-jose-winners-bloomberg-american-cities-climate-challenge/. Bolan, Richard S. 1980. "The Practitioner as Theorist." *Journal of the American Planning Association* 46, no. 3 (July): 261–74. https://doi.org/10.1080/01944368008977042.

——. 1999. "Rationality Revisited: An Alternative Perspective on Reason in Management and Planning." *Journal of Management History* 5, no. 2: 68–86. https://doi.org/10.1108/13552529910260082.

Boschma, Ron A. 2005. "Proximity and Innovation: A Critical Assessment." *Regional Studies* 39, no. 1: 61–74. https://doi.org/10.1080/0034340052000320887.

Boschma, Ron A., and Koen Frenken. 2006. "Why Is Economic Geography Not an Evolutionary Science? Towards an Evolutionary Economic Geography." *Journal of Economic Geography* 6, no. 3 (June 1): 273–302. https://doi.org/10.1093/jeg/lbi022.

Brenner, Neil, and Nikolas Theodore. 2002. "Cities and the Geographies of 'Actually Existing Neoliberalism.'" *Antipode* 34, no. 3 (June): 349–79. https://doi.org/10.1111/1467-8330.00246.

Bristow, Gillian. 2005. "Everyone's a 'Winner': Problematising the Discourse of Regional Competitiveness." *Journal of Economic Geography* 5, no. 3 (2005): 285–304.

Bulkeley, Harriet, and Michele M. Betsill. 2005. "Rethinking Sustainable Cities: Multilevel Governance and the 'Urban' Politics of Climate Change." *Environmental Politics* 14, no. 1 (February 1): 42–63. https://doi .org/10.1080/0964401042000310178.

——. 2013. "Revisiting the Urban Politics of Climate Change." *Environmental Politics* 22, no. 1136–54. https://doi.org/10.1080/09644016.2013.755797.

Bulkeley, Harriet, Pauline M. McGuirk, and Robyn Dowling. 2016. "Making a Smart City for the Smart Grid? The Urban Material Politics of Actualising Smart Electricity Networks." *Environment and Planning A: Economy and Space* 48, no. 9 (September): 1709–26. https://doi.org /10.1177/0308518X16648152.

Burns, Alexander. 2017. "Bloomberg's Next Anti-Washington Move: $200 Million Program for Mayors." Politics, *New York Times*, June 25, 2017. https://www.nytimes.com/2017/06/25/us/politics/michael-bloomberg -mayors-trump.html.

Burns, Janet. 2018. "New York Gives Uber Drivers Unemployment Rights in Blow to Nonemployee Model." *Forbes*, July 20, 2018. https://www.forbes .com/sites/janetwburns/2018/07/20/new-york-gives-uber-drivers -unemployment-rights-in-blow-to-non-employee-model/.

Camagni, Roberto, Lidia Daippi, and Giorgio Leonardi. 1986. "Urban Growth and Decline in a Hierarchical System: A Supply-Oriented Dynamic Approach." *Regional Science and Urban Economics* 16, no. 1: 145.

Carnoy, Martin, Manuel Castells, and Chris Benner. 1997. "Labour Markets and Employment Practices in the Age of Flexibility: A Case Study of Silicon Valley." *International Labour Review* 136, no. 1 (Spring): 27.

Caro, Robert A. 1975. *The Power Broker: Robert Moses and the Fall of New York*. New York: Vintage.

Carre, Francoise, Virginia duRivage, and Chris Tilly. 1994. "Representing the Part-Time and Contingent Workforce: Challenges for Unions and Public Policy." Pages 314–23 in *Restoring the Promise of American Labor Law*, ed. Sheldon Friedman et al.. Ithaca, NY: ILR Press.

Carriero, Rebecca. 2018. "Mike Bloomberg's Annual Letter on Philanthropy." Bloomberg Philanthropies, May 23, 2018. https://www.bloomberg.org /press/releases/mike-bloombergs-annual-letter-philanthropy-says -mayors-data-antidote-washingtons-divisive-assault-facts/.

Castells, Manuel, and Peter Hall. 1994. *Technopoles of the World: The Making of Twenty-First-Century Industrial Complexes*. London: Routledge.

Center for Open Data Enterprise. 2018. "Launching the U.S. Open Data Toolkit: Putting Government Data to Work." *Medium* (blog), July 24. https://medium.com/@odenterprise/launching-the-u-s-open-data -toolkit-putting-government-data-to-work-43207ba63af2.

Chaban, Matt A. V. 2015. "Unwelcome Mat Is Out at Some of New York's Privately Owned Public Spaces." *New York Times*, September 7, 2015. http://www.nytimes.com/2015/09/08/nyregion/unwelcome-mat-is-out -at-some-of-new-yorks-privately-owned-public-spaces.html.

Christopherson, Susan. 1989. "On Being Outside 'the Project.'" *Antipode* 21, no. 2: 83–89. https://doi.org/10.1111/j.1467-8330.1989.tb00181.x.

——. 1993. "Market Rules and Territorial Outcomes: The Case of the United States." *International Journal of Urban and Regional Research* 17, no. 2 (June): 274–88. https://doi.org/10.1111/j.1468-2427.1993.tb00481.x.

——. 2002. "Why Do National Labor Market Practices Continue to Diverge in the Global Economy? The 'Missing Link' of Investment Rules." *Economic Geography* 78, no. 1 (January): 1–20, https://doi.org /10.1111/j.1944-8287.2002.tb00173.x.

Christopherson, Susan, and Jennifer Clark. 2007a. "Power in Firm Networks: What It Means for Regional Innovation Systems." *Regional Studies* 41, no. 9: 1223–36.

——. 2007b. *Remaking Regional Economies: Power, Labor, and Firm Strategies in the Knowledge Economy*. Geography. New York: Routledge.

Christopherson, Susan, H. Garretsen, and R. Martin. 2008. "The World Is Not Flat: Putting Globalization in Its Place." *Cambridge Journal of Regions, Economy and Society* 1, no. 3 (November 1): 343–49. https://doi .org/10.1093/cjres/rsn023.

Christopherson, Susan, Michael Kitson, and Jonathan Michie. 2008. "Innovation, Networks and Knowledge Exchange." *Cambridge Journal of Regions, Economy and Society* 1, no. 2: 165–73. https://doi.org/10.1093/cjres/rsn015.

Clark, Don. 2019. "5G Is Coming This Year. Here's What You Need to Know." Technology, *New York Times*, January 1, 2019. https://www.nytimes.com /2018/12/31/technology/personaltech/5g-what-you-need-to-know.html.

Clark, Gordon. 1989. *Unions and Communities Under Siege: American Communities and the Crisis of Organized Labor.* Cambridge: Cambridge University Press.

Clark, Gordon, Maryann P. Feldman, Meric S. Gertler, and Dariusz Wójcik, eds. 2018. *The New Oxford Handbook of Economic Geography.* Oxford: Oxford University Press.

Clark, Jennifer. 2010. "Coordinating a Conscious Geography: The Role of Research Centers in Multi-Scalar Innovation Policy and Economic Development in the US and Canada." *Journal of Technology Transfer* 35, no. 5: 460–74. https://doi.org/10.1007/s10961-009-9137-z.

——. 2013. *Working Regions: Reconnecting Innovation and Production in the Knowledge Economy.* London: Routledge.

——. 2014. "Manufacturing by Design: The Rise of Regional Intermediaries and the Reemergence of Collective Action." *Cambridge Journal of Regions, Economy and Society* 7, no. 3: 433–48. https://doi.org/10.1093/cjres/rsu017.

——. 2014. "Siting 'Scientific Spaces" in the US: The Push and Pull of Regional Development Strategies and National Innovation Policies."" *Environment and Planning C: Government and Policy* 32, no. 5 (October): 880–95. https://doi.org/10.1068/c1271r.

——. 2015. "Hidden in Plain Sight: The North American Optics and Photonics Industry." In *The Handbook of Manufacturing Industries in the Global Economy*, ed. John Bryson, Jennifer Clark, and Vida Vanchan. Northampton, MA: Edward Elgar.

——. 2017a. "Designing the Smart City: A Programmatic Approach to Inclusive Innovation in Atlanta." *Atlanta Studies*, September 19, 2017. https://doi.org/10.18737/atls20170919.

——. 2017b. "Resilient Regions and Open Innovation: The Evolution of Smart Cities and Civic Entrepreneurship." Pages 109–22 in *Creating Resilient Economies: Entrepreneurship, Growth and Development in Uncertain Times*, ed. Tim Vorley and Nick Williams. Northampton, MA: Edward Elgar. http://www.e-elgar.com/shop/creating-resilient-economies.

——. 2018. "Policy Through Practice: Local Communities, Self-Organization, and Policy." In *The New Oxford Handbook of Economic Geography*, ed. Gordon L. Clark, Maryann P. Feldman, Meric S. Gertler, and Dariusz Wojcik, 2nd ed. Oxford: Oxford University Press.

——. 2019. "Remodeling Capitalism: A Return to Scale." *Environment and Planning A: Economy and Space* 51, no.5: 1178-80. https://doi.org/10.1177/0308518X19851320.

Clark, Jennifer, and David Bailey. 2018. "Labour, Work and Regional Resilience." *Regional Studies* 52, no. 6 (June 3, 2018): 741–44. https://doi.org/10.1080/00343404.2018.1448621.

Clark, Jennifer, and Susan Christopherson. 2009. "Integrating Investment and Equity: A Critical Regionalist Agenda for a Progressive Regionalism." *Journal of Planning Education and Research* 28, no. 3: 341. https://doi.org/10.1177/0739456X08327371.

Clark, Jennifer, and Marc Doussard. 2019. "Devolution, Disinvestment and Uneven Development: US Industrial Policy and Evolution of the National Network for Manufacturing Innovation." *Cambridge Journal of Regions, Economies, and Society* 12, no. 2 (July): 251–70, https://doi.org/10.1093/cjres/rsz009.

Clark, Jennifer, John Harrison, and Ernest Miguelez. 2018. "Connecting Cities, Revitalizing Regions: The Centrality of Cities to Regional Development." *Regional Studies* 52, no. 8 (August 3): 1025–28. https://doi.org/10.1080/00343404.2018.1453691.

Clark, Jennifer, Hsin-I. Huang, and John P. Walsh. 2010. "A Typology of Innovation Districts: What It Means for Regional Resilience." *Cambridge Journal of Regions, Economies, and Society* 3, no. 1: 121–37. https://doi.org/10.1093/cjres/rsp034.

Clark, Jennifer, and Supraja Sudharsan. 2019. "Firm Strategies and Path Dependencies: An Emerging Economic Geography of Industrial Data." *Regional Studies* July 3. https://doi.org/10.1080/00343404.2019.1619926.

Clarke, Susan E. 1984. "Neighborhood Policy Options: The Reagan Agenda." *Journal of the American Planning Association* 50, no. 4 (Autumn): 493–501. https://doi.org/10.1080/01944368408976782.

Clarke, Susan E., and Gary L. Gaile. 1998. *Work of Cities*. Minneapolis: University of Minnesota Press.

Clavel, Pierre. 1986. *The Progressive City: Planning and Participation, 1969–1984*. New Brunswick, NJ: Rutgers University Press, xviii, 262.

——. 1994. "The Evolution of Advocacy Planning." *Journal of the American Planning Association* 60, no. 2 (Spring): 146–49. https://doi.org/10.1080/01944369408975564.

——. 2010. *Activists in City Hall: The Progressive Response to the Reagan Era in Boston and Chicago*. Ithaca, NY: Cornell University Press.

Clavel, Pierre, and Robert Kraushaar. 1998. "On Being Unreasonable: Progressive Planning in Sheffield and Chicago." *International Planning Studies* 3, no. 2 (June): 143–62. https://doi.org/10.1080/13563479808721706.

Cohen, Patricia. 2019. "In Amazon Fight, Progressives Showed What They Want: A New Economic Agenda." Business, *New York Times*, February 17, 2019. https://www.nytimes.com/2019/02/16/business/amazon-economy-taxes.html.

Conradie, Peter, and Sunil Choenni. 2014. "On the Barriers for Local Government Releasing Open Data." *Government Information Quarterly* 31, suppl. 1: S10–S17. https://doi.org/10.1016/j.giq.2014.01.003.

Conroy, Maria Manta, and Jennifer Evans-Cowley. 2006. "E-Participation in Planning: An Analysis of Cities Adopting On-Line Citizen Participation Tools." *Environment and Planning C: Government and Policy* 24, no. 3 (June): 371–84. https://doi.org/10.1068/c1k.

Cook, Ian R., and Kevin Ward. 2011. "Trans-Urban Networks of Learning, Mega Events and Policy Tourism: The Case of Manchester's Commonwealth and Olympic Games Projects." *Urban Studies* 48, no. 12 (September): 2519–35. https://doi.org/10.1177/0042098011411941.

Craig, William J., Trevor M. Harris, and Daniel Weiner, eds. 2002. *Community Participation and Geographic Information Systems*. London: Taylor & Francis.

Crivello, Silvia. 2015. "Urban Policy Mobilities: The Case of Turin as a Smart City." *European Planning Studies* 23, no. 5 (May 4): 909–21. https://doi.org/10.1080/09654313.2014.891568.

Dalton, Craig M., Linnet Taylor, and Jim Thatcher. 2016. "Critical Data Studies: A Dialog on Data and Space." *Big Data & Society* 3, no. 1 (January 5). https://doi.org/10.1177/2053951716648346.

Dalton, Craig M., and Jim Thatcher. 2014. "What Does a Critical Data Studies Look like, and Why Do We Care?" *Society & Space*, May 12. http://societyandspace.org/2014/05/12/what-does-a-critical-data-studies-look-like-and-why-do-we-care-craig-dalton-and-jim-thatcher/.

De Monchaux, Nicholas. 2016. *Local Code: 3,659 Proposals About Data, Design & the Nature of Cities*. First edition. New York: Princeton Architectural Press.

Defilippis, James. 1997. "From a Public Re-Creation to Private Recreation: The Transformation of Public Space in South Street Seaport." *Journal of Urban Affairs* 19, no. 4: 405.

Dicken, Peter. 2015. *Global Shift: Mapping the Changing Contours of the World Economy*. 7th edition. New York: Guilford.

Doussard, Marc, Greg Schrock, and Laura Wolf-Powers. 2017. "The Maker Economy in Action: Entrepreneurship and Supportive Ecosystems in Chicago, New York and Portland." https://static1.squarespace.com/static /5812d937be6594b79f6b7c82/t/58177ff3197aea6c5f212446/1477935092051 /The+Maker+Economy+in+Action+--+Final+Report.pdf.

Dreier, Peter, John H. Mollenkopf, and Todd Swanstrom. 2014. *Place Matters: Metropolitics for the Twentyfirst Century*. Third edition. Lawrence: University Press of Kansas.

Drennan, Matthew P. 2002. *The Information Economy and American Cities*. Baltimore: Johns Hopkins University Press.

Dunford, Michael, and Weidong Liu. 2017. "Uneven and Combined Development." *Regional Studies* 51, no. 1 (January 2): 69–85. https://doi.org /10.1080/00343404.2016.1262946.

Dwoskin, Elizabeth. 2019. "Google Reaped Millions in Tax Breaks as It Secretly Expanded Its Real Estate Footprint Across the U.S." *Washington Post*. February 15. https://www.washingtonpost.com/business/economy /google-reaped-millions-of-tax-breaks-as-it-secretly-expanded-its -real-estate-footprint-across-the-us/2019/02/15/7912e10e-3136-11e9-813a -0ab2f17e305b_story.html.

Economics & Statistics Administration. 2015. "Open Data Impact: How Zillow Uses Open Data to Level the Playing Field for Consumers." Economic & Statistics Administration, U.S. Department of Commerce, October 27. http://www.esa.doc.gov/under-secretary-blog/open-data -impact-how-zillow-uses-open-data-level-playing-field-consumers.

ESRC (Economic and Social Research Council). 2018. "Why GDPR Matters for Research." *ESRC Blog* (blog), May 25. https://blog.esrc .ac.uk/2018/05/25/why-gdpr-matters-for-research/.

Etienne, Harley F. 2012. *Pushing Back the Gates: Neighborhood Perspectives on University-Driven Revitalization in West Philadelphia*. Philadelphia: Temple University Press.

Etzkowitz, Henry, and L. A. Leydesdorff. 1997. *Universities and the Global Knowledge Economy: A Triple Helix of University-Industry-Government Relations.* London: Pinter.

Evans, Angela M., and Adriana Campos. 2013. "Open Government Initiatives: Challenges of Citizen Participation." *Journal of Policy Analysis and Management* 32, no. 1: 172–203.

Fainstein, Norman I., and Susan S. Fainstein. 1987. "Economic Restructuring and the Politics of Land Use Planning in New York City." *Journal of the American Planning Association* 53, no. 2 (Spring):237–48, https://doi .org/10.1080/01944368708976658.

Fainstein, Susan. 2001. *The City Builders: Property Development in New York and London, 1980–2000.* Revised edition. Lawrence: University Press of Kansas.

Fainstein, Susan, and Ann Markusen. 1996. "The Urban Policy Challenge: Integrating Across Social and Economic Development Policy." In *Race, Poverty, and American Cities*, ed. John Boger and Judith Wegner. Chapel Hill: University of North Carolina Press.

Falco, Stefano de, Margarita Angelidou, and Jean-Paul D. Addie. 2019. "From the 'Smart City' to the 'Smart Metropolis'? Building Resilience in the Urban Periphery." *European Urban and Regional Studies* 26, no. 2 (April): 5–23. https://doi.org/10.1177/0969776418783813.

Feldman, Maryann P. 2000. "Where Science Comes to Life: University Bioscience, Commercial Spin-Offs, and Regional Economic Development." *Journal of Comparative Policy Analysis* 2, no. 3345–61. https:// doi.org/10.1080/13876980008412651.

Fitzgerald, Joan. 2006. *Moving Up in the New Economy.* Ithaca, NY: Cornell University Press.

Fitzgerald, Joan, and Nancey Green Leigh. 2002. *Economic Revitalization: Cases and Strategies for City and Suburb.* Thousand Oaks, CA: SAGE.

Fitzsimmons, Emma G. 2018. "New York City Caps Uber and Lyft Vehicles in a Crackdown." New York, *New York Times*, August 9, 2018. https:// www.nytimes.com/2018/08/08/nyregion/uber-vote-city-council-cap .html.

Flavelle, Christopher. 2019. "Rockefeller to Wind Down Biggest Private Climate Resilience Push." *Bloomberg News.* April 1. https://www.bloomberg .com/news/articles/2019-04-01/rockefeller-announces-end-of-major -climate-resilience-initiative.

Florida, Richard. 2002. *The Rise of the Creative Class: And How It's Transforming Work, Leisure, Community, and Everyday Life*. New York: Basic Books.

Flowers, Benjamin Sitton. 2009. *Skyscraper: The Politics and Power of Building New York City in the Twentieth Century*. Philadelphia: University of Pennsylvania Press.

———. 2017. *Sport and Architecture*. London: Routledge.

Forester, John. 1980. "Critical Theory and Planning Practice." *Journal of the American Planning Association* 46, no. 3 (July): 275–86. https://doi.org/10.1080/01944368008977043.

———. 1982. "Planning in the Face of Power." *Journal of the American Planning Association* 48, no. 1 (Winter): 67–80. https://doi.org/10.1080/01944368208976167.

———. 1994. "Bridging Interests and Community: Advocacy Planning and the Challenges of Deliberative Democracy." *Journal of the American Planning Association* 60, no. 2 (Spring): 153.

Frieden, Bernard J., and Lynne B. Sagalyn. 1991. *Downtown, Inc.: How America Rebuilds Cities*. Cambridge, MA: MIT Press, 1991.

Friedmann, John, and Clyde Weaver. 1979. *Territory and Function: The Evolution of Regional Planning*. London: E. Arnold.

Frug, Gerald. 2001. *City Making: Building Communities Without Building Walls*. Princeton, NJ: Princeton University Press.

———. 2013. *City Bound: How States Stifle Urban Innovation*. Ithaca, NY: Cornell University Press.

Fry, Richard. 2018. "Millennials Expected to Outnumber Boomers in 2019." Washington, DC: Pew Research Center, March 1. http://www.pewresearch.org/fact-tank/2018/03/01/millennials-overtake-baby-boomers/.

Galbraith, John Kenneth. 1967. *The New Industrial State*. 3rd ed., New York: Penguin.

———. 1977. *Age of Uncertainty*. Illustrated ed. London: Houghton.

Garreau, Joel. 1992. *Edge City: Life on the New Frontier*. New York: Anchor.

Gibson-Graham, J. K., Jenny Cameron, and Stephen Healy. 2013. *Take Back the Economy*. Minneapolis: University of Minnesota Press.

Giuffrida, Greg, Jennifer Clark, and Stephen Cross. 2015. "Putting Innovation in Place: Georgia Tech's Innovation Neighbourhood of 'Tech Square'" (unpublished manuscript, September). http://www.gatech.edu/sites/default/files/documents/ECIE-2015-Giuffrida-Clark-Cross.pdf.

Glaeser, Edward L. 2011. *Triumph of the City: How Our Greatest Invention Makes Us Richer, Smarter, Greener, Healthier, and Happier*. New York: Penguin.

Glasmeier, Amy, and Susan Christopherson. 2015. "Thinking About Smart Cities." *Cambridge Journal of Regions, Economy and Society* 8, no. 1 (March): 3–12. https://doi.org/10.1093/cjres/rsu034.

Goetz, Edward G. 1993. *Shelter Burden: Local Politics and Progressive Housing Policy*. Philadelphia: Temple University Press.

——. 2000. "Fair Share or Status Quo?: The Twin Cities Livable Communities Act." *Journal of Planning Education and Research* 20, no. 1 (September 1): 37–51. https://doi.org/10.1177/0739456001128992582.

Goetz, Edward G., Karen Chapple, and Barbara Lukermann. 2003. "Enabling Exclusion: The Retreat from Regional Fair Share Housing in the Implementation of the Minnesota Land Use Planning Act." *Journal of Planning Education and Research* 22, no. 3 (March 1): 213–25. https://doi.org/10.1177/0739456X02250304.

Goldsmith, Stephen, and Susan Crawford. 2014. *The Responsive City: Engaging Communities Through Data-Smart Governance*. San Francisco: Jossey-Bass.

Goldsmith, William W. 1982. "Enterprise Zones: If They Work, We're in Trouble." *International Journal of Urban and Regional Research* 6, no. 3 (September 1): 435–42. https://doi.org/10.1111/j.1468-2427.1982.tb00392.x.

——. 1997. "Who Cares About the Inner City?" *Journal of the American Planning Association* 63, no. 1 (Winter): 154.

Goldstein, Brett, and Lauren Dyson, eds. 2013. *Beyond Transparency: Open Data and the Future of Civic Innovation*. San Francisco: Code for America Press.

Goldstein, Matthew, and Patricia Cohen. 2017. "Public-Private Projects Where the Public Pays and Pays." DealBook, *New York Times*, June 6, 2017. https://www.nytimes.com/2017/06/06/business/dealbook/trump-infrastructure-plan-privatized-taxpayers.html.

Goodman, Peter S. 2018. "In Britain, Austerity Is Changing Everything." World, *New York Times*, May 28, 2018. https://www.nytimes.com/2018/05/28/world/europe/uk-austerity-poverty.html.

Goodman, Robert. 1972. *After the Planners*. New York: Simon & Schuster.

Goodspeed, Robert. 2015. "Smart Cities: Moving Beyond Urban Cybernetics to Tackle Wicked Problems." *Cambridge Journal of Regions, Economy and Society* 8, no. 1 (March 1): 79–92. https://doi.org/10.1093/cjres/rsu013.

Gordon, Eric, and Adriana de Souza e Silva. 2011. *Net Locality: Why Location Matters in a Networked World*. Chichester, UK: Wiley-Blackwell.

Gotlieb, Nate. 2017. "Neighborhood Groups Surprised by NRP Reallocation." Civic Beat, *Southwest Journal*. February 27, 2017. http://www.southwest journal.com/news/civic-beat/2017/02/minneapolis-nrp-phase-ii -reallocation/.

Green, Ben. 2019. *The Smart Enough City: Putting Technology in Its Place to Reclaim Our Urban Future*. Cambridge, MA: MIT Press.

Gregg, Melissa. 2010. "Available in Selected Metros Only: Rural Melancholy and the Promise of Online Connectivity." *Cultural Studies Review* 16, no. 1: 155–69. https://doi.org/10.5130/csr.v16i1.1450.

——. 2015. "Hack for Good: Speculative Labour, App Development and the Burden of Austerity." *Fibreculture Journal*, no. 25: 185–202. https://doi .org/10.15307/fcj.25.186.2015.

Griswold, Alison. 2016. "Uber Asked a Lot of Pittsburgh for Its Self-Driving Cars, and Offered Back Very Little." *Quartz*, December 29, 2016. https:// qz.com/874548/uber-asked-a-lot-of-pittsburgh-for-its-self-driving-cars -and-offered-back-very-little/.

Hackworth, Jason R. 2007. *The Neoliberal City: Governance, Ideology, and Development in American Urbanism*. Ithaca, NY: Cornell University Press. http://www.loc.gov/catdir/toc/ecip0617/2006023306.html.

Hall, Peter. 2014. *Cities of Tomorrow: An Intellectual History of Urban Planning and Design Since 1880*. 4th ed. Hoboken, NJ: Wiley-Blackwell.

Hand, David. 2012. "Open Data Is a Force for Good, but Not Without Risks." *Guardian*, July 10, 2012. https://www.theguardian.com/society/2012 /jul/10/open-data-force-for-good-risks.

Harrison, Bennett. 1994. *Lean and Mean: The Changing Landscape of Corporate Power in the Age of Flexibility*. New York: Basic Books.

Harrison, John, and Ivan Turok. 2017. "Universities, Knowledge and Regional Development." *Regional Studies* 51, no. 7 (July 3): 977–81. https://doi.org /10.1080/00343404.2017.1328189.

Harvey, David. 1989. "From Managerialism to Entrepreneurialism: The Transformation of Urban Governance in Late Capitalism." *Geographiska Annaler* 71, no. series b (1989): 3–17.

——. 2008. "The Right to the City." *New Left Review* 53, (September/ October):23–40. https://newleftreview.org/issues/II53/articles/david-harvey -the-right-to-the-city.

Hatch, Mark. 2013. *The Maker Movement Manifesto: Rules for Innovation in the New World of Crafters, Hackers, and Tinkerers.* New York: McGraw-Hill.

Hayden, Dolores. 1984. *Redesigning the American Dream: The Future of Housing, Work, and Family Life.* New York: Norton.

——. 1980. "What Would a Non-Sexist City Be like? Speculations on Housing, Urban Design, and Human Work." *Signs: Journal of Women in Culture and Society* 5, no. S3 (1980): S170–S187.

Hefetz, Amir, and Mildred Warner. 2007. "Beyond the Market Versus Planning Dichotomy: Understanding Privatisation and Its Reverse in US Cities." *Local Government Studies* 33, no. 4 (August 1): 555–72. https://doi.org/10.1080/03003930701417585.

Hefetz, Amir, Mildred E. Warner, and Eran Vigoda-Gadot. 2012. "Privatization and Intermunicipal Contracting: The US Local Government Experience 1992–2007." *Environment and Planning C: Government and Policy* 30, no. 4: 675–92. https://doi.org/10.1068/c11166.

Herd, Mike, and Murithi Mutiga. 2016. "100 Resilient Cities Announces Hundredth Member, but 'Work Is Only Just Beginning.'" Cities, *Guardian.* May 2016. https://www.theguardian.com/cities/2016/may/25/rockefeller-100-resilient-cities-washington-lagos-manchester-belfast.

Holdren, John P., Eric S. Lander, William Press, Maxine Savitz, Wanda M. Austin, Christopher Chyba, Rosina Bierbaum, et al. 2016. "Technology and the Future of Cities." Washington DC: Executive Office of the President, President's Council of Advisors on Science and Technology (PCAST).

Hollands, Robert. 2008. "Will the Real Smart City Please Stand Up? Intelligent, Progressive or Entrepreneurial?" *City* 12, no. 3: 303–20.

Holmes, Allan. 2018. "5G Cell Service Is Coming. Who Decides Where It Goes?" Technology, *New York Times*, March 2, 2018. https://www.nytimes.com/2018/03/02/technology/5g-cellular-service.html.

Homsy, George C., and Mildred E. Warner. 2015. "Cities and Sustainability: Polycentric Action and Multilevel Governance." *Urban Affairs Review* 51, no. 1 (January 1): 46–73. https://doi.org/10.1177/1078087414530545.

Hu, Winnie. 2018. "Congestion Pricing Falters in New York, Again." New York, *New York Times*, April 1, 2018. https://www.nytimes.com/2018/03/31/nyregion/congestion-pricing-new-york.html.

——. 2019. "Over $10 to Drive in Manhattan? What We Know About the Congestion Pricing Plan." New York, *New York Times*, March 28, 2019.

https://www.nytimes.com/2019/03/26/nyregion/what-is-congestion
-pricing.html.

Iammarino, Simona, Andres Rodríguez-Pose, and Michael Storper. 2018. "Regional Inequality in Europe: Evidence, Theory and Policy Implications." London: Centre for Economic Policy Research. https://cepr.org /active/publications/discussion_papers/dp.php?dpno=12841.

Imbroscio, David L. 2006. "Shaming the Inside Game: A Critique of the Liberal Expansionist Approach to Addressing Urban Problems." *Urban Affairs Review* 42, no. 2 (2006): 224.

Information Commissioner's Office. 2018. "Guide to the General Data Protection Regulation (GDPR)," May 25. https://ico.org.uk/for-organisations /guide-to-the-general-data-protection-regulation-gdpr/.

Irani, Lilly. 2015. "Hackathons and the Making of Entrepreneurial Citizenship." *Science, Technology & Human Values* 40, no. 5: 799–824, https:// doi.org/10.1177/0162243915578486.

Isard, Walter, Iwan Azis, Matthew Drennan, Ronald Miller, Sidney Saltzman, and Erik Thorbecke. 1998. *Methods of Interregional and Regional Analysis.* Aldershot, UK: Ashgate.

Jackson, Kenneth T. 1985. *Crabgrass Frontier: The Suburbanization of the United States.* New York: Oxford University Press.

Jacobs, Jane. 1961. *The Death and Life of Great American Cities.* New York: Vintage.

Johnson, Peter, and Pamela Robinson. 2014. "Civic Hackathons: Innovation, Procurement, or Civic Engagement?" *Review of Policy Research* 31, no. 4 (July 1): 349–57. https://doi.org/10.1111/ropr.12074.

Jonas, Andrew E. G. 1995. "The Formation of American Local Governments: Private Values in Public Institutions." *Journal of Regional Science* 35, no. 3 (August): 517.

Kang, Cecilia. 2017. "Pittsburgh Welcomed Uber's Driverless Car Experiment. Not Anymore." Technology, *New York Times*, May 21, 2017. https:// www.nytimes.com/2017/05/21/technology/pittsburgh-ubers-driverless -car-experiment.html.

Karvonen, Andrew, Federico Cugurullo, and Federico Caprotti, eds. 2019. *Inside Smart Cities: Place, Politics and Urban Innovation.* New York: Routledge.

Kastrenakes, Jacob. 2018. "AT&T's 5G Network Goes Live in 12 Cities—but You Can't Use It yet." *The Verge*, December 18, 2018. https://www.theverge .com/2018/12/18/18146246/att-5g-us-launch-hotspot-service-plan-price.

Katz, Bruce, and Julie Wagner. 2014. "The Rise of Innovation Districts: A New Geography of Innovation in America." Washington, DC: Brookings Institution.

Katz, Harry Charles, and Owen Darbishire. 1999. *Converging Divergences: Worldwide Changes in Employment Systems.* Ithaca, NY: Cornell University Press.

Kerner Commission. 1968. "Report of the National Advisory Commission on Civil Disorders." Washington, DC: National Advisory Commission on Civil Disorders.

Kirsch, Noah. 2018. "Michael Bloomberg Takes on Trump, Pledges $42 Million to U.S. Cities." *Forbes,* May 23, 2018. https://www.forbes.com/sites/noahkirsch/2018/05/23/michael-bloomberg-takes-on-trump-pledges-42-million-to-us-cities/.

Kitchin, Rob. 2014a. *The Data Revolution: Big Data, Open Data, Data Infrastructures and Their Consequences.* Thousand Oaks, CA: SAGE.

———. 2014b. "The Real-Time City? Big Data and Smart Urbanism." *GeoJournal* 79, no. 1 (February 1): 1–14. https://doi.org/10.1007/s10708-013-9516-8.

———. 2015. "Making Sense of Smart Cities: Addressing Present Shortcomings." *Cambridge Journal of Regions, Economy and Society* 8, no. 1 (March): 131–36. https://doi.org/10.1093/cjres/rsu027.

Klosterman, Richard E., Kerry Brooks, Joshua Drucker, Edward Feser, and Henry Renski. 2018. *Planning Support Methods: Urban and Regional Analysis and Projection.* Lanham, MD: Rowman & Littlefield.

Kofman, Ava. 2019. "Google's Sidewalk Labs Plans to Package and Sell Location Data on Millions of Cellphones." *The Intercept,* January 28, 2019. https://theintercept.com/2019/01/28/google-alphabet-sidewalk-labs-replica-cellphone-data/.

Kokalitcheva, Kia. 2019. "Uber and Lyft Race Google to Become the All-in-One Transit App." *Axios,* February 27, 2019. https://www.axios.com/the-race-to-become-the-all-in-one-transport-app-1726ef49-cd28-4ef2-b5cb-69b9ab458a11.html.

Kourtit, Karima, Peter Nijkamp, and John Steenbruggen. 2017. "The Significance of Digital Data Systems for Smart City Policy." In "Digital Support Tools for Smart Cities," ed. Peter Nijkamp, Roger Stough, and Karima Kourtit, special issue, *Socio-Economic Planning Sciences* 58, no. Supplement C (June 1): 13–21. https://doi.org/10.1016/j.seps.2016.10.001.

Kristensen, Peer Hull, and Jonathan Zeitlin. 2005. *Local Players in Global Games: The Strategic Constitution of a Multinational Corporation*. Oxford: Oxford University Press.

Krumholz, Norman. 1999. "Equitable Approaches to Local Economic Development." *Policy Studies Journal* 27, no. 1: 83–95. https://doi.org/10.1111/j.1541-0072.1999.tb01955.x.

Lakomaa, Erik, and Jan Kallberg. 2013. "Open Data as a Foundation for Innovation: The Enabling Effect of Free Public Sector Information for Entrepreneurs." *IEEE Access* 1558–63. http://ieeexplore.ieee.org/stamp/stamp.jsp?tp=&arnumber=6584732&isnumber=633654.

Lau, Wanda. 2019. "Q+A: What Is a Smart City? Three Experts Explain." *Architect*, January 14. https://www.architectmagazine.com/technology/q-a-what-is-a-smart-city-three-experts-explain_o.

Le Dantec, Christopher A. 2016. *Designing Publics*. Cambridge, MA: MIT Press.

Lefebvre, Henri. 2011. *The Production of Space*. Malden, MA: Blackwell.

LeRoy, Greg. 2018. "Public Auction, Private Dealings: Will Amazon's HQ2 Veer to Secrecy Create A Missed Opportunity for Inclusive, Accountable Development?" New York: Good Jobs First, April 2018.

LeRoy, Greg, and Maryann Feldman. 2018. "Cities Need to Stop Selling out to Big Tech Companies. There's a Better Way." Cities, *Guardian*, July 3, 2018. http://www.theguardian.com/cities/2018/jul/03/cities-need-to-stop-selling-out-to-big-tech-companies-theres-a-better-way.

Levine, Dan. 2015. "Uber Drivers Granted Class Action Status in Lawsuit Over Employment." *Reuters*, September 1, 2015. https://www.reuters.com/article/us-uber-tech-drivers-lawsuit/u-s-judge-gives-uber-drivers-class-action-status-idUSKCN0R14O920150901.

Lobao, Linda, Mia Gray, Kevin Cox, and Michael Kitson. 2018. "The Shrinking State? Understanding the Assault on the Public Sector." *Cambridge Journal of Regions, Economy and Society* 11, no. 3 (October 29): 389–408. https://doi.org/10.1093/cjres/rsy026.

Lodato, Thomas, and Carl DiSalvo. 2016. "Issue-Oriented Hackathons as Material Participation." *New Media & Society* 18, no. 4 (April 1): 539–57. https://doi.org/10.1177/1461444816629467.

Lodato, Thomas, Emma French, and Jennifer Clark. 2018. "Open Government Data in the Smart City: Interoperability, Urban Knowledge, and Linking Legacy Systems." *Journal of Urban Affairs*, October 16, 2018. https://doi.org/10.1080/07352166.2018.1511798.

Loukissas, Yanni A. 2019. *All Data Are Local: Thinking Critically in a Data-Driven Society*. Cambridge, MA: MIT Press.

Lowe, Nichola J., and Laura Wolf-Powers. 2018. "Who Works in a Working Region? Inclusive Innovation in the New Manufacturing Economy." *Regional Studies* 52, no. 6 (June 3): 828–39. https://doi.org/10.1080/00343404.2016.1263386.

MacKinnon, Danny, Andrew Cumbers, Andy Pike, Kean Birch, and Robert McMaster. 2009. "Evolution in Economic Geography: Institutions, Political Economy, and Adaptation." *Economic Geography* 85, no. 2: 129–50. https://doi.org/10.1111/j.1944-8287.2009.01017.x.

Malecki, Edward J. 1997. *Technology and Economic Development: The Dynamics of Local, Regional and National Competitiveness*. 2nd ed. Essex, UK: Longman.

——. 2004. "Jockeying for Position: What It Means and Why It Matters to Regional Development Policy When Places Compete." *Regional Studies* 38, no. 9 (December): 1101–20.

Manjoo, Farhad. 2018. "How Tech Companies Conquered America's Cities." Technology, *New York Times*, June 21, 2018. https://www.nytimes.com/2018/06/20/technology/tech-companies-conquered-cities.html.

Markusen, Ann. 2007. "A Consumption Base Theory of Development: An Application to the Rural Cultural Economy." *Agricultural and Resource Economics Review* 36, no. 1 9–23, https://doi.org/10.1017/S1068280500009412.

——. 1999. "Fuzzy Concepts, Scanty Evidence, Policy Distance: The Case for Rigour and Policy Relevance in Critical Regional Studies." *Regional Studies* 33, no. 9 (December): 869.

Marshall, Aarian. 2019. "The Age of Congestion Pricing May Finally Be Upon Us." *Wired*, March 1, 2019. https://www.wired.com/story/age-of-congestion-pricing-nyc/.

Martin, Ron, and Peter Sunley. 2016. "Toward a Developmental Turn in Evolutionary Economic Geography?" In *Evolutionary Economic Geography: Theoretical and Empirical Progress*.ed. Dieter F. Kogler, New York: Routledge.

Marvin, Simon, Andrés Luque-Ayala, and Colin McFarlane, eds. 2016. *Smart Urbanism: Utopian Vision or False Dawn?* London: Routledge; New York: Taylor & Francis.

Massey, Doreen. 1979. "In What Sense a Regional Problem?" *Regional Studies* 13, no. 2 (1979): 233–43. https://doi.org/10.1080/09595237900185191.

———. 1984. *Spatial Divisions of Labour: Social Structures and the Geography of Production.* London: Macmillan.

McCann, Eugene. 2011. "Urban Policy Mobilities and Global Circuits of Knowledge: Toward a Research Agenda." *Annals of the Association of American Geographers* 101, no. 1 (2011): 107–30.

McGreal, Chris. 2018. "Is Bezos Holding Seattle Hostage? The Cost of Being Amazon's Home." Cities, *Guardian*, July 4, 2018. http://www .theguardian.com/cities/2018/jul/04/is-bezos-holding-seattle-hostage -the-cost-of-being-amazons-home.

MetroLab Network, The. 2017. "First, Do No Harm: Ethical Guidelines for Applying Predictive Tools Within Human Services."Washington, DC: Data Science and Human Services Lab. https://metrolabnetwork.org /wp-content/uploads/2017/09/Ethical-Guidelines-for-Applying-Predictive -Tools-within-Human-Services_Sept-2017.pdf.

Miao, Julie T. 2018. "Parallelism and Evolution in Transnational Policy Transfer Networks: The Case of Sino-Singapore Suzhou Industrial Park (SIP)." *Regional Studies* 52, no. 9 (January 24): 1191–1200. https://doi.org /10.1080/00343404.2017.1418979.

Milkman, Ruth, and Ed Ott, eds. 2014. *New Labor in New York: Precarious Workers and the Future of the Labor Movement.* Ithaca, NY: ILR Press.

Mollenkopf, John H., and Manuel Castells. 1991. *Dual City: Restructuring New York.* New York: Russell Sage Foundation.

Morgan, Kevin. 2004. "The Exaggerated Death of Geography: Learning, Proximity and Territorial Innovation Systems." *Journal of Economic Geography* 4, no. 1 (January 1): 3–21. https://doi.org/10.1093/jeg/4.1.3.

Morrison, Andrea. 2008. "Gatekeepers of Knowledge within Industrial Districts: Who They Are, How They Interact." *Regional Studies* 42, no. 6 (2008): 817–35. https://doi.org/10.1080/00343400701654178.

Motoyama, Yasuyuki. 2012. *Global Companies, Local Innovations: Why the Engineering Aspects of Innovation Making Require Co-Location.* Surrey, UK: Ashgate.

Musulin, Kristin. 2018. "What Mary Meeker's 2018 Trends Report Signals for Smart Cities." *Smart Cities Dive.* https://www.smartcitiesdive.com/news /mary-meeker-2018-trends-report-smart-cities/525038/.

Nam, Taewoo, and Theresa A. Pardo. 2011. "Conceptualizing Smart City with Dimensions of Technology, People, and Institutions." Pages 282–91 in *Proceedings of the 12th Annual International Digital Government Research*

Conference: Digital Government Innovation in Challenging Times, Dg.o '11. New York: Association for Computing Machinery. https://doi.org/10.1145 /2037556.2037602.

Neumayer, Eric, and Richard Perkins. 2005. "Uneven Geographies of Organizational Practice: Explaining the Cross-National Transfer and Diffusion of ISO 9000." *Economic Geography* 81, no. 3: 237–59. https:// doi.org/10.1111/j.1944-8287.2005.tb00269.x.

New State Ice Co. v. Liebmann. 1932. 285 U.S. 262 (March 21).

O'Brien, Mike. 2016. "A New Law Is Letting Uber Drivers Unionize." *The Nation*, July 1, 2016. https://www.thenation.com/article/a-new-law -is-letting-uber-drivers-unionize/.

OECD. 2017. *SME and Entrepreneurship Policy in Canada*. Paris: OECD Publishing. http://www.oecd.org/publications/sme-and-entrepreneurship -policy-in-canada-9789264273467-en.htm.

Offenhuber, Dietmar. 2015. "Infrastructure Legibility—A Comparative Analysis of Open311-Based Citizen Feedback Systems." *Cambridge Journal of Regions, Economy and Society* 8, no. 1 (March 1): 93–112. https:// doi.org/10.1093/cjres/rsu001.

O'Mara, Margaret Pugh. 2005. *Cities of Knowledge: Cold War Science and the Search for the Next Silicon Valley*. Princeton, NJ: Princeton University Press.

Orfield, Myron. 1997. *Metropolitics: A Regional Agenda for Community and Stability*. Washington, DC: Brookings Institution Press.

O'Sullivan, Feargus. 2018. "In London, Uber Fights for Its License." *City Lab: The Atlantic*. https://www.citylab.com/amp/article/562322/?utm _source=twb&__twitter_impression=true.

Oved, Marco. 2019. "Google's Sidewalk Labs Plans Massive Expansion to Waterfront Vision." *Thestar.Com*, February 14, 2019. https://www.thestar .com/news/gta/2019/02/14/googles-sidewalk-labs-plans-massive-expansion -to-waterfront-vision.html.

Oved, Marco, and Paul Hunter. 2018. "Privacy Expert Steps down from Advisory Role with Sidewalk Labs." *Toronto Star*, October 20, 2018. https://www.thestar.com/news/gta/2018/10/20/privacy-expert-steps -down-from-advisory-role-with-sidewalk-labs.html.

Paroutis, Sotirios, Mark Bennett, and Loizos Heracleous. 2014. "A Strategic View on Smart City Technology: The Case of IBM Smarter Cities During a Recession." *Technological Forecasting and Social Change* 89 (November): 262–72. https://doi.org/10.1016/j.techfore.2013.08.041.

Pastor, Manuel. 2000. *Regions That Work: How Cities and Suburbs Can Grow Together*. Globalization and Community, vol. 6. Minneapolis: University of Minnesota Press.

Patton, Carl V., David S. Sawicki, and Jennifer Clark. 2013. *Basic Methods of Policy Analysis and Planning*. 3rd ed., Upper Saddle River, NJ: Routledge.

Peck, Jamie. 1992. "Labor and Agglomeration: Control and Flexibility in Local Labor Markets." *Economic Geography* 68, no. 4 (October 1992): 325–47.

——. 2002. "Labor, Zapped/Growth, Restored? Three Moments of Neoliberal Restructuring in the American Labor Market." *Journal of Economic Geography* 2, no. 2 (April 2002): 179.

——. 2017. *Offshore: Exploring the Worlds of Global Outsourcing*. Oxford: Oxford University Press.

——. 1996. *Work-Place: The Social Regulation of Labor Markets*. New York: Guilford.

Peck, Jamie, and Nikolas Theodore. 2010. "Mobilizing Policy: Models, Methods, and Mutations." *Geoforum*, Themed Issue: Mobilizing Policy, 41, no. 2 (March): 169–74. https://doi.org/10.1016/j.geoforum.2010.01.002.

——. 2015. *Fast Policy: Experimental Statecraft at the Thresholds of Neoliberalism*. Minneapolis: University of Minnesota Press.

Peck, Jamie, and Kevin Ward. 2002. *City of Revolution: Restructuring Manchester*. Manchester, UK: Manchester University Press.

Pendall, Rolf, Kathryn A. Foster, and Margaret Cowell. 2010. "Resilience and Regions: Building Understanding of the Metaphor." *Cambridge Journal of Regions, Economy and Society* 3, no. 1 (March 1): 71–84, https://doi.org/10.1093/cjres/rsp028.

Perry, Andre. 2018. "Opinion | Who Gets Left Out of the Urban Tech Boom?" Opinion, *New York Times*, July 21, 2018. https://www.nytimes.com/2018/07/19/opinion/amazon-hq2-google-pittsburgh-jobs.html.

Peterson, Paul E. 1981. *City Limits*. Chicago: University of Chicago Press.

Pike, Andy, Andrés Rodríguez-Pose, and John Tomaney. 2006. *Local and Regional Development*. New York: Routledge, 2006. http://www.loc.gov/catdir/enhancements/fy0654/2006005421-d.html.

Pollard, Jane S. 2004. "From Industrial District to 'Urban Village'? Manufacturing, Money and Consumption in Birmingham's Jewellery Quarter." *Urban Studies* 41, no. 1: 173–93. https://doi.org/10.1080/0042098032000155731.

Porter, Eduardo. 2019. "Tech Is Splitting the U.S. Work Force in Two." Business, *New York Times*, March 12, 2019. https://www.nytimes.com /2019/02/04/business/economy/productivity-inequality-wages.html.

——. 2017. "Why Big Cities Thrive, and Smaller Ones Are Being Left Behind." *New York Times*. October 10, 2017. https://www.nytimes.com/2017 /10/10/business/economy/big-cities.html.

Porter, Michael. 1990. *The Competitive Advantage of Nations*. New York: Free Press.

——. 1995. "The Competitive Advantage of the Inner City." *Harvard Business Review* 73, no. 3 (May 1995): 55.

Prince, Russell. 2012. "Policy Transfer, Consultants and the Geographies of Governance." *Progress in Human Geography* 36, no. 2 (April 1): 188–203. https://doi.org/10.1177/0309132511417659.

Puttick, Ruth, Peter Baeck, and Philip Colligan. 2014. "I-Teams: The Teams and Funds Making Innovation Happen in Governments Around the World." Nesta & Bloomberg Philanthropies, June. https://www.bbhub .io/dotorg/sites/2/2014/06/Nesta_2014_Report_final_webcombined.pdf.

Quintas, Paul, David Wield, and Doreen Massey. 1992. "Academic–Industry Links and Innovation: Questioning the Science Park Model." *Technovation* 12, no. 3 (April): 161–75. https://doi.org/10.1016/0166-4972(92)90033-E.

Rantisi, Norma M. 2010. "The Local Innovation System as a Source of 'Variety': Openness and Adaptability in New York City's Garment District." *Regional Studies* 36, no. 6 (August): 587–602. http://emoglen.law.columbia .edu/twiki/pub/LawNetSoc/CrystalMaoFirstPaper/RANTISI _-_innovation_communities.pdf.

Ratti, Carlo, and Matthew Claudel. 2016. *The City of Tomorrow: Sensors, Networks, Hackers, and the Future of Urban Life*. New Haven, CT: Yale University Press.

Rockefeller Foundation. 2018a. "Challenge Eligibility and Criteria." 100 Resilient Cities. http://www.100resilientcities.org/challenge-eligibility-criteria/.

——. 2018b. "What Is 100 Resilient Cities?" 100 Resilient Cities. http:// www.100resilientcities.org/about-us/.

Rosenblat, Alex. 2018. *Uberland: How Algorithms Are Rewriting the Rules of Work*. Oakland: University of California Press.

Rossi, Ugo. 2015. "The Variegated Economics and the Potential Politics of the Smart City." *Territory, Politics, Governance* 4, no. 3 (May 12): 337–53. https:// doi.org/10.1080/21622671.2015.1036913.

Rushe, Dominic. 2018a. "'It's a Huge Subsidy': The $4.8bn Gamble to Lure Foxconn to America." Cities, *Guardian*, July 2, 2018. http://www .theguardian.com/cities/2018/jul/02/its-a-huge-subsidy-the-48bn -gamble-to-lure-foxconn-to-america.

——. 2018b. "US Cities and States Give Big Tech $9.3bn in Subsidies in Five Years." Cities, *Guardian*, July 2, 2018. http://www.theguardian.com /cities/2018/jul/02/us-cities-and-states-give-big-tech-93bn-in-subsidies -in-five-years-tax-breaks.

Rusk, David. 1999. *Inside Game/Outside Game: Winning Strategies for Saving Urban America*. Washington, DC: Brookings Institution.

Sagalyn, Lynne B. 1997. "Negotiating for Public Benefits: The Bargaining Calculus of Public–Private Development." *Urban Studies* 34, no. 12 (December): 1955–70. https://doi.org/10.1080/0042098975169.

——. 2001. *Times Square Roulette: Remaking the City Icon*. Cambridge, MA: MIT Press.

——. 2007. "Public/Private Development: Lessons from History, Research, and Practice." *Journal of the American Planning Association* 73, no. 1 (March 31): 7–22. https://doi.org/10.1080/01944360708976133.

Sanchez, Kelly Vencill. 2018. "Will Smart Cities Make Life Easier for Everyone?" *Dwell* (July 20). https://www.dwell.com/article/smart-city -technology-mit-sensable-cities-lab-6b26d0a3.

Sassen, Saskia. 2001. *The Global City: New York, London, Tokyo*. Princeton, NJ: Princeton University Press.

Satariano, Adam. 2018. "Uber Claims to Have Changed. A London Judge Will Decide." Technology, *New York Times*, June 25, 2018. https://www .nytimes.com/2018/06/24/technology/uber-london-appeal.html.

Sbragia, Alberta M. 1996. *Debt Wish: Entrepreneurial Cities, U.S. Federalism, and Economic Development*. Pittsburgh: University of Pittsburgh Press.

Scheiber, Noam. 2019. "Labor Dept. Says Workers at a Gig Company Are Contractors." *New York Times*, April 29, 2019. https://www.nytimes.com /2019/04/29/business/economy/gig-economy-workers-contractors.html.

Schneider, Benjamin. 2017. "From the Ruins of a Retail Meltdown, Post-Industrial Playgrounds Emerge." *CityLab*, November 16, 2017. https:// www.citylab.com/life/2017/11/sears-warehouses-find-new-life-as-post -industrial-playgrounds/545936/.

Scott, Allen. 1998. *Regions and the World Economy: The Coming Shape of Global Production, Competition, and Political Order*. Oxford: Oxford University Press.

Scott, Allen, and Edward Soja. 1996. *The City: Los Angeles and Urban Theory at the End of the Twentieth Century*. Berkeley: University of California Press.

Shelton, Taylor, and Jennifer Clark. 2016. "Technocratic Values and Uneven Development in the 'Smart City.'" *Metropolitics* May 10, 2016. http://www.metropolitiques.eu/Technocratic-Values-and-Uneven.html.

Shelton, Taylor, and Ate Poorthuis. 2018. "The Nature of Neighborhoods: Using Big Data to Rethink the Geographies of Atlanta's Neighborhood Planning Unit System." October 25, 2018. https://doi.org/10.17605/OSF.IO/P9W2B.

Shelton, Taylor, Matthew Zook, and Alan Wiig. 2014. "The 'Actually Existing Smart City.'" *Cambridge Journal of Regions, Economy and Society* 8, no. 1 (October 27): 13–25. https://doi.org/10.1093/cjres/rsu026.

Sheppard, Eric S., Trevor J. Barnes, and Claire Pavlik. 1990. *The Capitalist Space Economy: Geographical Analysis After Ricardo, Marx and Sraffa*. London: Unwin Hyman.

Sibley, Mari. 2018. "AT&T, San Jose Sew Up Model Small Cell Deal." *Light Reading*, March 14, 2018. https://www.lightreading.com/smart-cities/atandt-san-jose-sew-up-model-small-cell-deal/d/d-id/743032.

Sieber, Renee. 2006. "Public Participation Geographic Information Systems: A Literature Review and Framework." *Annals of the Association of American Geographers* 96, no. 3 (September): 491–507. https://doi.org/10.1111/j.1467-8306.2006.00702.x.

Singleton, Royce A. Jr., and Bruce C. Straits. 2010. *Approaches to Social Research*. 5th ed. New York: Oxford University Press.

Smith, Neil. 1984. *Uneven Development: Nature, Capital, and the Production of Space*. New York: Blackwell.

Somerville, Heather. 2015. "Seattle Passes Law Letting Uber, Lyft Drivers Unionize." *Reuters*, December 15, 2015. https://www.reuters.com/article/us-washington-uber/seattle-passes-law-letting-uber-lyft-drivers-unionize-idUSKBN0TX2NO20151215.

State of California2018. Consumer Right to Privacy Act (CaCPA), 17–0039 Cal. Civ. Code § 1798.100 §.

Stone, Katherine. 2001. "The New Psychological Contract: Implications of the Changing Workplace for Labor and Employment Law." *UCLA Law Review* 48: 540–49.

——. 2004. *From Widgets to Digits: Employment Regulation for the Changing Workplace*. New York: Cambridge University Press.

Storper, Michael. 1997. *The Regional World: Territorial Development in a Global Economy*. New York: Guilford.

Storper, Michael, Thomas Kemeny, Naji Makarem, and Taner Osman. 2016. *The Rise and Fall of Urban Economies: Lessons from San Francisco and Los Angeles*. Stanford: Stanford Business Books.

Storper, Michael, and Anthony J. Venables. 2004. "Buzz: Face-to-Face Contact and the Urban Economy." *Journal of Economic Geography* 4, no. 4: 351–70, https://doi.org/10.1093/jnlecg/lbh027.

Kendra Strauss, "Precarious Work and Winner-Take-All Economies" Pages 1–11 in *The New Oxford Handbook of Economic Geography*, ed. Gordon L. Clark et al. Oxford: Oxford University Press. https://www.oxfordhandbooks.com/view/10.1093/oxfordhb/9780198755609.001.0001/oxfordhb-9780198755609-e-22.

Streitfeld, David, and Claire Ballentine. 2018. "Seattle Officials Repeal Tax That Upset Amazon." Technology, *New York Times*, June 12, 2018. https://www.nytimes.com/2018/06/12/technology/seattle-tax-amazon.html.

Taylor, Linnet, Christine Richter, Shazade Jameson, Perez de Pulgar, and Carmen Perez de Pulgar. 2016. "Customers, Users or Citizens? Inclusion, Spatial Data and Governance in the Smart City." SSRN Scholarly Paper. Rochester, NY: Social Science Research Network, June 9. http://papers.ssrn.com/abstract=2792565.

Taylor, Peter, and Ben Derudder. 2015. *World City Network: A Global Urban Analysis*. 2nd ed. Abingdon, UK: Routledge.

Thatcher, Jim. 2017. "You Are Where You Go, the Commodification of Daily Life Through 'Location.'" *Environment and Planning A* 49, no. 12 (December): 2702–17. https://doi.org/10.1177/0308518X17730580.

"The Uber Workplace in DC." 2019. Washington DC: Kalmanovitz Initiative for Labor and the Working Poor, Georgetown University, April. https://lwp.georgetown.edu/wp-content/uploads/Uber-Workplace.pdf.

"The World's Most Valuable Resource Is No Longer Oil, but Data." 2017. *The Economist*, May 6, 2017. https://www.economist.com/leaders/2017/05/06/the-worlds-most-valuable-resource-is-no-longer-oil-but-data.

Tiebout, Charles M. 1956. "A Pure Theory of Local Expenditures." *Journal of Political Economy* 64, no. 5 (1956): 416.

Todtling, Franz. 1994. "Regional Networks of High-Technology Firms—The Case of the Greater Boston Region." *Technovation* 14, no. 5: 323.

Todtling, Franz, and Michaela Trippl. 2007. "Knowledge Links in High-Technology Industries: Markets, Networks or Milieu? The Case of the Vienna Biotechnology Cluster." *International Journal of Entrepreneurship and Innovation Management* 7, no. 2–5: 345.

——. 2004. "Like Phoenix from the Ashes? The Renewal of Clusters in Old Industrial Areas." *Urban Studies* 41, no. 5–6: 1175–95. https://doi.org/10.1080/0042098041001675788.

Townsend, Anthony M. 2013. *Smart Cities: Big Data, Civic Hackers, and the Quest for a New Utopia.* New York: Norton.

Treado, Carey Durkin. 2010. "Pittsburgh's Evolving Steel Legacy and the Steel Technology Cluster." *Cambridge Journal of Regions, Economy and Society* 3, no. 1 (2010): 105–20. https://doi.org/10.1093/cjres/rsp027.

Turok, Ivan, David Bailey, Jennifer Clark, Jun Du, Ugo Fratesi, Michael Fritsch, John Harrison, et al. 2017. "Global Reversal, Regional Revival?" *Regional Studies* 51, no. 1 (January 2): 1–8. https://doi.org/10.1080/00343404.2016.1255720.

U.S. Department of Transportation. 2017. "Smart City Challenge: Lessons for Building Cities of the Future." Washington, DC: U.S. Department of Transportation. https://www.transportation.gov/sites/dot.gov/files/docs/Smart%20City%20Challenge%20Lessons%20Learned.pdf.

U.S. National Science Foundation. 2018. "Smart and Connected Communities (S&CC)." 2018.. https://www.nsf.gov/funding/pgm_summ.jsp?pims_id=505364.

Valderrama, Alisa, and Larry Levine. 2012. "Financing Stormwater Retrofits in Philadelphia and Beyond." Washington, DC: Natural Resources Defense Council February. https://www.nrdc.org/sites/default/files/StormwaterFinancing-report.pdf.

Village of Euclid, Ohio v. Ambler Realty Co. 1926. 272 U.S. 365.

Wakabayashi, Daisuke. 2018. "California Passes Sweeping Law to Protect Online Privacy." Technology, *New York Times,* July 30, 2018. https://www.nytimes.com/2018/06/28/technology/california-online-privacy-law.html.

Walker, Richard. 2018. *Pictures of a Gone City: Tech and the Dark Side of Prosperity in the San Francisco Bay Area.* Oakland, CA: PM Press.

Warner, Mildred E. 2013. "Private Finance for Public Goods: Social Impact Bonds." *Journal of Economic Policy Reform* 16, no. 4 (December): 303–19. https://doi.org/10.1080/17487870.2013.835727.

Warner, Mildred E., and Robert Hebdon. 2001. "Local Government Restructuring: Privatization and Its Alternatives." *Journal of Policy Analysis and Management* 20, no. 2: 315–36. https://doi.org/10.1002/pam.2027.

Weber, Rachel. 2002. "Extracting Value from the City: Neoliberalism and Urban Redevelopment." *Antipode* 34, no. 3 (July 1): 519–40. https://doi.org/10.1111/1467-8330.00253.

———. 2015. *From Boom to Bubble: How Finance Built the New Chicago.* Chicago: University of Chicago Press.

Whyte, William Hollingsworth. 1988. *City: Rediscovering the Center.* New York: Doubleday.

Wiig, Alan. 2015. "IBM's Smart City as Techno-Utopian Policy Mobility." *City* 19, no. 2–3 (May 4): 258–73. https://doi.org/10.1080/13604813.2015.1016275.

Wilson, William Julius. 1990. *The Truly Disadvantaged: The Inner City, the Underclass, and Public Policy.* Reprint ed., Chicago: University of Chicago Press, 1990.

Wines, Michael. 2018. "Drive Against Gerrymandering Finds New Life in Ballot Initiatives." U.S., *New York Times*, July 23, 2018. https://www.nytimes.com/2018/07/23/us/gerrymandering-states.html.

Wingfield, Nick. 2018. "Amazon Chooses 20 Finalists for Second Headquarters." Technology, *New York Times*, January 19, 2018. https://www.nytimes.com/2018/01/18/technology/amazon-finalists-headquarters.html.

Wolf-Powers, Laura, Marc Doussard, Greg Schrock, Charles Heying, Max Eisenburger, and Stephen Marotta. 2017. "The Maker Movement and Urban Economic Development." *Journal of the American Planning Association* 83, no. 4 (October 2): 365–76. https://doi.org/10.1080/01944363.2017.1360787.

Wolman, Harold, and Gerry Stoker. 1992. "Understanding Local Economic Development in a Comparative Context." *Economic Development Quarterly* 6, no. 4 (November): 406–17. https://doi.org/10.1177/089124249200600407.

Zervas, Georgios, Davide Proserpio, and John W. Byers. 2015. "The Impact of the Sharing Economy on the Hotel Industry: Evidence from Airbnb's Entry Into the Texas Market." Page 637 in *Proceedings of the Sixteenth ACM Conference on Economics and Computation*, EC '15. New York: Association for Computing Machinery. https://doi.org/10.1145/2764468.2764524.

Zook, Matthew A. 2002. "Grounded Capital: Venture Financing and the Geography of the Internet Industry, 1994–2000." *Journal of Economic Geography* 2, no. 2 (April 1): 151–77. https://doi.org/10.1093/jeg/2.2.151.

Zukin, Sharon. 2009. "Changing Landscapes of Power: Opulence and the Urge for Authenticity." *International Journal of Urban and Regional Research* 33, no. 2 (June): 543–53. https://doi.org/10.1111/j.1468-2427.2009.00867.x.

———. 2011. *Naked City: The Death and Life of Authentic Urban Places.* Reprint ed., Oxford: Oxford University Press.

INDEX

Page numbers in *italics* refer to figures or tables.

GPSR Authorized Representative: Easy Access System Europe, Mustamäe tee
50, 10621 Tallinn, Estonia, gpsr.requests@easproject.com

www.ingramcontent.com/pod-product-compliance
Lightning Source LLC
Chambersburg PA
CBHW022138020426
42334CB00015B/944